Guides to Japanese Culture

Guides to Japanese Culture

Japan Culture Institute

A word to those who read Japanese: a Japanese-language edition of this book is also available. We feel that comparison of the subtle differences in expression necessitated by the English and Japanese languages should in itself afford valuable data to those concerned with the problems of culture and cultural exchange.

Edited
by
Murakami Hyôe and Edward G. Seidensticker

First printing, 1977
Published by the Japan Culture Institute
201 Park Avenue, 20, Sendagaya 1 chôme, Shibuya-ku, Tokyo
Designed by Ikeda Masuo
Printed by the Toppan Printing Co., Ltd.
Distributor: Japan Publications Trading Co., Ltd.
20 Clearbrook Road, Elmsford, N.Y. 10523, U.S.A.
P.O. Box 5030 Tokyo International, Tokyo 101-31, Japan
ISBN: 0-87040-403-2
Printed in Japan

CONTENTS

Preface

Throughout the world people today are searching earnestly for ways to live together in mutual peace and prosperity. It has become more than ever necessary for each nation and each people to understand other nations and peoples. Undoubtedly understanding of others' economic and political systems is important; but of most basic importance is knowledge of one another's traditions, life styles, ways of thinking and feeling – in short, all that is generally known as "culture."

This is easy to say, of course, but extremely difficult to accomplish. We all bear a weight of cultural tradition stretching back over thousands of years, and so deeply ingrained that we ourselves are scarcely aware of it.

Let us consider Japan. What were its geography and climate like ten thousand years ago, and how did they affect the inhabitants of these islands? How was the Japanese language, the "orphan of the world," formed and what are the distinguishing characteristics of its expression of logic and feeling? What is the actuality of Shinto and Buddhism, so deeply rooted in Japanese life even today, and how do they function? What is the true meaning of the Japanese reverence for nature, of so-called ancestor worship, of Zen? What are the distinctive ideas of Nishida Kitarô and other thinkers who have knit these diverse cultural strands into original philosophical systems? What is the nature of Japanese society and human relationships? Of Japan's history, literature, and arts? And finally, how do the Japanese perceive the West and the world in general?

The editorial staff of the Japan Culture Institute has endeavored to answer such questions with this book, through concise yet comprehensive summaries and commentaries introducing forty-five works by modern Japanese scholars and thinkers. *Guides to Japanese Culture* is first and foremost an introduction to Japanese culture, a compendium of representative modern Japanese achievement hitherto accessible only to the relative few who can read Japanese. And for those who do read Japanese, it is our hope that this book will serve as a useful bibliographic guide to further study , whatever one's field of interest.

The forty-five works outlined herein were chosen on the basis of the opinions of over 120 distinguished Japanese scholars, writers, and artists.

Use was also made of the *Bibliography of Standard Reference Books for Japanese Studies with Descriptive Notes*, compiled by the Kokusai Bunka Shinkôkai (Tokyo: University of Tokyo Press, 1965-73). The staff of the Japan Culture Institute under the guidance of the writer and critic Murakami Hyôe carefully made the final selection from among the hundreds of candidates. The English translations were edited by the eminent translator Professor Edward G. Seidensticker of the University of Michigan.

Guides to Japanese Culture was compiled in order to present authoritative views of the Japanese themselves concerning the major areas of their culture. But the discerning reader will note a still more important purpose underlying this book: to show that becoming acquainted with another culture serves in the end to deepen and renew one's understanding of the place of one's own tradition among the many cultures comprising the world of humankind.

Editors' Note

The completion of any book depends on the cooperation of many individuals. The editors wish to express their deep gratitude to all who have helped make the publication of this book possible, especially the authors of the forty-five works selected and the translators of the essays: Richard Bowring, Hugh Burleson, Edward Fowler, Don Kenny, David Lemon, Charles Terry, and Suzanne Trumbull. They worked long and patiently with the Japan Culture Institute editorial staff at the demanding task of rendering into English the essence of Japanese culture as expressed in Japanese.

The Hepburn system of romanization is used for Japanese terms, which are italicized except for words included in the second edition of *Webster's New World Dictionary*.

Summaries and Commentaries

I
Land and People

1. NATURE IN JAPAN

Nihon no Shizen By Nakano Takamasa, Kobayashi Kunio
Tokyo: Iwanami Shinsho #346, Iwanami Shoten, 1959.

In December, 1943, at the foot of Mt. Usudake in Hokkaido, there occurred a momentous event. The earth started to rumble and the whole area was shaken by a series of tremors. They continued for some months at a rate of over one hundred per day. The railway line was pushed upwards and a small hill was formed, about twenty-four meters high. Large cracks appeared in the fields, wells ran dry, and as the earth writhed almost hourly the inhabitants of the area spent their days and nights in fear of what might happen next. In June of the next year smoke started to pour from the field which had shown the greatest upheaval, and by the end of that year the field had risen 150 meters. Gradually there appeared from the top of this new volcano a black cone which grew sixty centimeters a day until it was about four hundred meters high. It was this lava cone that had been the cause of the tremors and the convulsions.

There are so many different volcanoes in Japan that the country might well be called, as is the Auvergne in the Massif Central, a museum. There are, if we include Mt. Fuji, over forty live volcanoes, accounting for roughly a tenth of the world's total; and in addition volcanic activity can often be observed on the spot, making Japan a kind of natural laboratory. Japan is also at the top when it comes to the frequency of earth tremors. Tokyo experiences anything from forty to fifty sensible tremors a year, and a destructive earthquake occurs somewhere in Japan on an average of once every two years. It is also worth remembering that when earthquakes do occur in Japan they often bring with them tidal waves (*tsunami*). On the outer perimeter of the Japanese archipelago lies an earthquake belt, part of the orogenetic circum-Pacific belt, which is volcanically unstable and where submarine quakes often cause tidal waves.

But perhaps in recompense for its volcanoes, earthquakes, tidal waves, typhoons, floods, and other such unpleasant phenomena, Japan is blessed with many places of great scenic beauty and with many hot springs. They have been used for their medicinal properties since ancient times. According to 1954 statistics there are 1,133 such areas and 8,452 actual springs.

"Now in the mountains/now by the beach/out across the iron bridge/back into the tunnel/out of the darkness onto the plains." This song about a train ride, which every Japanese child knows, illustrates how Japan, with its mountains, plains and enclosed valleys, offers a rich variety of scenery in a comparatively small area. Small though the scale may be, it contains units of widely differing geological age and includes areas which are even now undergoing constant change, upheaval, subsidence, and folding – a mosaic in miniature. And yet despite its size this small island country has unusually high mountains.

The Japanese archipelago lies in a north-to-south arc along the eastern side of the Asian continental mass, and because of its mountainous nature it has a rich variety of climatic conditions, not only regionally but also seasonally, there being a remarkable contrast between summer and winter. The range of temperature throughout the year is very great and the change in the seasons is clearly marked. Compared with Central Europe, for example, where spring and autumn are short and summer and winter long, there is a subtle gradation of the seasons in Japan and the colorful procession of flowers and trees emphasizes this sense of season. Winter snow and spring blossoms, the fresh green of early summer and the dark green of high summer, maple leaves in early autumn and falling leaves in late autumn, they all play their part. Here too, perhaps, we can find a reason for the emergence of such seasonal poetry as haiku. Being part of the monsoon belt Japan has a high rainfall. Summer is hot and humid, more uncomfortable, some say, than in the Amazon jungle; autumn is the typhoon season, and in winter enough snow falls in the northwest to bury the houses. Cherry blossoms open in March in the south and in early June in the far north, and it is possible if one follows them northwards to enjoy three months of spring. In winter to travel from Tokyo to Niigata is to experience the contrast between the dry east and the heavy snows of the Japan Sea coast. Japan is indeed a storehouse of seasons.

The rain and snow that fall on the high mountains flow in clear torrents, eating deep into valleys, creating a delicate network of V-shaped valleys large and small that have a beauty all their own. When the rivers emerge from the mountains, particularly in time of flood, they bring with them a heavy sediment of sand and gravel, and these deposits fan out to form alluvial plains. But unlike the wide eroded plains of Europe they are always fairly small and the sea is never far away. They are, in a sense, mere adjuncts to the mountains. But owing to high population density these plains, although they hardly merit the name, have for long been fully utilized by man, and people have always lived cheek by jowl. Such a population throughout history has changed the nature of these plains almost out of recognition, and in the process of creating paddies not only on the plains but also on the tablelands the rivers too have been turned to human purposes. The hand of man is yet another factor in the diversity not only of the topography, the distribution of subsurface water and the characteristics of flora, but also of the soil itself. In most parts of the world climatic and soil conditions are correlated, but in Japan this is not necessarily the case. In areas of paddy, for instance, it is rare to find the soil in its natural state. Wet rice is originally a tropical plant, but by dint of human endeavor in Japan it is cultivated even in cold latitudes, and in the central mountain ranges in cool altitudes of 1,300 meters and more. This is a phenomenon not found elsewhere in the world. Rice is the plant closest to the hearts of the Japanese people. It is an important index when investigating the relationship between man and nature.

Generally speaking vegetation in Japan is not as nature designed it. The Musashino plain in the Kantô area and the grassland at the foothills of volcanoes in other areas are the product of human labor, and the woods that we now see from the carriage window are also man made. Natural forest can only be found deep in the mountains or imagined from the feel of the precincts of old shrines. And yet for all that many of Japan's high mountains are covered in forest which ranges from subtropical through temperate to near arctic. The climate too changes according to altitude, and so the vertical distribution of flora in Japan is similar to the latitudinal spread.

It has already been mentioned how the change in the seasons is perceived in the change of temperature and the color of the leaves, but another sign is migrant birds. When the young branches send forth buds and all is a fresh green, Japan is visited by a large variety of birds. The country forms a kind of corridor and resting place for birds flying north to south and the reverse: summer birds such as the swallow and the cuckoo, winter birds such as the swans and thrushes which come to escape the bitter cold of the lands to the north, and nomadic birds which move over a fairly limited area such as the bush warbler. They fly the same paths every year and visit each part of the country. They too have been celebrated in song and poetry since ancient times.

Commentary

Japanese scenery is often compared to a "miniature landscape." A miniature landscape is the recreation, in a small space, of mountains, rivers, forests and houses – a landscape produced by the combined efforts of nature and man. The very fact that this children's pastime exists is symbolic of the complex yet compact nature of the Japanese scene. As this book shows us, Japan is a storehouse of the seasons and has abundant natural variety. With this in mind the authors discuss the special characteristics of Japanese mountains, plains, and rivers, the sea, the lakes, the climate, and the flora and fauna, and give many concrete examples while seeking also to generalize. They include the latest findings of geological and physical research and also of human geography. The book is scientifically sound and at the same time lucidly written for the layman.

After dealing with the "natural formation of the Japanese Archipelago," this book shows how Japanese have reacted to nature throughout their history. The reason for listing it as a guide to Japan should be clear from the fact that "Japanese nature is of the greatest significance as the environment in which we live." Both authors are geography experts but they also deal competently with the cultural effects of nature. They point out that the plight of the poorer Japanese in winter is given expression in the famous "Dailogue on Poverty" by Yamanoue no Okura in the *Manyô-shû*, and also that a strong sense of seasonal change is reflected in such nature poetry as haiku.

Nature has great influence over man; through what man makes of nature and his way of life it affects his emotions, his language and many other aspects of his existence. This book is a useful introduction to the study of Japanese geography, and it is basic as well to an understanding of Japanese culture.

2. A TREATISE ON JAPANESE CULTURE

Nihon Bunka Ron By Ishida Eiichirô
Tokyo: Chikuma Shobô, 1969.

Formation of the Japanese Race

If they who made Japanese culture their own through the medium of the Japanese language are to be considered the original Japanese, the formation of the Japanese race took place during the Yayoi period (200

B.C.-300 A.D.). The islands of Japan were inhabited much earlier, but it was during this period that rice farming began and most of the agricultural techniques that support the life of the Japanese village were developed.

Earlier there was the Jômon (10,000 B.C.-200 B.C.) culture, supported by gathering and hunting, though comparatively sedentary. The new culture probably resulted from large-scale movements on the Asian Continent. Yayoi culture was founded upon Jômon culture.

The importation of continental culture was intermittent, but the actual number of immigrants seems to have been so small that intermarriage with the Jômon people finally resulted in complete absorption. There are various theories as to where the immigrants came from and how they reached Japan, but there is no definite proof for any of them. The culture of the period is characterized by peaceful farming and festivals.

Formation of the Japanese Nation

During about the third century of the Christian era, a group of priests began to assume political and economic leadership, forming small theocracies, between which rivalries arose, sometimes of a warlike nature. The tumulus period (when rulers were buried in gigantic mounds) extended from the third to the seventh century. The roots of the imperial system were taking shape in the Yamato court, which unified the country and created the nation of Japan.

The change from the ceremonial to the warlike indicates that heterogeneous elements entered Japan from abroad. Indications of a change appeared around the end of the fourth century, and were in full evidence by the fifth. According to Egami Namio's *Mounted Nomadic Peoples* (*Kiba Minzoku Kokka*), the transition took place when a northern nomadic line of Wa kings moved from the Korean Peninsula to Japan. This small group of warriors was soon absorbed linguistically and culturally into the Japanese race. Thus the "core personality" of the Japanese was firmly established long before a refined continental culture was introduced.

Idiosyncrasies of Japanese Culture

The Japanese as a race have been forced to deal with the geographical reality of the Tsushima Straits. In antiquity, Japan and Korea were very closely related. At one point in history they were a part of the same cultural area. Today they have their own unique and separate cultures. While there are examples of "things" which came across the Tsushima Straits to Kyushu and western Japan and became a part of Japanese culture, but which no longer exist on the continent, there are also many "things" that spread as far as the southern tip of the Korean Peninsula and never crossed to Japan.

Utensils of horn that are common in Korea have never been used in Japan. An earthen vessel shaped like a leather bag is very much a part of Korean life, but, except for a few examples from the tumulus period, there is no evidence of its ever having been used in Japan. The custom of having the housewife hold all the keys, which makes the key almost a symbol of the housewife in China and Korea, never came across the Tsushima Straits to Japan, where the symbol of the housewife is the wooden ladle (*shamoji*). Compared with Korea, the roots of Christianity and Confucianism are very shallow in Japan. While Confucianism did indeed make its way into the military class during the Edo period, there is little or no evidence of an appreciable influence on the life of the masses, and, especially the farm population.

A remarkable example of an institution that did not enter Japan is the eunuch system (the use of castrated men at court). Deriving from the practice of castrating animals among pastoral peoples, the system spread from China to western Europe and to Korea, but never reached Japan.

There are two clues to the idiosyncrasies of Japanese culture. The first is rice planting. Historically, the rice-planting zone has its center in southern China, and spreads through the warm, humid monsoon areas of India, Indonesia, Okinawa, Japan, and Korea. The cultural idiosyncrasies common to all these races include a life centered upon planting techniques, formal observances related to rice planting and an animistic concept of the origins of life. Yet we must once more take note of the line drawn by the Tsushima Straits.

Archaeologically, southern Korea and western Japan were very similar in the Yayoi period and the tumulus period. More recent differences resulted from Jômon influences and the later histories of the two nations. Thus the first clue to the idiosyncrasies of Japanese culture can be discovered by considering Japanese farm life and agricultural methods.

The second clue can be found in an unbroken tradition restricted to the Japanese Islands for more than a thousand years. There were no foreign invasions. Japanese culture itself was sealed off from outside disturbances. The secret of the vigor of the Japanese people may well lie in a continuing willingness to import foreign culture into circumstances of racial and cultural endogamy. Since Japan is a basically endogamous society, there has been no necessity for volubility and eloquence, and so logic and rhetoric have not flourished.

Japan and the Occident

Since the Meiji period, the Japanese have taken an inordinate interest in Europe and America. Under the belief that Japan was an underdeveloped nation, Occidental civilization and culture have been introduced at an alarmingly fast rate.

Due to extremely close contacts with the West since the end of the Pacific War, new theories of Occidental culture and civilization have begun to appear which contrast strongly with the Meiji and prewar views. Aida Yûji's writings are representative of this trend (see Aida Yûji's *Anatomy of Japanese Consciousness*).

Murakami Hyôe recently wrote of a trip to Europe in the monthly magazine *Chûô Kôron* (December, 1965). The following are some of his points.

In European civilization, the instinct for protecting position and personal rights is extremely strong. It is the backbone of European nationalism. While a Japanese may use the same words, the meaning is far more good-natured and easy-going.

A memorial stone was erected at Hiroshima bearing the words, "We shall not make this mistake again." Another stone was erected at the northernmost point on Hokkaido informing tourists that it is "the northern tip of Japan." It predates the peace treaty in relinquishing claim to territories beyond. Nothing of the sort would happen in Europe.

A stroll through any European city reveals an extremely large number of well-trained dogs. The development of animal training is an aspect of European culture, as opposed to the Japanese ability to raise plants. In horticulture, one must subordinate oneself to plants, while in the training of animals, one exacts obedience by the use of sweets and the whip.

These observations are pertinent. An effective index for the comparison of European and Japanese culture is found in looking upon the former as a pastoral culture developed in a dry climate, and the latter as a farming culture developed in a humid environment. The recognition of the fact that the raising of animals is not an intrinsic aspect of traditional Japanese life provides an important clue for the understanding of Japanese culture.

Commentary

This book is based on a series of lectures delivered in 1966. Ishida is a pioneer cultural anthropologist. Working in the traditions of Japanese ethnology developed by Yanagita Kunio, he has sought a methodology for the study of comparative culture. In this book he expresses his opinions on the origins of the Japanese people and nation and the idiosyncrasies of Japanese culture, based on long years of research, for a popular readership.

The origins of a race cannot be explored without the cooperation of such sciences as anthropology, archaeology, comparative linguistics, and ethnology. Ishida has actually contributed a great deal to the development of such studies. The tendency in Japanese historical and archaeological studies has been to think of a single race of Japanese since the Stone Age. Ishida places great emphasis on contacts and mixtures with outside elements. Concerning the diffusion of rice planting, he rejects Yanagita's theory of dissemination from the Ryukyu Islands, maintaining that rice culture was brought to Japan from southern Korea. Also he supports Egami's theory of the founding of the Yamato dynasty by mounted nomads.

Nihon Bunka Ron has been translated into English by Kachi Teruko as *Japanese Culture: A Study of Origins and Characteristics* (Tokyo: University of Tokyo Press, 1974).

3. THE LAURISYLVAN CULTURE

Shôyôjurin Bunka Edited By Ueyama Shunpei
Tokyo: Chûkô Shinsho #201, Chûô Kôron-sha, 1969.

Introduction

This book centers on discussions by five scholars seeking to recapture the Jômon culture, which is presumed to be the earliest Japanese culture. The five are Nakao Sasuke (plant culture and genetic breeding), Kira Tatsuo (plant physiology), Okazaki Takashi (Chinese archaeology), Iwata Keiji (cultural anthropology) and the editor Ueyama Shunpei (philosophy).

Superficially, there is in Japan today a culture with a strong European coloration traceable to the industrial revolution. Yet if one layer is removed, an agricultural society is revealed, strongly colored by Chinese culture and yet uniquely original. Even deeper there sleeps a pre-agricultural hunting and gathering culture known as Jômon.

The expression "sleeping" is not precisely correct. The old culture still lives, though altered in many ways. In all parts of Japan are to be found the native religious establishments called shrines (*jinja*), with annual festivals. The rites of that native religion are to be observed at opening ceremonies for super-express trunk railways and express highways and at dedication ceremonies for high-rise buildings. The Shinto religion is not something that began in the Yayoi period, as is popularly believed. Its roots are thought to go back to Jômon.

What are Laurisylvan (Glossy-leafed) Woods?

The Jômon culture, which produced the world's most ancient earthenware vessels, is believed to be one of the cultures that developed in the zone of glossy-leafed woods – laurisylva.* The laurisylvan zone is one of the floral climatic divisions, the zone in the temperate region where evergreen broad-leafed woods predominate. It spans Nepal, the area south of the Yangtze River, and Japan. The trees characteristic of this zone are evergreens of the beech family, including many varieties of nut trees. They are distinguished by thick leaves against the cold of winter. They differ from the sclerophyllic (hard-leafed evergreen) woods of the Mediterranean littoral, even though they are a part of the same temperate region. Representative of the latter are the olive and cork oak, which can withstand the dry heat of summer.

Farming in the Laurisylvan Zone

Heretofore, it has popularly been held that Jômon was a culture of hunting and gathering, and that farming began with the rice cultivation of the Yayoi period. It may be correctly surmised, however, that farming in some form may have existed from the middle of the Jômon period. This farming we may call "semi-cultivation." We may assume that there were fixed abodes and, besides wild nuts and fruits, deer and boars, there were nut orchards, sometimes of improved varieties producing large nuts. Such rootstocks (or root crops) as yams (*Dioscorea japonica*), arrowroot and adder's tongue lily were staple foods and were processed into starch with the development of soaking techniques. We may call that way of living "the early laurisylvan culture complex."

In the late Jômon period, there came cultivation of small grains and such legumes as soy beans and adzuki beans by slash-and-burn methods. We may call this slash-and-burn cultivation "the laurisylvan culture complex." Most of these cultivated plants are thought to have come in from the west. We may speculate boldly that they came to Japan from the

Southwest China via the Yangtze River – through the laurisylvan zone.

The Laurisylvan Woods and Jômon Culture

According to radiocarbon dating, earthenware appeared in Japan about ten thousand years ago, after the Würm glacial epoch. (It is called Jômon – rope-figured – earthenware due to the characteristic rope imprinting.) The uses of the earthenware were, broadly, three: storage, transporting and boiling; but for early Jômon earthenware such a division of functions is not found. The bottom was pointed, and all functions seem to have been performed by each vessel. The vessels for storage tended to have their surfaces beautifully polished – very distinctly so in the late Jômon period. The foods stored were mainly nuts. The starch taken from these nuts and the yam rootstock was boiled and eaten.

The culture of gathering and semi-cultivation continued for almost ten thousand years. Grass cereals were slow to make their appearance. The cultural pattern of this period may be called a northern variant of the "rootstock cultivation culture"* which centered on the use of yams.

The Japanese laurisylvan woods thus provided men with an abundance of rootstock and nuts; and yet, because the blessings of nature were few as compared to the tropics, a higher technology developed. Earthenware was early produced, and there were large communities and fixed abodes. In the late Jômon period, laurisylvan farming culture came in from South China. Its produce had for staples such grains as foxtail millet, Chinese millet, finger millet; soy beans and adzuki beans; and also a melon (*Cucumis melo* var. *makuwa*) and the bottle gourd (*hyôtan*). Of these, finger millet and the bottle gourd were of African origin, so that the produce of aboriginal African farming came into the laurisylvan farming culture. It is possible that at this time upland rice also came in – ahead of paddy rice; but there still is no conclusive evidence. We must also consider the possibility that with the cultivation of the small grains stone knives came in for cutting grain heads. There is still no generally accepted opinion as to whether or not the stone blade implements excavated from the late Jômon sites were such tools.

In the last stages of the Jômon period, paddy-rice cultivation entered western Japan. Through the Yayoi period the Japanese adapted this cultivated plant of the tropics as far as the colder Tôhoku region (northern Honshu). That endeavor continued right into historical times. In the Yayoi period, however, life had not come to depend entirely on paddy-rice cultivation. It is clear from the excavations of Yayoi-period sites that semi-cultivated plants such as nuts and rootstock continued to be important foods. From the Middle Ages and into the Edo period, nuts were gathered for food in times of bad rice harvests. This was even true in the times of critical food shortages during World War II.

The Native Religion of the Laurisylvan Zone

It is not certain whether the religious forms of the mountain tribes of Southeast Asia, the peoples who live in the laurisylvan zone, (1) have continued unchanged from ancient times, (2) entered with religions originating in India or elsewhere when they accepted rice cultivation, or (3) both comingled. Nevertheless, in the case of the Khmer people, for example, the rice god and ancestral god intermix in the same religious rites. With the Thai, the demarcation between the ancestral god and the local god is unknown. In the case of Japan, it is said that the process of blending the rice god, the ancestral god and the local god is farthest advanced.

If shamanism in the religion of ancient Japan originated in the north, coming from Siberia through the Korean Peninsula, then we must also note that there is also shamanism among the Southeast Asian peoples. We cannot conclude that Japanese shamanism was of northern derivation.

Commentary

Where should the oldest strata of Japanese culture be sought? The five scholars assume that it is in the Jômon culture; and each tries from his own field of specialization to hypothesize as much as possible on how the people of that age lived. The common premise of the participants establishes the climatic zone on the basis of the vegetation of the laurisylvan wooded zone and takes Jômon as a culture that developed in such an environment. We may thus assume that it had affinities running from Japan to the southwest.

The reason that such discussion attracts attention is that the origins of the Japanese are not truly known; and yet it is recognized archaeologically that an old culture having earthenware and going back more than ten thousand years developed almost independently in the Japanese archipelago, in a way that cannot clarify its relationships to continental cultures.

It had previously been thought that Japanese farming began with rice growing in the Yayoi period. The scholars in this symposium hypothesize that in the middle Jômon period, prior to rice cultivation, there already was "semi-cultivation," and that in the late Jômon period there was slash-and-burn agriculture of the same form as in the laurisylvan zone eastward from the south slopes of the Himalayas. They argue further that rice growing was soon accepted and developed rapidly.

Nakao Sasuke's *The Origins of Cultivated Plants and Farming* (*Saibai Shokubutsu to Nôkô no Kigen*, Tokyo: Iwanami Shinsho #583, Iwanami Shoten, 1966) discusses the world-wide origins of farming. In one chapter he describes the laurisylvan culture.

[NOTES]

*Laurisylva. *Laurisilvae* in Latin; *Lorbeerwälder* in German.

*Rootstock cultivation culture. Nakao classifies Old World farming cultures into three types, in terms of "cultivated plants and the rise of farming": the "rootstock cultivation culture" originating in Southeast Asia, the "savannah cultivation culture" originating in Africa, and the farming culture of areas bordering the Mediterranean Sea, where winters are rainy.

4. THE FORGOTTEN JAPAN

Wasurerareta Nihon By Okamoto Tarô

Tokyo: Chûô Kôron-sha, 1961.

In Okinawa, there are no actual physical "objects" that leave a deep impression. I first went to Okinawa vaguely expecting to find a concrete cultural heritage and objects of art. When I got there and saw the grave at Urazoe of one of the Shô kings, the royal cemetery called Tamaudon, the relics of the old royal family, Tsuboya pottery, and *bingata* dyeing, they all seemed very pleasant, but something was missing. I continued traveling around Okinawa, wondering if there might not be something impressive yet to be found. It was not until I had gone all the way to the Yaeyama Islands at the far end of the Ryukyus, and had become quite sure that there was indeed nothing to be found, that my heart leaped for joy. I suddenly felt that it is this complete lack of the concrete that is the important thing about Okinawan culture.

I said that nothing really struck me, that there was nothing I could put my finger on; but all during my trip through the Ryukyus, I did feel a deeply resounding response to several things. First of all, there were the stone walls – chunks of coral awkwardly piled one on another, seem heavy and rugged, under the violent light of the midday sun and later, in the dying light of the evening sun, they become strangely weightless and seem to have the gentleness of human skin. These stone walls left a very strong impression. Then there were the bare feet. The bare feet of the people walking along the roads are intensely appealing. The lithe, sturdy ankles of people whose fate is to live with the earth to the end. Life resounds directly off the land itself. The straw hats and baskets, the mats woven of pandanus leaves, the woven lids of the huge pots in which yams are boiled, and the boats. There are any number of such interesting objects. These shapes, refined naturally, are perfect forms. And they are all beautiful. Their beauty was not created consciously – it is not beauty for the sake of beauty. They were born of the bare necessities of life. They came into being through a sense of necessity – nothing more nor less – and through repeated use in daily life.

It is easy to lose the awareness that is at the very base of what we know as "culture," and herein lies a serious problem. It is this base that has grown and extended itself to become the very foundation of all Japanese culture. When we speak of "culture," we think in terms of its most refined products, such as the temples and sculpture of Egypt, Greece, and Rome, or the bronze ware of the Yin and Chou dynasties – fine treasures of the past. These objects were made purely for display, and they have a splendor of their own that is entirely divorced from daily life. On the other hand, the simple articles mentioned earlier have the splendor and beauty of the bare necessities of vital everyday life. I do not wish to maintain that one is of more intrinsic value than the other. I simply wish to point out that what we generally refer to as "culture" includes vastly different things, and that we must differentiate between these extremes in a consideration of the term. I wish to call attention to the following problem – the history of this group of tiny islands, which seem to have been negligently tossed into the waters of the Pacific Ocean, and left there on the outermost edge of Oriental culture to fend for themselves, has been supported over a very long period of time, without any room for surplus or vanity, by no more than the final desperate sparks of life of the people who live there. Japan itself is in a similar situation. A ripping away of the skin of the aristocratic culture that was imported from China would probably reveal the poignant reality of the culture that is an expression of our basic life force – the legacy from our oldest ancestors.

Western European culture finds its original motivation in the cultures of the ancient Middle and Near East and the Mediterranean. It passed through the Middle Ages and the Renaissance, and reached a kind of perfection. It is a world view that takes the solidity of stone as its foundation, and is intrinsically a magic formula for the immortality of culture. Firmness is of the essence. Its texture is rough, and yet it is elegant.

In the culture of Okinawa we find something quite different – an entirely different disposition. Throughout its long history, Okinawa has lived on in its natural state, like a plant that clings to the ground. Blown about by the mighty typhoon winds, torn apart, decaying, and efflorescing naturally, but always sprouting forth anew from beneath the ruins gently to grow and prosper once more, and going on to repeat the cycle again. Its textures are pliant and delicate. It seems naive, brittle, and transitory, but it is, in fact, strong and tenacious. Its strength is of an entirely different sort from that of Mediterranean culture. I somehow feel that the essence of Japanese culture is alive in Okinawa. There is no doubting the solid sensation one receives from the touch of the original impulses of Japanese life. I feel that I must go so far as to say that the culture of Okinawa and Japan is not oriental culture. Geographically, we are a part of Asia, but we do not have the same fate as the Asian Continent, and should be considered a part of Pacific island culture.

I am deeply moved by the many songs and tales of the cruel drama of the poll tax in the Yaeyama Islands.

– There were two young lovers. The young man was to be sent far away in a forced emigration. They pleaded to be sent away together, but in vain, however much they begged, for they were from different villages. On the night before they were to be parted forever, they climbed a mountain, and spent the night in lamenting, seated on the rock where they had met secretly. They beat their hands upon the rock as they shed hopeless tears. When the sun arose, it revealed two indentations in the rock, where they had beat out their sorrow with their fists. The mark of the young woman's hand was the deeper of the two. . .

I have never before heard such a pure tale of sadness. What casual simplicity! How insignificant and humble is this tiny indentation, when compared with the wailing and cursing that seems to move heaven and earth in the Greek tragedy! And this is the reason that the tales of Okinawa are so poignant. They are of the most extreme simplicity and innocence, but the grief they portray is desperately vivid.

It is said that the pain and grief of Yaeyama farmers was so intense that their wails became songs. They wept as they continued to bear the cruel load of forced labor. But the songs gave meaning to their lives. If the songs had only expressed despair, they would not have been sung so often. Does not the fact that these desperately mournful melodies have been sung and resung hundreds and thousands of times prove that while they express negative ideas and emotions, they reaffirmed the very fact of life and gave the singers something to live for ?

Okinawa is a land of dance. Throughout the four seasons of the year, all the various performing arts of the regular festivals, as well as weddings, birthdays, and especially the sixtieth and seventieth birthdays, the completion of buildings, and departure upon a journey, they call for special dances. When a ship sails, relatives gather on the shore or in the homes of the travelers and, dancing in a circle, sing of them. Since song and dance are so much a part of daily life, the Okinawans are able to dance without formal instruction. I saw a middle-aged woman, the owner of a fighting bull, dance in the bull ring. She waved her hands lightly in the air and stamped her feet. More than a dance, it was an expression of joy making use of her entire body. More than an expression of joy, it was, after all, a dance. This was the most simple and direct expression that I saw in all the dances of Okinawa. They are not formal or ceremonial. They are expressions of shared joy that simply come flowing out. I immediately sensed a candid physical rhythm. There is no doubt that all of us once had this power to express of vibrantly living movement. When and why did we lose this gracefully simple expression of life?

In Okinawa, a set of beliefs very similar to the old Shintoism of Japan is still alive. Women called *noro* are the mystic priests or shamans. The festivals are held in sacred places called *utaki* by these women only. There is nothing that represents the body of the god, no image, no iconography of any kind. There is only a stone that is called the censer or incense burner, before which the god can be worshipped. The god descends here, where there is no concrete object of any kind, to stand face to face with human beings. When the ceremony begins, the *utaki*, precisely because it contains nothing tangible, is suddenly metamorphosed into an austerely holy place. Was not the place of the gods in ancient Japan even so – a pure, empty space? Probably the beliefs of our ancestors and the emotions and sense of the absolute that sustained their everyday lives were of the same quality. Why otherwise would this sacred place, completely lacking in concrete points of reference, impress itself so strongly upon my physical being? I felt here a sort of contact-detonating device. Something in our Japanese blood, in our traditions, set off a strong response. It came to me in this sacred place as a sudden shock, and aroused a strong feeling of nostalgia.

Commentary

This book tells of the shock experienced by Okamoto Tarô, a well-known artist, upon his first meeting with the culture of Okinawa. He does not speak only of Okinawan culture, but of the deeper levels of all Japanese culture; hence the title, "The Forgotten Japan."

If the reader expects to find a concrete discussion of the similarities between Japanese and Okinawan culture, he will be disappointed. Coming upon the primitive roots of Japanese culture in Okinawa, the author did not pursue his discovery with the eyes of a cultural anthropologist. Nor did he take the cultural aspects of various relics he found in Okinawa as the subject of his discussion. It is true that many of the classical elements of Japanese culture can be found in Okinawa. It is said that the language of Okinawa preserves many elements of ancient Japanese. But what Okamoto has done here is look at the birthplace of the culture and interpret the life forces and sensations he finds there through the eyes of an artist.

Okamoto begins this book with a quotation from Yanagita Kunio's "Mountain Life," in *Japanese Tales of Cruelty* (*Nihon Zankoku Monogatari*). Okamoto claims that it is the essential beauty of extreme cruelty, which he calls "the violent gentleness of life," that has sustained Japan and the lands near by. It is this essential element that he discovered in Okinawa.

In 1609, Okinawa was conquered by Lord Shimazu of Satsuma (Kagoshima Prefecture) and plundered most cruelly. Especially heavy demands were made on the outlying Yaeyama Islands. A poll tax was levied on all men and women between the ages of fifteen and fifty, along with other heavy taxes.

What Okamoto found in this "world of poverty and forced labor" was a complete lack of anything concrete, and a wealth of intangibles – the songs and dances and the *utaki* shrines. Okamoto maintains that it was there that he found the true essence of Japanese culture. And he goes on to argue that the things generally considered expressions of Japanese culture, such as classical dance, the samisen, and the aesthetics of *wabi* and *sabi* austerity, are sheer modern decadence.

As the standard bearer of a new movement in art, Okamoto has continually called the Japanese taste for such intangible qualities of stillness and elegance as *yûgen*, *wabi* and *sabi* false traditionalism. He discovered the vigorous beauty of Jômon pottery. And he has made great efforts to break down the rural inferiority complex which believes that culture is to be found only in Tokyo, Paris, and New York, and once more bring to the fore the everyday life that is the source of art. This book is an extension of Okamoto's efforts in this cause.

5. IN SEARCH OF THE COMMON MAN

Shomin no Hakken By Miyamoto Tsuneichi
Tokyo: Miraisha, 1961.

Whenever I travel on the Sanyô Line I experience a feeling of deep affection for the Japanese countryside, where life is in such order, peace and harmony. I have a particular love of the scenery from Mihara over the Saijô Highlands. Here and there in the terraced paddies are the houses with their beautiful thatch or reddish-brown tiles, their slender supports, their verandas, innumerable screens and only an occasional solid wall. There is little fear of being molested, although the houses are scattered everywhere, and in summer the inhabitants give no second thought to sleeping with the doors wide open. If there is no peace and people cannot trust each other such a life is not possible.

Their forefathers who first opened up this land are honored, they say, at the graves that stand here and there in the fields, and there each family has buried its kin ever since. The men who heaped up stones on these steep hillsides and created new paddies one by one with the sweat of their brow must have been strongly attached to their land, and as a result they took care of the world in which they found themselves, and did their utmost to make it a pleasant one.

The village of Nishi-shiwa lies in a hollow in the hills at the farthest end of the valley formed by a tributary of the River Ôta. In the past the paddies were so waterlogged it was almost a swamp; when planting out the rice seedlings they had to lay down large logs on which to stand. Reaping in the autumn was backbreaking work and the harvest was meager. They were literally bogged down in their dismal existence. In 1885, when the emigration agreement with Hawaii was signed, many Japanese crossed the seas, but whether they left or whether they stayed behind, those who had been born and brought up in this village retained their affection for it, despite the toil in the mud. But the villagers did not just accept the situation and resign themselves to their lot; they were always ready and willing to improve their land and make it more productive. Maruyama Kawaru was one such man.

Maruyama's family was of no particular importance in the village and it was the best he could do to finish primary school. Thereafter, as was the custom for the eldest son, he succeeded his father as head of the family and started work as a farmer. But he wanted to improve his farming as best he could, and so no sooner was the day's work done and the evening meal finished than off he would go to study under a technical expert at the experimental station at Saijô. It was a round trip of sixteen kilometers and there was no bus; if he had walked it would have taken all night, and so he ran there and back every evening. This he did for four years; nor was he the only farmer to do so, for there was a deeply rooted tenacity of purpose in their lives.

As a result of these four years of study Maruyama not only learned that the land in his own village, if improved, would create excellent paddy, but he also learned how to effect this improvement and was determined to put this knowledge to good use. He became a teacher himself in village evening classes, and in the winter after the harvest he and twelve of his students marked off a portion of the fields as a test area and started to construct a complicated system of irrigation. It entailed much hardship and great labor, but a few years later four hundred hectares of unproductive land were reborn as fertile paddy. Now that the fields were improved there was an increased demand for an adequate supply of water in the summer months, and so they built up the banks of the local pond to store water in greater quantity. As the villagers all wanted to own this good land, tenant farmers saved and saved until they could afford to become independent. Maruyama planned with his fellow farmers and they began straightening out the winding pathways and laying out the paddies in neat squares. As life became a little easier they turned their attention to matters that previously had been totally disregarded, such as redesigning the kitchens in their houses, and to plan their lives more efficiently they learned bookkeeping. The work of improving the village which Maruyama had begun continued without pause and his own responsibilities grew. Thirty years passed, and eventually he was elected head of the village. He continued to help and guide the rest. He is, to me, an example of all that is best in the Japanese farmer.

I have visited Maruyama's home twice since World War II. The first time was an evening in March and I was greeted by the spectacle of huge fires burning here and there in the paddies. Later in the evening we went for a stroll outside. It was very cool and still. A slightly acrid smell hung over the earth, and I could see the smoke rising from the paddies. They had been burning straw. By covering the scorching earth with soil they would be able to rejuvenate the land. The smell seemed to pervade all my senses.

The second visit I made was in the autumn when the land glowed with the color of ripening grain. We talked late into the evening and shared the same room that night, but I felt strangely unsettled and was unable to sleep. It must have been about two o'clock in the morning when someone arrived and Maruyama had to get up. I heard their voices for a long time, and then it seemed that Maruyama had gone out. Day was just breaking. Still sleepless, I got up and went for a walk along the country paths. Maruyama returned carrying a large bundle of grass which he had just cut as fodder for the oxen, a daily task that is no longer necessary in this age of mechanization. It appeared that he had had no sleep at all that night. The visitor had been a farmer from the village and they had discussed how, because of the postwar agrarian reforms, land that had been handed down from generation to generation was being taken over by tenant farmers. The son of the house had gone off to fight in the war and left them short handed, and so they had called on the tenant farmers for help. After the war the land reform had given priority of ownership to the actual cultivator. According to Maruyama such visitors came almost every evening.

Everyone thinks of farming people as narrow minded and superstitious, but I cannot agree. On the contrary they must be passionately committed and courageous, and have a sense of responsibility and perseverance if they are thus to put their ideals into practice.

Once, on a walking tour of the villages in the Saijô Highlands, I caught the sound of metal striking stone in the sharp, clear autumn air. I walked toward the sound and came upon a party of stone-cutters working in the river. As I stood watching they came up to the bank for a rest, and I took the opportunity to talk for a while about their life and work.

"We do it for the money and I wouldn't recommend it," said one. "Working in the river in the depth of winter is a terrible experience. I wouldn't want my son to have to do a job like this, but I intend to carry on for the rest of my life. It gives me real pleasure when going around the countryside to come across a beautiful retaining wall built against the side of a small paddy that you wouldn't give a second glance to. I always try my hardest to make a good strong wall that will never collapse. To do good work is always satisfying."

"Sometimes on piecework we skimp a little for reasons of economy, but after it's finished I can't sleep at nights for fear it might collapse in a downpour. If you do a bad job then those who follow you will produce shoddy work as well. But if you do your own job properly it doesn't matter what the weather is like, you can always sleep soundly, secure in the knowledge that anything you've done will stand up to a lot more than a bit of rain. I'm a firm believer that the man who takes over such work will carry on in the same spirit."

What they said was quite ordinary, but they had their own particular brand of home-spun philosophy, and it was this, I felt, that really kept the world going.

"There's nothing quite like doing a good job and getting due praise for it. Mind, you feel like producing good work regardless."

They had learned the value of being their own masters through their own work, rather than being dictated to by someone else. They were compliant in the face of authority but unyielding in the face of mere power. They understood instinctively that one should respect authority and truth above all things. For me the sum total of their attitudes is embodied in the everyday "tangible culture" we see before us.

A fisherman from the Ondo Straits in the Inland Sea used to come to the farm, on the island of Ôshima, where I was born and bred. After the war, when food was in short supply, he would occasionally bring conger eel and ask for sweet potatoes in return. The first time he came we had none, but persuaded certain relatives to sell some cheaply. From then on we became very friendly. I suggested that he save up and buy a motor boat, as he could only take a small catch in the row boat he was using. But he replied that he could not save anything from the money he made. The number of fish in the sea seemed to be dwindling too. One day he brought some eel and goby fish in a basket and asked for some rice in return, for he had not eaten any in a very long time. After he had left I noticed that the tails of the goby had been cut off; these fish had been in fact part of his bait, I realized. It would have been rude of me to have sent them back, and so I had my son take some *miso* and soy sauce down to the beach and invited him up for a hot bath that evening. But he never came. It began to rain and I thought of him that night sleeping in his boat in the open.

Months later he suddenly appeared with a large heap of eels. He had come to say thank you, he said, and although he did not ask for any provisions, I gave him some rice and sweet potatoes. "Actually, I've bought a motor boat," he said. I went down to the beach and there lay his brand-new boat, his wife standing there with a happy smile on her face. He had just wanted to show it to me. He started the engine and put out to sea. I have a great affection for the sea which provides a livelihood for such men.

Commentary

This book is a collection of eight essays written by the author in the late 1950s. The first four chapters deal with the way of life of various ordinary country people whom the author has met on his travels. The main point of this section is that "Japanese farming and fishing villages have always been poor, but they have always done their best in the midst of adversity and have never really allowed themselves to be overwhelmed by poverty. This is because they have in their own way conquered their difficulties in an atmosphere of mutual cooperation."

In the last four chapters the author discusses the attitudes which form such a way of life, how these attitudes are transmitted, and how subsequent generations receive and improve on such knowledge.

In the words of the farmer, the stone-cutters and the fisherman in the above abstract, the image of the common man who has unceasingly battled poverty over the ages is brought into relief. Taking peace and mutual trust as almost a foregone conclusion, these people born in poor villages have tried to improve their own lot and that of their villages as best they can. It is this latent energy of the common people and their way of life that the author has sought and found.

Miyamoto was inspired by his forerunners in Japanese folk studies, Yanagita Kunio and Shibusawa Keizô, and for over thirty years he has traveled to farming and fishing villages in all parts of Japan, recording his impressions and his findings. He has been particularly active in advising on the development of poor areas and outlying islands. This book, written by someone who has great affection for and knowledge of the common people, can teach us much about the kind of men and women who have been forgotten or disregarded in present-day Japan.

II
Language

6. LANGUAGE AND CULTURE

Kotoba to Bunka By Suzuki Takao
Tokyo: Iwanami Shinsho #858, Iwanami Shoten, 1973.

When people encounter a foreign culture, they are apt to make the mistake of generalizing on the basis of limited experience. Moreover, these generalizations invariably comply with the structure of their own culture, and from this arise all manner of misunderstandings.

In the area of language, for example, the English word *drink* generally corresponds to the Japanese word *nomu.* But the verb *nomu* not only applies to drinking water, tea, coffee, and the like, but is also used in such expressions as "to swallow powdered medicine" and "to smoke a cigarette." We can define the English verb *drink* as "the action of taking into the body through the mouth liquids that help sustain the body," whereas *nomu* can best be explained as "the action of taking something into the body through the mouth *without chewing.*" This kind of subtle difference in meaning is seldom noticed, and so understanding becomes difficult.

In speaking of culture, we can differentiate what are known as "overt culture" and "covert culture." For example, the Japanese eat with chopsticks, while Westerners use knife, fork, and spoon. This sort of phenomenon is part of overt culture. Though today Japanese often eat with spoon and fork, their way of handling a spoon differs subtly from that of Westerners. A Japanese holds the spoon more or less parallel to the line of his shoulders and sucks from it, whereas a Westerner holds it at an angle almost perpendicular to the line of his shoulders and drinks from the tip. He pours the liquid down rather than sucks it up. This kind of difference belongs to covert culture. Culture thus consists of the accumulation of countless little habits and customs of which the individual himself is unaware. Becoming aware of this hidden area is the key to understanding a foreign culture. The actual physical action described by the words "He drank soup" differs in different cultures. The portion of reality that can be conceptualized through words always represents only the tip of the iceberg.

In most European languages, the device for indicating the speaker and the person spoken to is essentially the same: first- and second-person pronouns. But in the case of the Japanese language, we cannot completely explain such words as *watakushi* or *boku* (I) and *anata* or *kimi* (you) by the term "personal pronoun." The Japanese show a clear tendency to avoid using such words as far as possible. Whether indicating oneself or a second person, words expressing the relationship of the two in terms of kinship, status, and location are widely used in preference to so-called personal pronouns. Words designating profession also are often employed to refer to a second or third person.

In Indo-European languages, the same words have been used consistently as first-person pronouns for thousands of years. The history of second-person pronouns is somewhat more complicated, but limiting the field to those languages that retain words of the *tu* type, we can say that the same usage has continued over thousands of years. The short life span of Japanese pronominal terms stands in sharp contrast. Not only can we not trace back to antiquity the so-called first-person pronouns of contemporary standard Japanese, such as *watakushi* and *boku*; the use of *boku* in the spoken language began only a little over a hundred years ago. Nor can such terms indicating second person as *kimi, omae, anata,* and *kisama* be traced back to ancient times as personal pronouns. From the beginning of Japanese history, pronominal terms indicating first and second person have changed at a dizzying rate, and the newer terms coming into use have always been adapted from substantive words originally bearing specific denotations. This pattern of change possesses certain consistent features. Every first-person pronoun, when it first came into use, in some way expressed humility toward the person addressed. In the course of long use it gradually came to show the assumption of an attitude of superiority over the person spoken to, until finally it became a word used only to indicate the inferiority of the one addressed, and fell out of common use. A classic example is the first-person pronoun *boku*. This word, used mainly in *kanbun* (written Japanese in the classical Chinese style) during the Edo period (1603-1867) and meaning "your servant," gained currency as a spoken term in the Meiji period (1868-1912), and is today best avoided when addressing a superior or in formal situations. In contrast, exactly the opposite transformation is seen in terms of address. *Kisama,* for example, literally meaning "august or noble personage," was originally used to show respect toward the person addressed. But by degrees it came to express condescension and has finally become a word whose use is sanctioned only as a rough term of scorn and contempt – or between extremely close friends.

If taking the example of a certain forty-year-old male primary-school teacher, we examine the terms for self and terms of address that he uses we find seven terms for self and, in addition to the second-person pronouns *anata, kimi, omae,* and so on, such terms of address as *sensei* (teacher), *otôsan* (father), *niisan* (big brother), and *bôya* (boy, son). Examining a number of such examples, we can discern fairly systematic rules of usage. Fundamentally supporting this regularity is the contrastive concept of *me-ue* (one of higher position vis-à-vis the speaker) and *meshita* (one of lower position vis-à-vis the speaker).

Moreover, we can regard all dialogue between Japanese, even that occurring in a social context, as ultimately a magnification of the pattern of dialogue between kin. At the same time, the fictive use of kinship terminology is extremely well developed (for example, a child will call a male adult living nearby *ojisan,* "uncle"). This is true not only of terms of address; we can show that a person will also use kinship terminology in referring to himself when talking to non-family members (for example, a male adult will call himself *ojisan* rather than "I" in addressing children).

Usually kinship terms are "egocentric particulars"; the same person will be called by different terms according to the differing standpoints of the various people related to him. But kinship terms as used in Japanese conversation are often employed not as egocentric particulars but in a very special fashion. For example, we see that a woman whose daughter has children will call her own daughter *mama.* A married woman with children will call her husband *otôsan,* "father." In both cases the speaker is making an empathetic identification, the grandmother taking the standpoint or viewpoint of her grandchildren, the wife that of her children.

Though a married couple may call each other by first name to begin with, once children are born they address each other as *papa* and *mama.* Japanese couples almost never make overt declarations of love, nor do they have saccharine terms like "honey" and "darling." For them the state of marriage is not a dynamic, contractual relationship whose mutual love is maintained through constant reaffirmation. It is rather a static, unchanging relationship: a parent-child relationship whose denial or dissolution is impossible by definition, and which is understood as a "presented" or "given" relationship. Any personal uncertainty lingering in the depths of their hearts is stabilized and resolved with the birth of children, and the world begins to revolve around their children.

The function of the first-person pronoun is to express clearly in words that one is the speaker. In Indo-European languages the speaker's verbal self-identification is effected voluntarily and independently, without relationship to the person addressed or to the circumstances of the immediate environment. First there is "I," then the second person is identified. In Japanese, on the contrary, identification of the second person precedes self-identification. One first identifies the person spoken to as son, colleague, elder, and so on, then chooses a corresponding term for self. Therefore a Japanese confronted with a complete stranger is, even linguistically, placed in an insecure position, lacking fixed coordinates, until he has grasped the other person's actual status (neighbor, influential member of one's firm, younger graduate of the same school, relative). From this stems the Japanese behavior pattern reflected in the dislike of engaging in casual conversation with strangers. At the same time, this type of self-identification depending on the object also absorbs one into the object and gives rise to the peculiar psychology seen in the strong tendency to try to dissolve the distinction between self and other. Instead of asserting himself in a clear-cut manner, a Japanese swiftly takes into consideration the feelings and thoughts of others. Even before another person has clearly expressed his opinions or wishes in words, a Japanese immediately senses them and sets about adjusting his behavior accordingly. The origin of this marked tendency to try to blend and harmonize separate individuals lies, of course, in the fact that the Japanese have always lived within a homogeneous culture.

Commentary

In this book the linguist Suzuki Takao, comparing Japanese with Indo-European languages, especially English, begins by showing how the structure of language differs in different cultures. He also demonstrates, through a wealth of easily understood, concrete examples, that even the things described by what are considered equivalent words, as well as the scope of the words, differ according to culture. In the author's view, things do not exist for people as things per se; people invest things with existence by representing them in words.

From these two starting points, the author proceeds to invite the reader to participate in the central debate: "What is language?" The invitation is extended not by means of abstract philosophical arguments but through an abundance of fresh, intriguing and concrete examples. The reader will thus come to perceive the meaning and function of language from angles hitherto overlooked.

The final chapter, "Words Indicating People," is both the longest and the most noteworthy section of the book. Herein are discussed Japanese terms for self and terms of address. Such terms and their usage in Japanese display striking idiosyncrasies in comparison with Indo-European languages. What we have presented in the summary of the book comprises only a portion of this discussion.

Distinguishing the special characteristics of a language becomes possible only through comparison with other languages. At the same time, the measure of the value and rationality of a language is to be found only within the culture to which that language belongs. Language being an essential part of culture, the reader who has understood this chapter of Suzuki's book will surely have been enabled to grasp many aspects of Japanese psychology and behavior from within.

7. THE LOGIC OF JAPANESE

Nihongo no Ronri By Toyama Shigehiko
Tokyo: Chûô Kôron-sha, 1973.

The Logic of Japanese

Ever since Japan came into contact with western European culture in the mid-nineteenth century, Japanese intellectuals have been haunted by a sense of inferiority in the matter of logic. Many Japanese hold the belief that the Japanese language is illogical. Is this really so?

One origin of the impression that Japanese is illogical as compared with European languages lies in "translation Japanese." The Japanese intellectual tradition since the Meiji period has been, in a word, "translation culture." Even today, Japan is one of the leading publishers of translated works. A tremendous volume of translations has been produced, and these have had a powerful influence on Japanese society. The language of translation Japanese is generally thought to be awkward and hard to understand. It is not unusual for a translation to be incomprehensible upon the first reading; sometimes it is even easier to understand a work in the original language. This sort of impenetrable translation is not often seen in literary works, but it is common in philosophy, ideas and the social sciences, all of which are supposed to be logical.

Japanese intellectuals have long considered that translated works, even though some portions may be incomprehensible, contain matters important and indeed the guiding principles of advanced societies, which must be learned. Instead of criticizing translations for their awkwardness, intellectuals have often chosen the course of concluding that the Japanese language itself is not logical.

In the matter of technical problems of translation, we may say that it has been thought that translation is possible by putting Japanese equivalents into a Japanese word order. The order of words within sentences is changed, but not the order of sentences. If it is true that one cannot produce Japanese without changing word order, however, then it should also hold true that without skillfully changing the sequence of sentences one cannot produce natural Japanese. A frequent cause of obscurity has been translation in which the sentence order is not altered. This is inadequate translation; and to assert on the basis of such translation that Japanese is not logical is hardly fair.

If it is true that the immediate cause of an awareness of the logic of Japanese – or in this case, its supposed want of logic – lies in the comparison of Japanese with foreign languages and in methods of translation, then it is necessary to reassess the relationship of the logic of language to translation. Might it not be that what the Japanese consider logic is that peculiar logic suited to the expression of European languages and to their representation in writing? If so, it is quite natural that such a logic cannot be expressed perfectly in Japanese. In other words, logic cannot be divorced from the language that expresses it. The Japanese language, then, should have a logic of its own.

Let us now consider the fundamentals of human linguistic activity. The logic of the language of daily life is extremely informal; nevertheless, communication is not established unless the words follow a certain route. The logicality intrinsic to language may be thought of as a line. The listener proceeds toward understanding what the speaker says as he follows the route of the speaker's words; but the way the speaker marks out his route differs according to his degree of familiarity with the listener. With complete strangers, the route is solidly paved and the listener must take care not to stray from its bounds. Logic must be rigorously organized. A classic example is in legal language. Its clarity is probably due to the fact that it is directed at unspecified persons in varied situations, who may even read laws from a standpoint of outright opposition. Though to a lesser extent than with legal language, one must in communication with strangers be sure that the mode of expression leaves no room for misunderstanding. A rigorous linguistic logic results.

By contrast, one may communicate with close friends by expressing only the gist of what is to be said. Greater economy is possible.

Among friends, what is known in the science of logic as formal logic is disliked. A typical example is conversation within the family. Family members use a language full of abbreviated expressions and leaps of logic. An outsider cannot follow at all, but the family members understand one another perfectly. They are using a logic different from "formal" logic. The language route, in such intimate relationships, need not always constitute a perfect line. Except for major points it weathers away, so to speak, so that gaps appear in the line and a series of points results.

All human beings possess the ability to link together such points and perceive them as a line. In situations where this "point logic" is understood, the stiff formality of linear logic is scorned. Highly abbreviated expressions, allowing a diversity of interpretations, are thought more interesting and richer in implication. The process of comprehension through linking points into a line is itself a kind of linguistic creation.

Japanese is characterized by "point logic." European languages developed in countries bordered by other lands, while the Japanese language evolved in an island nation. When a homogeneous people with unified customs uses a single language over an extended period of time, the degree of mutual comprehension attains an extremely high level. In effect, we may say that the logic of language as used within the family here prevails throughout society. The logic of the Japanese language is basically not of a linear type, but one whose points are much more highly developed.

The Japanese language is considered illogical because it is measured by the yardstick of the linear logic of European languages. If the principle that "point logic" develops in mature linguistic societies is granted, then it should be recognized that the Japanese language possesses its own logic.

The Aesthetics of Nonconformity in Haiku

Haiku, a short verse form of unparalleled sophistication, could only have developed from a language of "point logic." Poetry is not achieved by arranging words according to the flow of logic characteristic of prose. Haiku does not arrange disconnected short words by making them conform but instead places them so that they collide; we might say that haiku is rooted in the aesthetics of nonconformity. Striving to gain the unified image of a single verse from this group of nonconforming words, the reader is to leap to a higher harmony.

An old pond
A frog jumps in.
The sound of water

In this well-known verse by Bashô, the pond and the frog present the stillness of nature and the motion of a small animal. When the reader ventures to link the two, there is a clash between stillness and motion which is resolved as the two converge in a higher realm in which their contradictions are sublimated. Then comes "the sound of water," and, on yet another plane, the process of confrontation, blending, and harmony unfolds. From stillness to motion, then to sound: through non-consecutive, nonconforming expressions is established the sense of the unique polyphony of haiku.

Commentary

The foregoing is from the first chapter of "The Logic of Japanese," and chapter four, "The Aesthetics of Nonconformity." The book also contains very interesting discussions of the relationship between the Japanese language and creativity of foreign languages, and of the relationship between visual images and language. The author's opinions on the logic of the Japanese languages are reiterated in *The Sensibility of Japanese* (*Nihongo no Kankaku*; Tokyo: Chûô Kôron-sha, 1975):

"In a mature linguistic society, there is a tendency for linear expression to 'weather' so that the units of expression become isolated and become a series of points. This may be said of any language, but it is especially true of the language of an insular and homogeneous people. In Japanese, leaps occur from one point to another, but the points are still linked. It is a poetic progression. Poetics in Europe is akin to symbolic expression; but in Japanese a symbolism of a high level is in common use. The Japanese language is often ambiguous, but this very ambiguity permits diversity of interpretation, richness of implication, and depth, the most important elements in symbolic poetics."

The author is a professor of English, and his opinions concerning Japanese are based on comparison with foreign languages, especially English. When he discusses the peculiar character of Japanese, he emphasizes repeatedly that it must be measured against the totality of the Japanese language. His thinking is close to that of Suzuki Takao and Watanabe Shôichi, who are especially active in theory and debate on the Japanese language.

8. THE ORIGIN OF THE JAPANESE LANGUAGE

Nihongo no Kigen By Ôno Susumu

Tokyo: Iwanami Shinsho #289, Iwanami Shoten, 1957.

In 1949, man-made stone artifacts were discovered in a stratum of red clay in a cliff overlooking a road in Iwajuku, Gunma Prefecture, in the Kantô region of eastern Japan. Until then the oldest known artifacts had been pottery articles found directly above the stratum in which the stone artifacts were discovered. Red-clay strata in the Kantô region are said to have formed as the result of eruptions of Mount Fuji more than ten thousand years ago. Until the 1949 discovery, no one had thought that human beings inhabited Japan in such ancient times. The Iwajuku artifacts, undoubtedly the work of human hands, represented a major discovery. Eventually it became clear that the makers had no pottery articles, only simple stone implements, and so their culture is called pre-pottery culture.

Its artifacts include hand-axes and stone knives. It is thought that cultures with hand-axes derive from southern Asia and southern China, while those with stone knives are related to the cultures of Siberia and northern China. In considering the origin of the Japanese people, the fact that stone tools characteristic of both southern Asia and Siberia appear in Japan from the time of the earliest known culture is highly suggestive. However, it is still not clear whether Japan was continuously inhabited from the time of the pre-pottery culture to that of the succeeding Jômon culture or whether the pre-pottery people died out and Jômon represented a new influx.

The Jômon period was succeeded by the Yayoi, beginning around 300 B.C. In the latter period came wet-rice cultivation, looms and metal implements, burial urns in tombs marked by huge stones, and other manufactures different from those of the previous period. The original stimulus for this development came from without, from southern Korea. We find clear evidence in the language. For example, the fact that the modern Japanese words *hata*, field (ancient Japanese *pata* – ancient Korean *pat*), *suki*, plow (*pera* – *pyöt*), and many other agricultural terms are similar in Japanese and Korean shows clearly that Japanese agriculture introduced techniques from Korea. It is easy to find similar terms in the two languages pertaining to clothing and ornaments and to crafts. *Hataori*, loom (*pata* – *poit'ïl*), *hari*, needle (*pari* – *panʌl*), *koromo*, robe (*ösupi* – *os*), and *kama*, kiln (*kama* – *kama*) are good examples.

But here we encounter a problem: whether sweeping changes that revolutionized life could only have been due to the introduction of a new culture from abroad. Did the bearers of this new culture actually come from overseas or not? Opinions diverge widely.

Yayoi-style pottery of the oldest type has not been found in Korea. The source of the outstanding hallmark of the Yayoi culture, wet-rice cultivation, has not yet [1957] been confirmed. Moreover, changes in human bone structure between the end of the Jômon period and the beginning of the historical period in Japan do not show the major alterations that would be expected in the case of conquest by an alien people. We can interpret the changes in bone structure that are seen as the natural alterations that would accompany changes in life style. In addition, boat-building techniques were not sufficiently advanced for the massive migration that would have been necessary had Yayoi people crossed to Japan by sea, conquered the preceding Jômon people by force, and established a new colony. Even changes in pottery shapes can be regarded as reflecting a natural transition from Jômon to Yayoi ware.

When we consider the firing of pottery, however, a different opinion is advanced. The red polished ware that is one of the distinctive features of Yayoi pottery was fired at a higher temperature than Jômon pottery; and we must not ignore the fact that the colors and shapes of this Yayoi pottery are similar to those of Korean ware in general. Moreover, the use of great flat stones placed so as to form tablelike dolmens and of rectangular coffins and burial urns was customary in Korea, and similar objects have been discovered in great numbers in northern Kyushu. Artifacts that may be regarded as the prototypes of the bronze swords, spears, and *dôtaku* (large bell-shaped bronze objects) of Japan are also found in Korea.

On the basis of the above, the author advances the following views. The culture of the Yayoi period brought with it to Japan the loom, the wet-rice cultivation of the south, and the bronze swords and spears and dolmens of the north. Furthermore, these were all transmitted to Japan by a people living in southern Korea. The rice-cultivating culture that is thought to have migrated from southern China along the coast via the mouth of the Yangtze River, finally arriving in southern Korea, remained there for several hundred years. During that time southern Korea came under the domination of a Tungusic people from the north and became a composite culture. Thus when the wet-rice cultivation of the south reached Japan it was accompanied by strong northern elements. The Tungusic culture featured a sky god and a patrilineal system, while the southern culture emphasized an earth-mother deity and a matrilineal system. To distinguish these two cultural strands and discern how they interacted to form the culture of ancient Japan is the basis of understanding the essence of Japanese culture.

On the basis of the above observations, let us examine the relationship of the Japanese and Korean languages. It is not known certainly what degree of conflict, if any, there was between the people who migrated to Japan from Korea and those already living in the islands. However, we can surmise from linguistic similarities that the people from Korea held political sway, or at least looked to Korea for their political model. For example, we can cite the common features of words defining units of political land division, such as *kôri*, district (*kopori* – *kopor*), and *mura*, village (*mura* – *maïl*); words designating units of weight and measure, such as *masu*, a unit of dry measure (*masu* – *mal*), and *hiro*, fathom (*pirö* – *pal*); and the word signifying tax collection, *hataru* (*pataru* – *pat*). In the area of word structure, too, we see the following similarities in Korean and Japanese: (1) no change in word ending to indicate change of person; (2) no distinction between *r* and *l*; (3) division of pronouns into three categories indicating degree of proximity (i.e., Japanese *kore,* this; *sore,* that; *are,* that over there); and (4) accent determined by high and low pitch. Nevertheless, one cannot necessarily infer common origin from structural similarities. When and how, then, was the Japanese language formed?

Important data are afforded by correspondences between Korean and Japanese terms for parts of the body. Though we cannot find exactly equivalent terms, we do see cases in which Korean nouns correspond to Japanese verbs. However, there are more than a dozen Japanese body terms for which we can find no corresponding words in Korea; most of these words are not to be found in any of the Altaic languages, which include Turkish, Mongolian, and Manchurian as well as Korean. Equivalents for such archaic Japanese words as *ta* (hand, arm), *kaho* (face), *hitahi* (forehead), *ma* (eye), *shita* (tongue), *wata* (entrails), *kimo* (liver, gall bladder), *heso* (navel), and *karada* (body) have been discovered instead in the languages of southern peoples. This fact indicates the inadequacy of seeking the derivation of the Japanese language in correspondences with either northern or southern languages alone.

The author reasons that in the Jômon period a language of southern derivation was in use. When the Yayoi culture was introduced to Japan, it brought with it an Altaic language from southern Korea. But the introduction of this new language was not accompanied by a massive migration of people. Although the new language was able to change the grammatical pattern of the language earlier prevalent in Japan, a portion of the older vocabulary remained unchanged. Thus we can detect words of southern derivation indicating parts of the body. If questioned about the derivation of the Japanese language we should reply that it belongs to the Altaic family of languages. But because of the influence of an earlier culture and language, we can find only slight similarities to Altaic languages in Japanese words. One reason for this is that the language brought to Japan came via southern Korea, where it had already assimilated many words not of Altaic derivation but belonging to a people whose culture included many southern elements. It is possible that differences in vocabulary from such languages of Altaic derivation as Mongolian and Tungusic became increasingly pronounced as a result. We must not overlook the fact that correspondences between Japanese and Korean words include not only northern elements but also factors of southern origin.

Commentary

How and when did the Japanese language come to be spoken in the islands of Japan? Elucidation of the problem demands a wide and deep knowledge of the origin of Japanese culture. But scholarship in this area was slow to develop, and while the question of Japanese origins became a major focus of interest among Japanese linguists from the Meiji period onward, scholarship remained inadequate.

However, the dramatic advances in anthropology, archaeology, and ethnology following World War II have begun to clarify the circumstances of ancient Japanese culture. The author, on the basis of the fruits of such scholarship, has carried out a thorough and meticulous examination from the standpoint of comparative linguistics, and has attempted to present a unified interpretation of various discoveries in Japanese linguistic research.

The author places considerable weight on the southern elements in Japanese culture, pointing out that these elements were strongly established and widespread in western Japan, where the Japanese nation first took form. He also emphasizes that these southern factors were already deeply rooted as early as the Jômon period. In particular, he considers the Polynesian languages noteworthy for their phonological similarities to Japanese, and has advanced the hypothesis that a southern language of Polynesian derivation was in use in Japan in the Jômon period. In the succeeding Yayoi period, the prototype of the Japanese language emerged with the advent of a people from southern Korea who had inherited a southern rice-cultivating culture but were under the political domination of a northern Tungusic people.

The author's methods of comparison and his views on the rules of phonology do not necessarily have the support of the entire academic community. He uses his analysis of the pronunciation of words in the oldest extant Japanese documents, such as the eighth-century *Kojiki* and *Manyôshû,* as shown in the phonetic readings of Chinese ideographs, as important evidence of the relationship of Japanese with northern languages. There are also strong arguments in opposition to his analysis. While the author's theory of the origin of the Japanese language cannot be said to represent the view generally accepted in academic circles, it has attracted attention as an ambitious attempt to elucidate the origin of Japanese culture on the basis of linguistics.

Nihongo no Kigen has been translated into English under the title *The Origin of the Japanese Language* (Tokyo: Kokusai Bunka Shinkôkai, 1970).

III
Spiritual Life

9. THE JAPANESE FESTIVAL

Nihon no Matsuri By Yanagita Kunio
Tokyo: Kadokawa Bunko, white series #83, Kadokawa Shoten, 1956.

It is only through familiarity with the ceremonial observances known as *matsuri*, "festivals" that an understanding of the religious beliefs peculiar to Japan is to be gained, in terms of their original forms, and the alterations that have been made through the years. When compared with such organized religions as Buddhism and Christianity, the most immediately obvious characteristic is that they are not derived from or based on a canon of sacred writings. Nor have there ever been preachers, or evangelism, apart from the ceremonies and observances themselves. In the past there were no full-time priests, and of course, no seminaries or similar training programs for the clergy. While there were, in actual fact, a large number of men in positions of leadership for each shrine, the passing on of doctrine was effected more by living example than through verbal daily instruction. In fact, specific verbal instruction was deferentially avoided. Only through regular participation in the various annual festivals was the deepening, and renewal, of religious experience and knowledge thought possible. Thus the festival was the one way to religious enlightenment in the national religion known as Shinto.

Japan is a country where festivals abound. There is a festival being held almost every day of the year somewhere in Japan. Festivals are generally thought of as being showy and highly animated, but they were originally extremely modest affairs in which only the small number of villagers directly attached to the shrine would gather for offerings and sacred sake. The word *matsuri* itself means "to be in the presence of and to render service to a deity."

The erection of some sort of wooden pole was long a special characteristic of Shinto festivals. It served as a guide for the deity, who was believed to descend from above during the festival. It was decorated with sacred folded paper, strands of hemp, or strips of cloth, and at night a fire was built nearby for illumination. In earliest times, a straight and tall live tree was chosen as the sacred spot for the deity to descend. Later, after the construction of shrine buildings became popular, it was believed that the deity resided in the shrine at all times. There are still numbers of great festivals, such as that of the famous Suwa Shrine in Nagano Prefecture, in which a post or pole is still erected.

In ancient times, the Japanese day began at approximately six o'clock in the evening. A festival day commenced with the evening meal and was completed with breakfast the following morning. The festival itself was held indoors, with torches or bonfires burning outside in the garden or courtyard. The main event of the festival was a sort of all night "cloistering," during which the participants shut themselves up in the shrine, entertained the deity with sacred sake and specially prepared foods, and awaited his appearance or his message, after which all would partake of the offerings.

The wine and food for the festival were originally prepared so as to insure absolute purity, and only those members of the community who had gone through a strict regimen of fasting and abstinence, to rid them of all defilement, were thought worthy to participate. The abstinence was a set period of deference in preparation for worship. It was believed that unless it was fully observed, the deity would not only refuse to recognize the festival, but might also be angered. Such asceticism was observed by all who participated in festivals, and there are still places today where the custom of sleeping during the day and staying awake all night for several days prior to the festival is observed. Every effort is made to spend the time in near-complete silence. In most places, it is now the custom today for only the immediate family of the man responsible for the festival to observe all the abstinence requirements. They vary from district to district and from shrine to shrine. In some areas, the home of the festival headman is thoroughly cleaned, and no one but the headman himself is allowed to enter the main room, which has been designated as the sacred abode of the deity. The headman is not allowed to visit the homes of others, and he must allow no one into his house during the period of abstinence. He is also required to light a torch and sprinkle himself with salt water every day. In other cases, he is permitted to make visits, but must not accept food or drink away from home. He must also abstain from sexual intercourse, and he must not drink tea or smoke.

In Buddhism, all animal foods are forbidden during periods of fasting, while Shinto only forbids the consumption of animal flesh and blood. Shinto is very strict concerning the use of fire. For instance, fire must not be accepted from a defiled house (meaning the house of a recently bereaved family), and great importance is laid on water purification. A remnant of the custom of washing the entire body before approaching the presence of a deity remains in the ceremonial basins found before Shinto shrines today.

Festive preparations for entertaining the deity were very much like preparations to receive any other eminent guest. The best foods (among which something from the sea was always included) and wines were set out in the most attractive possible manner. There were competitions in most of the traditional sports and entertainments, such as sumo wrestling, rope-pulling, cock-fighting, and bull-baiting.

Sacred Shinto performances known as *kagura* are thought to have originally been not dances but rather recitations or chants, to which gestures and movements were added later. Dance came into being when worshippers faced their god and concentrated upon chants of praise and adoration. "We do not doubt that you will come to us in time of need and make unto us holy revelations"; and presently there came a state of religious ecstasy between the realms of god and man. Since the annual festival was the opportunity to calm the heart of the deity and receive his blessings, it was not considered sufficient to sing his praises. The believers faced their god and uttered words of deep respect at the moment when it was thought that he would be most satisfied. "Have you not done these things for us since ancient times? We remember these sayings from generations past." And again: "We know of the covenant with our ancestors to listen to our prayers and answer them." The chanters were presently moved to intense awareness and to dance-like rhythms and gestures.

In the Noh drama, there are still remnants of this recitation and dance. It is thought that the turning and whirling of the performers in village *kagura* dances are also a remnant, although both dancer and audience have come to think of them as set dance forms, and their specific significance was forgotten long ago. The people and their gods were in a far more intimate relationship, and worshipers welcomed the deity to the festival in much more the manner of an honored guest than is the case today.

The single most important change appears to be the development of a group that may be termed "spectators." There appeared among the participants a group whose only purpose was to observe the proceedings from a purely aesthetic point of view. While this introduced a showy, spectacular aspect, it also resulted in a certain separation from the shrine as the absolute center of religious life. Though they too lived in the villages, the festivals was for them merely something to observe. This is not a recent phenomenon. It was already in evidence before the Meiji Restoration of 1868. As the agricultural villages became affluent; there arose the desire to please this new group. Believers, however, did not abandon the covenant made by their ancestors. Thus a large number of ceremonies, old and new, have all been brought under the single term "festival."

Commentary

Japan is a country where festivals abound in very great variety and number. Almost every day of the year there is a festival somewhere in Japan. Counting only major festivals, the annual number is estimated to be around fifty thousand.

Yanagita attempts to search through a great variety of festivals to discover their basic elements. He finds the following five to be common denominators: 1) a festival site; 2) a family whose head presides over the ceremonies; 3) a unified ritual that serves as the nucleus of the festival (the presentation of offerings, a *kagura* dance, or a parade to escort the deity from the shrine to the festival site); 4) votive offerings; and 5) a special festival day or days which relate directly to a season (spring and autumn festivals are for the purpose of praying for or giving thanks for a rich harvest; summer festivals are generally held in urban areas to exorcise epidemics and floods; and winter festivals usually center upon the winter solstice and have to do with rites of purification, such as the burning of sacred objects, and fasting).

Yanagita also attempts at some length to clarify the origins of festivals, and places great importance upon fasting and abstinence, which earlier writers tended to treat rather lightly.

Yanagita Kunio (1875-1962) accepted a position with the Ministry of Agriculture and Commerce after graduation from the University of Tokyo. During his youth he was associated with literary circles. He wrote poerty and worked to introduce foreign literature. In his thirties, he traveled widely as a labor organizer. His travels finally led him to concentration on Japanese folklore. He was publisher for the magazine *Ethnology* (*Minzoku*), and he directed the "Folklore Society" (Minkan Denshô no Kai), which later became the "Japan Folklore Association" (Nihon Minzoku Gakkai), and which has worked toward the definition and preservation of Japanese ethnology. He wrote more than one hundred books on Japanese ethnology.

10. THE CONCEPT OF HELL

Jigoku no Shisô By Umehara Takeshi
Tokyo: Chûkô Shinsho #134, Chûô Kôron-sha, 1967.

At the mention of hell, many Japanese think at once of paradise and mock both as Buddhist superstitions calculated to arouse moral fear. But the concept of hell and that of paradise belong to two entirely different lineages. Belief in hell was widespread in the India of Sakyamuni, the historical Buddha and founder of Buddhism. But Sakyamuni, a highly intellectual thinker, made no definite pronouncements on the subject of hell. He believed that life is suffering, that desire is the source of suffering, and that desire must therefore be abolished.

After the death of Sakyamuni, many Buddhist sects developed from his teachings. All of them inherited his view that life is suffering. From this it followed that the world in which we live is a place of suffering, or, in other words, hell. It was taught that living beings transmigrate among six worlds – hell; the worlds of hungry spirits, animals, warlike demons (*asura*); human beings and heaven. Hell, interpreted as one of the six worlds, was said to have actual existence below this earth. Descriptions and portrayals of hell acquired detail from age to age.

The teachings of Sakyamuni emphasized negation and were highly pessimistic. As time passed, there came a reaction against this pessimism. The Mahayana School of Buddhism was a result. Mahayana is more liberal than the older school – sometimes called the Hinayana School – and incorporates the merciful ideal of the bodhisattva, a being who has reached enlightenment and who is eligible for Nirvana but who postpones his entry into that state in order to be of help to other living beings. The Buddhism that was introduced into Japan in the sixth century of the Christian Era was of the Mahayana School. It was a religion which recognized the dark aspects of life and sang bright hymns in praise of life as well. It seems probable that the early Japanese lived optimistically in affirmation of life and in the worship of nature gods. Into this world, Buddhism introduced simultaneously a speculative, negative philosophy and an affirmative philosophy. Although Confucianism was later to become popular, and still later Japan was to undergo modernization and Westernization, Buddhist sentiments still retain a strong hold on the Japanese mind.

Buddhism has split into many sects. An element common to them all has had a strong influence on Japanese culture. If I might venture a hypothesis, I would suggest that three concepts have remained constant in Buddhism and have accounted for its continuing influence: the concept of life, the concept of mind, and the concept of hell.

The Concept of Life

The ancient indigenous religion of Japan is Shinto, a worship of life in natural phenomena. Esoteric Buddhist thought, influenced by magical tantric and yoga ideas, was introduced into Japan by two great priests, Saichô (767-822) and Kûkai (774-835). Esoteric Buddhism teaches belief in the Cosmic Buddha (*Mahâvairocana-tathâgata*) as a god of universal life and as a nature god who gives forth unlimited life. It took root in Japan because of an element of nature worship that it shares with the native Shinto. A reverence for life seems to be central to the Japanese view of the world.

The Concept of Mind

During the Nara period (710-794), the Buddhist teaching of consciousness (*vijñapti-mâtratâ*), which includes a detailed and subtle analysis of the operations of the mind, was popular in Japan and exerted a great influence on Japanese thought. The Chinese character *hsin* (transliterated *shin* for Japanese) is used to write the native Japanese word *kokoro,* which is variously translated as "mind," "spirit," "the heart," or "the moral nature" but which is used in this text only in the first sense. It does not occur often in the eighth-century *Records of Ancient Matters* (*Kojiki*). It occurs with striking frequency, however, in the famous eleventh-century romance *The Tale of Genji* (*Genji Monogatari*). From the Heian period, the word *kokoro* becomes of central importance in all Japanese literature. This development would have been unthinkable without the influence of the Buddhist teachings of consciousness expounded by the Kegon and other Nara sects.

The Concept of Hell

Chih-i (538-597), who founded the school of Buddhism known as T'ien-t'ai and who lived in China in a time of warfare and strife, devoted intense thought to the idea of hell. Saichô brought Chih-i's teachings to Japan, where they became the foundation of the Japanese sect known as Tendai. Together with Shingon, which was founded by Kûkai, Tendai was very important during the Heian period. The basic teachings of T'ien-t'ai and Tendai are a profound analysis of the human condition into ten states of existence. Of these ten, six are called the delusive states, experienced by those who have not attained enlightenment. Tendai insists that one must always be aware of human suffering, delusion and demonic action. Further, one must realize their emptiness and try to break all ties with them.

The Tendai sect employed the idea of hell as a means of spreading its beliefs. In his *Essentials of Salvation* (*Ôjô Yôshû*) the Tendai priest Genshin (942-1017) related the idea of hell to that of paradise. Genshin taught that this world is one of suffering and defilement and that man ought to strive to abandon it and attain the future world of paradise.

The concept of paradise, or the Pure Land (*Sukhâvatî*), derives from the teachings of the Jôdo or Pure Land sect of Buddhism, which is thought to have arisen in India in the first century of the Christian Era. It passed into China and entered Japan in the seventh century. The Buddha revered by this sect is called Amida (his name is a combination of *Amitâyus* – Buddha of Infinite Life – and *Amitâbha* – Buddha of Infinite Light). The sect holds that all who call on his name will be reborn in his Western Paradise, which is called the Pure Land, and will become Buddhas themselves. Genshin related the idea of the Pure Land to the Tendai concept of hell. In Japan the Pure Land teaching became the foundation for the Jôdo sect and the Jôdo-shin sect or True Sect of Pure Land Buddhism, which teach that man should look directly at human suffering, to understand values other than worldly ones, to advance the cause of good, to cease doing evil, and to find salvation from the fear of death.

Shinran (1173-1262), the founder of the Jôdo-shin sect, abolished the idea of a hell in the future by insisting that Amida Buddha saves even the wickedest. Jôdo-shin makes provisions for two Pure Lands, graded according to the purity or impurity of the person's faith, and rejects hell as a place, though it admits that hell can exist in the individual.

In Shinran, the Japanese found a way out of hell to a realm of joy in boundless life. According to Christian beliefs, he who accepts Christ is saved. As long as Buddhist thought insists that human life is basically suffering, however, hell is inescapable. Buddhism thus stimulates man to see the truth of the human situation.

In the following paragraphs, comments will be made on representative writings to illustrate the influence of the concept of hell on Japanese literature.

The Tale of Genji: Demons of Passion

Though a paean to the ecstasies of passion, this famous book is at the same time a lament for the deep suffering arising from those same passions. As a devout Buddhist, Murasaki Shikibu, the court lady who wrote the tale and who lived in the tenth and eleventh centuries, was a close observer of the hell that human beings harbor within themselves.

The Tales of the Heike: World of Warlike Demons

The military romance called *The Tales of the Heike* (*Heike Monogatari*) consists of twelve volumes and an additional volume known as the *Kanchô-no-maki,* which recounts the last years of Kenreimon-In. This lady, the mother of the child emperor Antoku, barely escaped from the battle of Dannoura (1185), in which the Heike (Taira clan) was decisively defeated by the Genji (Minamoto clan). She lived in straitened retirement as a nun. In the *Kanchô-no-maki*, she is depicted as reflecting on her past life and telling how she has known the six delusive states of human existence. *The Tale of Genji* depicts sufferings from the hell within us. *The Tales of the Heike*, on the other hand, is a historical romance in which the external world is seen as hell. *The Tales of the Heike* achieved tremendous popularity and was recited to lute accompaniment. This particular version of hell thus gained common acceptance.

The World of Zeami: Deluded Spirits

Zeami (1363-1443) was one of the great masters of the Noh drama and among the most important aestheticians of Japan. When the Noh was in its formative stage in Japan, a Chinese dramatic form called the Yüan drama (the *yüan-ch'u*) was also in formation. A comparison between the two reveals a characteristic of Japanese culture. The Yüan plays, created under the affirmative and practical influence of Confucian thought, present stories in which virtue is rewarded and wickedness punished. The Noh, which was influenced by Buddhism, deals with the complaints of spirits who are unable to find salvation. Although Buddhism teaches that the same kind of life is common throughout the universe, it also teaches that actualities are empty and transitory. The Noh drama deals with the superhuman and the fantastic. The genius of Zeami succeeded in giving artistic representation to the idea that hell is to be found within the human heart.

The World of Chikamatsu Monzaemon: Elopement to Death

Both the Japanese puppet theatre and the Kabuki rely heavily on two major dramatic forms: *jidaimono*, historical plays performed in a highly stylized fashion; and *sewamono* performed in a more natural style and based on everyday matters. The plays of Chikamatsu Monzaemon (1653-1724) in the *sewamono* style frequently end with the suicide of a pair of lovers. The eye of the playwright is fixed on life; but life is a pathway to death. Some found life a hell from which there was no hope of escape in this world. Deciding to risk everything on the hope of happiness in the next world, they sometimes elected to kill themselves. It was about them that Chikamatsu wrote.

Later Writers

Concern with hell is to be found in the works of many men of letters since the Meiji Restoration of 1868. Most notable among them are Miyazawa Kenji (1896-1933), who was a believer in the teachings of the Lotus Sutra, and Dazai Osamu (1909-1948), who was haunted by a picture of hell that he saw as a child.

Commentary

It is impossible to think of Japanese philosophy and culture apart from Buddhism. In an attempt to make concrete investigations of the influence of Buddhism on Japanese life, the author, an authority on Buddhist philosophy, develops his argument on "The Concept of Hell." He divides his material into two sections. The first, treated in his first five chapters, traces the concept of hell from Sakyamuni through Chinese T'ien-t'ai philosophy and the work of Genshin and that of Shinran.

In the first part of the book, the following comment is of special importance. "To people near death, Genshin said, 'You are about to go to a wonderful place.' But no matter how assiduously he spoke of the beautiful paradise of the Pure Land, Genshin found that his words only saddened the person to whom he said them. There were both bitterness and sweetness in the sentiments Genshin expressed to the dying. This bitter-sweet quality can be considered the prototype of Japanese sentimentalism. Many Buddhist hymns have been written about it. The same feelings are reflected in the *jôruri* ballads that accompany the traditional puppet theatre, in shorter ballads, and even in the modern popular song. Much of the greatness of Genshin lay in his creating this prototypical Japanese sentiment."

The priest Shinran (1173-1262) founded the Jôdo-shin sect of Buddhism, which was given organized form by Kakunyo (1270-1351). Jôdo-shin became the most popular of all Japanese Buddhist sects. Under the slogan "Hate and abandon this polluted world and seek happiness in the next world," it came in frequent conflict with the feudal government. Because of its role in the peasant uprisings of the fifteenth and sixteenth centuries, Jôdo-shin became a rallying point for the commoner in the open expression of his dissatisfactions. Before the development of Jôdo-shin, Buddhist teachings had been primarily for the ruling classes. Jôdo-shin carried Buddhist thought to the common people, who came to understand the concept of hell in human life that Shinran evolved.

The second half of Umehara's book (chapters six through eleven) analyzes representative literary works from *The Tale of Genji* to the novels of Dazai Osamu, who died in 1948. The analysis traces the concept of hell through the centuries.

Umehara's highly individual interpretations of great literary works is a break with tradition. Thus he criticizes the great Edo-period scholar and critic Motoori Norinaga (1730-1801) for saying that *The Tale of Genji* depicts the emotions exactly as they were. He objects to dismissing *The Tales of the Heike* as dealing with transitoriness and nothing more. He sees it rather as the story of the hell created by the selfish and inordinately ambitious Taira no Kiyomori, the head of the clan, to whom is attributed the remark that the Taira contain all that is possible to humanity.

Umehara shows that Japanese culture is not one of beautified death. It is rather a culture of life, making life more strikingly vivid by the consciousness of death. The book ends with this admonition: "Look directly at the hell latent in human life because only thus is it possible to find the path to paradise. This is the truth of Buddhism."

11. ZEN AND JAPANESE CULTURE

Zen to Nihon Bunka By Suzuki Daisetsu
Tokyo: Iwanami Shinsho #75, Iwanami Shoten, 1940.

Zen is a form of Buddhism which was introduced from India into China in the first century A.D. and flourished there around the eighth century, and which was introduced into Japan in the twelfth century. Through the practice of Zen one seeks enlightenment to the essence of Buddhism, which is *prajñâ* (transcendental wisdom) and *karunâ* (love, compassion). To attain to *prajñâ* is to grasp the significance of life and the world. Thus enlightened, one is no longer caught up in individual concerns, whether of gain or loss, pleasure or pain, but realizes in their place *karunâ*, which is the desire to bring others to enlightenment. Zen seeks to awaken a person to the *prajñâ* which resides dormant within himself but which is encumbered by *avidyâ* (ignorance) and *karma*, both the slaves of intellection.

Zen rejects intellection, that is, verbalism and logic, and indeed, negates any act of conceptualization. Words are not the thing itself, and Zen insists that a person experience the thing itself – the reality, in other words, not the empty abstraction.

There are three kinds of knowledge: that which one attains to through verbal communication, such as reading or listening; that which one attains to through scientific inquiry – observation, experiment, analysis, and inference; and that which one attains to only through intuitive understanding. The practitioner of Zen seeks to attain to this third kind of knowledge, which comes from deep within his own being.

Zen and Japanese Art

A Chinese artist thus described to his disciples the secret of painting (followed religiously by Japanese artists as well): "Draw a bamboo for ten years, become a bamboo, then forget all about bamboos when you are drawing. Once in possession of an infallible technique, you place yourself at the mercy of inspiration."

To become a bamboo, to forget even that you are one with it while drawing it – this is the Zen of the bamboo. This is the moving with the "rhythmic movement of the spirit" which resides in the bamboo as well as in the artist himself. What is now required is to have a firm hold upon this spirit and yet not be conscious of the fact. It is a very difficult task achieved only after long spiritual training. The Eastern peoples have been taught since very early times to subject themselves to this discipline if they want to accomplish something in the world of art and religion. Zen has thus given expression to it: "One in All and All in One." In the statement is creative genius. It is to be understood as an expression of the intuitive way in which Zen grasps the world, not as a theory of knowledge. The "All" and "One" are not to be conceptually analyzed, nor to be taken separately. "One in All and All in One" is to be understood simply as the perfect expression of *prajñâ*.

One of the commonest Zen sayings has it: "Willows are green and flowers red." It takes each aspect of reality for what it is, and no more. We could also say, "Bamboos are straight and pines are gnarled." Facts of experience are accepted as they are. Experience is the absolute reality. Those who proceed to analyze the experience and try to establish a theory of knowledge are not students of Zen.

Imbalance, asymmetry, extreme economy of brush stroke, *wabi, sabi,* simplification, and cognate ideas make up the most conspicuous and characteristic features of Japanese art and all Japanese culture. They emanate from one central perception of the truth of Zen, which sees all things as things in themselves and at the same time sees the one in the many and the many in the one.

A painting of a solitary bird on a dead branch, for example, in which not a line, not a shade, not a mass is wasted, is enough to show the desolate mood of autumn, when the days grow short and chilly and nature begins to recall once again her display of luxurious summer vegetation. It makes one feel somewhat pensive, but it also gives an opportunity to turn the attention inwards. The inner life, given proper attention, spreads out its rich treasures in full view.

From it comes an appreciation of what is known as *wabi* in the dictionary of Japanese cultural terms. *Wabi* means spiritual richness in poverty. Stated in terms of practical everyday life, *wabi* is life in a little hut, like the log cabin of Thoreau; meager fare, such as a dish of vegetables picked in the neighboring fields; an existence close to nature that rejoices even in the pattering of a gentle spring rain. *Wabi* represents one of the ways in which the Japanese, and all Eastern peoples, attempt to grasp life from within, not from without.

One of the virtues of the Japanese sensibility is that it does not conceive of things logically and philosophically but grasps the deepest truths intuitively. It then represents them symbolically in palpable, realistic forms.

This artistic sensibility effects aloofness from conventional rules. Where a line or mass or balancing element might be expected, there is none. It is missed, and yet this very lack awakens unexpected feelings of pleasure. What would normally be taken as an obvious deficiency or shortcoming, is not felt it to be so. Imperfection becomes in itself a form of perfection. Beauty does not necessarily spell perfection of form. This has been one of the favorite tricks of Japanese artists – to find beauty in imperfection and even ugliness. And when this beauty of imperfection is accompanied by antiquity, rustic unpretentiousness, or the subtle richness of withered, monochrome nature, we have a glimpse of *sabi,* so prized by Japanese connoisseurs.

Zen and the Samurai

Zen became intimately related with the life of the samurai from its beginnings in Japan. It sustained the samurai both morally and philosophically: morally, because as a religion it allows no distractions once a course of action has been embarked upon: philosophically, because it treats life and death without distinction. Zen is a religion of the will, and because it rejects intellection and values intuition it has appealed to the warrior and soldier. Zen discipline is simple, direct, self-reliant, and self-denying, and its ascetic tradition was congenial to the fighting spirit. It has been historically linked to the military classes. It was taken up by the Hôjô, noted for the severe frugality and moral discipline with which they ruled Japan from the end of the elegant, refined, even effeminate Heian period (794-1185). When Tokiyori (1227-63) and Tokimune (1251-84), two Hôjô regents, became followers of Zen, its influence was felt throughout the entire country.

The problem of death is a most pressing one for all of us, and especially for the warrior, whose life is precarious. The very notion of death extends the consciousness beyond the limitations of this finite life, and simultaneously, makes it worth taking seriously. Zen rejected any appeal to learning or moral training or ritual. This was a great attraction to the relatively unsophisticated mind of the samurai, who turned to Zen with the idea of mastering death. Zen simply urged a warrior to go ahead with whatever decision, rational or irrational, he had arrived at, and to act without looking backward once he had made the decision. It also taught him to attain to a certain state known in Zen teaching as "no-mind" (*mushin*), beyond the duality of life and death.

The Zen attitude toward death has affected all Japanese. To die resolutely, bravely, and with no regrets is one of the thoughts dearest to the Japanese. He will forgive the criminal his crime if he dies thus. The ideal is to be blown away like cherry blossoms before the wind. There is possibly no Japanese philosophy of life, but there is a philosophy of death. It may at times appear reckless, but it has urged the ultimate sacrifice for a cause thought worthy.

Zen and Swordsmanship

The sword was most intimately linked with the life of the samurai. It became the symbol of loyalty and self-sacrifice and an object of universal reverence, endowed with a certain mystical quality. When making a sword, the swordsmith invokes the aid of his guardian deity and commences his work only after purifying both himself and his workshop. He exerts himself to the limit of his mental, physical and spiritual powers to create a sword that is a true work of art, something that appeals to the soul, and may be seen not as a weapon of destruction but as a source of inspiration.

The samurai always carried with him two swords, a longer one for attack and defense, and a shorter one to direct against himself if the need arose. The sword was the supreme symbol of dignity and honor, contributing to moral and spiritual advancement. The Way of the Sword was in harmony, then, with the Way of Zen. The samurai reached the ultimate stage of swordsmanship when he attained to the state known as "no-mind."

Commentary

Zen to Nihon Bunka was first published in 1938 under the title *Zen Buddhism and Its Influence on Japanese Culture*. Suzuki wrote for a non-Japanese audience, although many of his works, including the one under discussion, have subsequently been translated into Japanese. He presents his ideas on Zen and its relation to Japanese culture under these general headings: "What is Zen?," "Japanese Art Culture," "Zen and the Study of Confucianism," "Zen and the Samurai," "Zen and Swordsmanship," "Zen and Haiku," "Zen and the Art of Tea," and "Love of Nature."

Suzuki stresses several themes in his book. First, Zen disregards ritual and focuses on the spiritual. Zen requires one to go beyond theoretical and verbal interpretations and to rely instead on direct, intuitive experience. Second, Zen is intimately related to art, but not to morality; it is artistic in its sensibility, and yet amoral. Third, Zen and Nature are of the same world. Zen training takes place as a rule in monasteries deep in the mountains, and it stresses the bond with Nature. Zen tells us to enter into the very object of contemplation; and this emphasis has made artists seek to express the spirit of an object in a painting.

Zen is also intimately related to the art of tea, which is an artistic expression of man's deeply felt desire to return to Nature and become one with it.

Despite the considerable influence of Zen in the past, it is very difficult to say just how much the Japanese of today practices Zen in his own everyday life, or just how much of the spirit of Zen remains in ancient traditions. Still, we cannot afford to forget its influence on Japanese culture.

12. ANCESTOR WORSHIP

Sosen Sûhai By Takeda Chôshû

Kyoto: Heirakuji Shoten, 1957.

"Ancestor worship" refers to the worship of one's ancestors or to a worshipful feeling directed toward one's ancestors, an emotion held by most Japanese. At any rate, it is considered abnormal to rebel against this custom and feeling. Very few people, however, can determine either the inner meaning of such worship or the identity of their own ancestors. How indeed did such a peculiar phenomenon arise?

Ancestor worship in Japan is formed from a blending of the social factor of the *ie* and the religious factor of ancestral spirits. Although the word *ie* is usually translated as "family," its actual meaning is quite different. An *ie* can include more than one pair of married couples or none at all; furthermore, an *ie* continues over the generations, transcending time. The concept of the *ie* includes the following: (1) consanguineous relatives in lineal descent and their families (grandparents, parents, sons and their wives, grandsons and their wives, and so on); (2) collateral consanguineous relatives and their families (siblings and their spouses, nephews and nieces and their spouses, and so on); (3) nonconsanguineous, or "fictive," relatives in lineal descent and their families (an adopted son and his family, the families of servants or employees); and (4) nonconsanguineous collateral "fictive" relatives and their families (the families of hereditary servants or employees). Some or all of these patterns may be included in the *ie* either simultaneously or at different times.

Severance of blood lineage does not of itself mean discontinuation of the *ie*. When severance of the lineage is foreseen, its continuation is secured through the adoption of an heir. And even if the lineage should be broken, it can be revived by designating a successor. In this way the demand that the *ie* be perpetuated is considered a natural obligation by the Japanese, all of whom, of course, belong to an *ie*.

Ancestor worship tends to be popularly thought of as something established on the basis of blood lineage. But if that were so, we could not explain why it is that ancestors are reckoned only through the paternal line, ignoring the maternal line; nor could we explain the fact that although the progenitor of a line must himself have had parents, the latter are not recognized by the *ie* as being among its ancestors. The *ie* is established at a specific time, and the inheritance by the head of the household of the right and duty to command the *ie* is the basis of its continuation. Because the concept of veneration of blood ties becomes closely associated with this in a secondary fashion, outwardly the *ie* appears to be based on consanguineal linear succession.

The origin of the feeling that it is an obligation to perpetuate the *ie* is closely linked to the fact or idea of the genesis of the *ie*; this is the focus of concern. The origin of the *ie* being all-important, its progenitor must be a figure possessed of absolute value. For this reason the succession of the *ie* is insisted upon as an absolute. Here lies the actual basis for ancestor worship. All members of the *ie* must worship the ancestors; to deny them is to be guilty of rebellion and immorality against the *ie*. This has to do with the ethics of the Japanese *ie*, which in this way differs fundamentally from religious beliefs left to individual preference.

Excluding cases like the imperial family or the ancient Fujiwara clan, few people can trace their lineage back over dozens of generations and identify its actual historical progenitor. But within those families that today bear the responsibility for their *ie*, it is taken for granted that at some time the *ie* did have a progenitor; thus for most people the progenitor exists as a spirit. Even when the actual progenitor is clearly known, his identity blends with the distinctive Japanese concept of spirit, as will be seen below, and in practice ancestor worship takes the form of a sort of religious belief in ancestors and ancestral spirits.

Let us now consider the character of the extended kinship group known as the *dôzoku*. Associations of several *ie* based on geographical ties are of two kinds: horizontally linked alliances and *dôzoku* alliances. The families (*ie*) comprising the former are equal in status and are on an equal footing; the *dôzoku*, by contrast, bears the striking characteristic of being centered on a main family, to which branch families are connected in a vertical relationship. In most *dôzoku* the surname and house crest are the same for all member families, and the alliance extends over all aspects of daily life – farm management, partnership in cooperative labor organizations, and common ownership of certain property.

As interfamilial relationships, *dôzoku* persist over the generations. The consanguineous lineal branch family founded by a younger son is the usual type, but nonconsanguineous, or "fictive," branches, such as those founded by loyal servants or employees, are not uncommon. Again, a branch may be established originally on the basis of consanguineous lineage, but while the blood tie will weaken with successive generations, there is no change in the principles underlying the structure of the *dôzoku* itself. We can regard the *dôzoku* as an extended or enlarged *ie*.

The inseparable relationship between the *ie* and ancestor worship applies to the *dôzoku* in exactly the same way on a larger scale. Two striking characteristics mark *dôzoku* rites. First, the enshrined spirits, whether identified as Shinto *kami* ("deity" or "spirit") or as buddhas, are of many and diverse types, and the rites themselves are performed in as many different ways as there are *dôzoku*. Second, despite this diversity all *dôzoku* are exactly alike in that while all individuals outside the *dôzoku* are strictly excluded from participation, for *dôzoku* members participation is both a right and a duty.

The *kami* of the *dôzoku* may be identified as the agricultural deity Inari, the warrior god Hachiman, or any other of a variety of Shinto or Buddhist deities. Moreover, if the *dôzoku* deity is Inari, for example, the fact that a particular member of the *dôzoku* does not subscribe to the Inari cult does not excuse him from participation in the *dôzoku* rites. Likewise, no matter how fervent a devotee of Inari a person may be, if he is not a member of the *dôzoku* he is not permitted to take part in ritual activities at that shrine. This phenomenon of exclusiveness arises because the original *dôzoku* deity is considered to be the progenitor of that *dôzoku*. In other words, it suffices that the progenitor is an entity to be venerated; its powers or spiritual efficacy are not at issue. This entity is easily assimilated to and blended with various other *kami*, buddhas, and other spirits, a factor that imparts a religious appearance to *dôzoku* rites.

That its ancestor or progenitor thus becomes the object of worship of an *ie* or *dôzoku* without reference to a specifically identified progenitor or ancestral line is closely allied to the general Japanese concept of spirits: the spirit of a dead person is gradually purified with the passage of time, shedding its individuality in the process and eventually becoming apotheosized and assimilated into the collective entity known as the sacred "ancestral spirit."

This process is strongly suggested by the dual-tomb system. The common practice is to erect a tombstone over the burial site; this is known as the single-tomb system. But in the older dual-tomb system a second tombstone is raised at a different site from that of the actual burial, the second tombstone marking a purely ritual site. In usual practice, pilgrimages to the burial tomb cease after a certain length of time. This is because during the period in which it is enshrined in the burial tomb, that is, while a degree of taboo pollution and individuality adheres to it, the spirit of the dead person is gradually apotheosized and unites with the ancestral spirits; when this process is complete, the spirit comes to be enshrined in the ritual tomb, or pilgrimage tomb.

The transformation from spirit of the dead to ancestral spirit, seen in the dual-tomb system, is shown still more clearly in the custom whereby the thirty-third anniversary of a death (or the fiftieth anniversary in some areas) is called the "cessation of mourning," and marks the end of Buddhist memorial services for the spirit of the deceased. At this time the spirit is purified and becomes a *kami.* Because an ancestral spirit is an entity lacking substance or individuality, it is enshrined as an "ancestor" or "progenitor" and so its identity is easily interchanged with that of a particular *kami* or buddha.

The world in which the spirit of a dead person comes to rest when it has been purified to the status of an ancestral spirit must be, above all, a pure and sacred realm completely divorced from the polluted world of daily life. Since ancient times the Japanese people have identified this spirit realm with mountains. It is extremely noteworthy that in all regions of Japan, most of the temples famous as "sacred places" are purposely located in mountainous areas. The concept of ancestral spirits being secluded in the mountains is suggested by the fact that most places closely related to funerary rites are found in mountain areas and that most pilgrimage tombs and sites enshrining *dôzoku* deities are set up in raised areas near mountains.

The ancestral spirits, situated in the mountains from where they watch over their descendants' daily lives, are believed to visit their families at the midsummer Bon festival and at Shôgatsu (New Year), when they converse happily with the family. The Bon festival has been subjected to heavy Buddhist influence, and with the switch from the old lunar calendar to the solar calendar the festival has changed drastically from its original form, which centered on the fifteenth day of the seventh lunar month. The diffusion of the new calendar has also caused New Year festivities to shift from an original form centered on the fifteenth day of the first lunar month to one centered on January 1. This has strengthened the character of Shôgatsu as a year-opening observance.

Despite these later accretions, we can still discern in both Bon and Shôgatsu the common function of welcoming those who visit the home (*ie*) from without. At Shôgatsu the pine and at Bon mountain flowers serve as the ancestral spirits' abode for the duration of their visit, as the spirits are considered to descend from the mountains. Once received, the ancestral spirits are entertained with rites and food at the household altar until they are sent off with fire at the end of the festival period. Shôgatsu and Bon correspond to the full moon at the time of spring planting and the fall harvest, respectively.

Commentary

The concept of venerating one's ancestors has always occupied an important place in the spiritual life of Japan. But there has been almost no attempt to examine scientifically its substance, structure, and formative process.

The present work, which represents such an attempt, is divided into three major parts: (1) "The Structural Relationship Between the *Ie* and Ancestor Worship," (2) "Various Forms of Ancestor Worship as Seen in History," and (3) "Ancestor Worship and the Japanization of Buddhist Thought." Here we have introduced portions of part one, which demonstrates how the structure of the Japanese *ie* gave rise to ancestor worship and further points out the exact correspondence of this phenomenon with the Japanese concept of spirits.

Part two considers, in a historical context, the development of the *ie* and how ancestor worship came to be expressed in terms of this development. The final part analyzes, from the viewpoint of the Japanization of Buddhist teachings, how the religion as transmitted to Japan was transformed into and assimilated as popular Buddhism and fused with ancestor worship.

Most Japanese people think of themselves as Buddhists. But a Buddhism so deeply intermeshed with ancestor worship is unique even among the Buddhist countries of East Asia. The Shinto *kami* and buddhas of folk belief were frequently treated as one and the same from the medieval period onward, until the Meiji government forcibly separated the two. The same sacred entity was both *kami* and buddha, and often also ancestor. After World War II the traditional Japanese *ie* all but disintegrated, and the feeling for ancestor worship was greatly weakened. Nevertheless, in comparison with other peoples around the world, ancestor worship can be seen to have left a rich legacy in Japan.

In elucidating the *ie* system and the Buddhism peculiar to Japan through examining ancestor worship, this work is an excellent guide to understanding both the form and the inner meaning of the traditional Japanese way of life.

13. JAPANESE FOLK BELIEFS

Minkan Shinkô By Hori Ichirô
Tokyo: Iwanami Zensho #151, Iwanami Shoten, 1951.

Primitive Japanese culture was a complex blending of the so-called southern cultures borne on the Black Current and the western and northern cultures introduced from the Asian Continent. With the passage of time highly developed cultures entered Japan from the continent in overlapping waves. None of these elements was rejected; all were accepted, coexisted, and still survive, albeit in changed form. In European society, a few ancient beliefs survive as mere superstitions or popular beliefs. But in Japan, ancient beliefs have retained something of their original function in certain areas of contemporary society. They have been passed down as living realities.

The great art critic Okakura Tenshin (1862-1913) once described Japan as "the art museum of the Far East." This image can be applied to religion as well.

Japanese folk beliefs include such variations as the following: remnants of ancient beliefs that survive in an undeveloped form; such beliefs in a warped or distorted form; remnants of beliefs predating organized religion; beliefs once subsumed under a higher religion but later discarded; and degenerate remnants of early religions that were thrust aside by the incursion of higher religions. All these demonstrate specific aspects of beliefs that were assimilated into daily life at various stages in the history of the Japanese people. They also express the fundamental character and consciousness of the nation. There is even some doubt whether Shinto should be called a religion. It retains many vestiges of a nature religion in its rituals and beliefs and has much in common with folklore.

We must first observe the circumstances of folk beliefs in Japanese agrarian society and extract common elements. Among the beliefs operative in the daily life of groups linked by lineage or geography in village society, we note faith in the *ujigami*, or tutelary clan deity (the deity of the ancestors of the *uji*, or clan), and in the *ubusunagami* (the guardian deity of the birthplace; since the sixteenth century this has been treated as synonymous with the *ujigami*). Second, there are rites and beliefs connected with ancestors and the dead in general, linking household Buddhist altars, graveyards, and the Buddhist temples enshrining the spirits of deceased members of the same blood lineage. These communal, social, group beliefs are enjoined by the environment; they are not a matter of free choice. Third, there are individual, private beliefs originally derived from or annexed to beliefs of the first two types, which have spread and gained acceptance over a relatively wide area.

S Village in Nagano Prefecture is a typical farming village. According to a survey made in 1944, it consisted of 682 families comprising thirteen *ôaza* (large subvillage units) and thirty-three *koaza* (smaller subvillage sections). Susuki-no-miya is the shrine of the guardian deity (*ubusunagami*) of the village as a whole, enshrining two mythical *kami*. Observation of shrine rituals reveals the influence of the famous shrine of Suwa

Myôjin at nearby Lake Suwa. Traces can also be seen of Buddhist image once installed as a "shrine treasure." This is thought to reflect the influence of the Nenbutsu (Amidist or Pure Land) pietism of the powerful Zenkô-ji temple in Nagano.

While the villagers consider this shrine to be that of their guardian deity, within the community there are also small groups centered on the extended kinship association known as the *dôzoku*; in this way, a double ritual sphere is established. In fact, there are as many as ninety-one of these private *dôzoku* shrines, and the deities enshrined are extremely varied in nature. The most common deity (forty-two shrines) is Inari. The tendency to enshrine Inari as a household deity in both farming villages and cities, beginning in the sixteenth century, is especially prevalent in the Kantô and Chûbu regions of central Honshu. This cult is of two types: that originating with wandering or resident female shamans who act as oracles and mediums, and that based on the "messenger of the *kami*" cults growing out of village agricultural rites. In addition we note twenty-seven other *kami,* buddhas, and sundry spirits. Six private shrines enshrine tutelary deities and ancestral spirits, suggesting that the prototype of private-shrine rites grew out of *dôzoku* rituals.

In the sphere of private-shrine rites, about two-thirds of these shrines feature one shrine per family, or sixty-three shrines. This indicates the disintegration of *dôzoku*-based rites and the gradual change to a system characterized by family or household gods. However, the remaining twenty-eight private shrines retain the character of *dôzoku* shrines, since they are used by two to thirty families respectively. In these group rites the head of the main family of the *dôzoku* holds what may be called ritual rights, and we see that such rites serve to strengthen and renew the consolidation of the *dôzoku*. Most of the ceremonies conform to a simple pattern: the head of the main family leads the rites, with the heads of the other families of the *dôzoku* gathering at the main family; when the ceremonies are over, all partake in a common meal and then disperse. In about half the cases a Shinto priest is called in to recite formal prayers.

We must not overlook the existence, parallel with or overlapping the private-shrine system, of the numerous religious associations known as *kô* and of the worship of miniature stone towers, linga, and other stone roadside images and markers of a phallic or protective nature. There are 144 such stone images and markers in S Village, of which the greatest number depict the Kôshin deity or are Nenbutsu stones.

The content of the Kôshin cult varies greatly from region to region and from *kô* to *kô*. Kôshin is commonly regarded as a god of agriculture, guardian against disasters, god of luck, deity of the locale, or god of various arts; very rarely, he is worshiped as guardian of horses, god of felicitous human relations, especially marriage or protector of children. The rites related to his worship usually follow the *tôya* system, whereby families are chosen by lot or rotation to take charge. On a fixed day one member of each family belonging to the *kô* goes to the *tôya*, or duty house; all line up before the altar to offer prayers and read a portion of a designated sutra, then eat and drink together well into the night. The *tôya* serves in addition as a meeting place for general discussion and consultation. Members of the *kô* also contribute to a reserve fund. While such rites are in a sense religious, they also provide recreation, exchange of knowledge, mutual aid, and consolidation of the village consensus. Village lore is also passed down within such gatherings.

Kô can be of various kinds: a particular community may form a *kô*, within the community there may be additional *kô* based on locality, and there may be various other *kô* for women only or children only; in addition there may be an association embracing the entire community. An example is the so-called Ise *kô,* where a fund is accumulated to allow groups to make pilgrimages to the Ise Grand Shrines in rotation. S Village also has Nenbutsu *kô*, one of which is said to have been formed to venerate and pray for the repose of the spirits of the victims of the Edo-period agricultural uprisings.

On the basis of the above data we can make certain deductions. First, the private-shrine form, illustrating the smallest possible cult group, and within that especially the ritual pattern of the *dôzoku*, was once the smallest in-group of the village structure. Shrine cults arose as folkways within this primitive community.

Moreover, in the beliefs of the inhabitants of a given village the coexistence of dissimilar beliefs and the overlapping juxtaposition of similar beliefs can be seen. These are remnants of beliefs that have been upheld to a greater or lesser extent depending on communal consciousness within the village. These beliefs do not result from the importation of alien faiths, but have arisen from outside pressures and development and expansion from within; in this formative process foreign elements have fused with traditional beliefs. Furthermore, villagers have had no strong consciousness of the separateness or individuality of imported faiths but have accepted them as if they were indigenous beliefs. The only difference concerned the degree to which beliefs were of a private or a public nature.

To recapitulate: the source imbuing the village as an administrative unit with the awareness of being a single communal society is the guardian deity of the geographical locale, the *ubusunagami*. Beneath this are the shrine beliefs, similar in nature and form, which define the "natural villages" whose units are the *ôaza* and *koaza*. *Dôzoku* cults, also similar in nature and form, exist as subgroups. This configuration of overlapping beliefs of similar nature and form is the typical pattern of Japanese agrarian society.

Commentary

While Japan is a highly developed civilization, at the base of Japanese society are ancient beliefs that may be called "natural religion," which have persisted through the ages like an underground conduit. In this respect Japan differs greatly from European society, where a powerful religion like Christianity, with its developed doctrinal and evangelical systems, either exterminated ancient beliefs or absorbed them into the religious life of Christian believers.

In his major work *A Study of the History of Japanese Folk Religion* (*Wagakuni Minkan Shinkô-shi no Kenkyû* [Tokyo: Tokyo Sôgen-sha, 1955]), Hori describes Japanese modes of belief as follows: "In Japan there exist indigenous beliefs of most ancient times and northern shamanism, which are similar in nature; the various religious elements of the southern tradition; the imported continental faiths of Buddhism, Onmyô-dô [yin-yan magic], and Taoism; and in the premodern period, various Christian beliefs and religious forms. Some elements have co-existed as independent entities, while others have become partially fused; some have been absorbed, while others have yielded to a particular interpretation and have developed into new patterns of belief. In any investigation of the actual spiritual life of the Japanese people all these factors must be seen as constituting a single living entity. Religious beliefs are originally one with daily life, and it is inappropriate to consider them in the abstract, apart from this context."

Japanese Folk Beliefs, the work of a great scholar of religious ethnology, is a well-documented study indispensable for an understanding of Japanese society.

Here we have focused on Shinto-based beliefs. Today the general disintegration of rural agrarian communities is disturbing the traditional configuration of beliefs. But the long history of the belief patterns described in this book has undoubtedly exerted a profound influence on the social consciousness and behavior patterns of the Japanese people.

A significant portion of the book deals with an important aspect of Japanese folk religion omitted from our summary: the beliefs and rites connected with ancestors and the dead as these have been merged with Buddhism. (For a discussion of this subject see the essay on *Ancestor*

Worship [*Sosen Sûhai*] by Takeda Chôshû.)

Published in English: *Folk Religion in Japan*, edited by Joseph K. Kitagawa and Alan L. Miller (Chicago: The University of Chicago Press, 1968).

IV
Intellectual Tradition

14. THE WAY OF THINKING OF THE JAPANESE PEOPLE

Nihonjin no Shii Hôhô By Nakamura Hajime

Tôyôjin no Shii Hôhô vol.3; *Nakamura Hajime Senshû* vol.3
Tokyo: Shunjûsha, 1962.

The Phenomenal World and the Absolute

One of the outstanding characteristics of the Japanese way of thinking is the affirmation of the world as it is. The Japanese regard this world, with its diverse phenomena, as in itself absolute, and tend to reject viewpoints that seek the absolute in some realm beyond phenomena. The genesis of this way of thinking is extremely ancient. In addition to believing that all things are invested with spirit, the ancient Japanese personified even nonhuman *kami* (spirits or deities) and considered human *kami* the primary entity, or *hontai,* of *kami* in general. This way of thinking is seen throughout the history of the indigenous Shinto religion.

The Japanese also assimilated Buddhism to this way of thinking. Japanese Buddhism differs from that of India and China. As an example let us consider the Buddhist concept known in Japanese as *hongaku*. In India, where Buddhism originated, it signified the ultimate enlightenment that exists in a realm transcending the phenomenal world; but the Japanese interpreted the concept to mean "innate Buddha-nature" or "original Buddhahood," thus bringing it down to the phenomenal world. They felt that there was nothing intrinsically hidden from man; the world of phenomena in itself was the absolute. They saw even nonsentient natural phenomena as manifestations of Buddha-nature.

The Japanese had a great love of nature. They decorated their clothing with designs of flowers, birds, and grasses, and favored a cuisine that remained as close to nature as possible. They placed ikebana and bonsai in their alcoves (*tokonoma*), and painted stylized flowers and birds on the sliding partitions known as *fusuma*. Their literature, too, is closely bound up with a warm love of nature. If all the poems on nature were removed from the poetry anthologies, how much would remain?

The fact that the Japanese climate is generally temperate and the scenery beautiful can be regarded as a latent reason for the Japanese love of nature and perception of the phenomenal world as the absolute. The humid climate of the monsoon region causes vegetation to flourish. This does not strike the Japanese as oppressive but gives them instead a sense of kinship with nature. Nature is perceived not as hostile to man but as a continuum of which man is an integral part.

Secularism

Most religions tend to think of this world as impure and to see in the hereafter a pure and unsullied paradise, but the primitive Shinto religion of Japan unequivocally affirmed the value of the present world. When Buddhism was introduced to Japan, not only did the Japanese not amend their secularism – they transformed Buddhism itself into a world-centered religion. The Japanese assimilated the teachings of Buddhism by discarding their world-transcending aspects and adopting only the world-centered aspects appended to a small portion of the scriptures. The view of life and death among Indian Buddhists held that human beings transmigrate among the six states of existence (hell, hungry spirits, animals, angry or martial spirits, human beings, and the heavens) through the force of *karma,* but the Japanese believed that even ordinary, undistinguished people could be reborn in the human world if they but had faith.

Affirmation of Human Nature

Linked with acknowledgment of the significance of the natural world as it stands is the affirmation of human desires and emotions. The Japanese tend not to suppress such feelings. The ancient Japanese composed love poems expressing their emotions frankly and joyfully. This tendency has persisted down to the present. Even with the flowering of austere Confucianism in the Edo period, Japanese Confucians sometimes taught that we should not look for ethical significance in poetry.

A similar tendency was at work in the Japanese assimilation of Buddhism. A striking example is the abandonment of Buddhist moral and disciplinary precepts, a phenomenon never seen in India or China. Buddhist sects with especially strict precepts were not generally accepted by the Japanese. In Indian Buddhism, the aspirant was supposed to extinguish all attachment to emotions both pleasant and unpleasant; but in Japan, the fiery reformer Nichiren (1222-82) confessed, "I shed tears when happy, I shed tears when sad." The Japanese could easily identify with this kind of fervent and highly emotional teaching. Again, the priest

Onkô (1718-1804) taught, "Morality consists in obeying one's natural, true nature."

Nor did Japanese Buddhism rigorously enforce precepts against drinking intoxicants, eating meat, or sexual activity. In contrast to the Indians and the Chinese, who separated the realms of religion and human desires and placed the two in opposition, the Japanese had a strong tendency to perceive religion and desire as belonging to a single realm. Sexual and emotional love was affirmed as not inconsistent with religion.

Emphasis on Human Love

The Japanese way of thinking, with its regard for the natural human condition, went a step further to emphasize love. A purified love for others is called *karunâ,* or compassion, in Buddhism. This concept was especially emphasized in Japanese Buddhism, and generally accepted. Even warriors considered it a major virtue.

In Japan too there were frequent wars. When the fighting was over, however, it was customary for the victors to pray for the repose of not only their own fallen warriors but also the enemy dead. Even at the time of the Mongol invasions in the late thirteenth century Hôjô Tokimune, regent of the military government then ruling Japan, had prayers offered for the Japanese and enemy dead together. Similar ceremonies were held at the time of the Russo-Japanese War of 1904-5. That all people, friend and foe alike, are saved by the compassion of the Buddha is a signal tenet of Buddhist thought. It may well be that this concept took such firm root among the Japanese because it was congenial to their traditional nature.

Spirit of Tolerance and Appeasement

In the history of Japan, fellowship and harmony are much more strongly manifested than are relationships of dominance and submission. This is not to say that such relationships have not existed. Social restrictions and pressures on the individual may indeed have been stronger in Japan than in many other countries. Nevertheless, a spirit of fellowship and tolerance deeply permeated the subjective awareness of the individual Japanese.

The Japanese were unable to abhor offenders. As an example we can cite the fact that in ancient times there were no truly cruel criminal penalties. Crucifixion first appeared in Japan in the *sengoku* (warring provinces) period of civil strife (c. 1467-1568), and is thought to be due to the influence of Christianity. There appears to be a single recorded instance of burning at the stake in ancient times, after which it was not repeated for centuries. Throughout the four hundred years of the Heian period (794-1185) the death penalty was never invoked.

The concept of eternal punishment was difficult for the Japanese, with their love of tolerance, to comprehend. Even in assimilating Buddhism, they finally arrived at the belief that anyone, no matter how wicked, would be saved after death. Even the most depraved of persons was not to be held responsible after death for his deeds. All the dead were called *hotoke,* "buddha." There even occurred the peculiar phenomenon of enshrining exceptionally wicked people after death as entities of extraordinary spiritual power, with endless streams of pilgrims visiting their graves.

The Japanese spirit of tolerance is also seen in the merging of *kami* and buddhas. Japanese Buddhism was tolerant of the *kami* from the time of its introduction, and the idea of the essential identity of *kami* and buddhas presently evolved. Such a way of thinking was made possible by the nature of Buddhism itself, of course, but also by the traditional Japanese idea of the nature of *kami*. To the Japanese, any religion was acceptable provided that it did not disrupt the social order or the laws regulating human relationships.

The Japanese have a marked tendency, when adopting universal religions from abroad, to interpret them in accordance with the traditions of Japanese society and the circumstances of the times. This is a way of thinking that perceives universal principles only as they are manifested in particular or specific forms. Most sects of Buddhism in Japan consider religion something that must be suited to the times. Confucian thinkers of the Edo period, too, often denied those teachings that did not suit Japanese ways.

This tendency in the Japanese way of thinking harbors two dangers. When people become estranged from universality and overemphasize temporal particulars, it becomes easy to adopt an opportunism that compromises with specific circumstances or situations. And when spatial particulars are overemphasized, it is easy to lapse into a narrow ethnocentrism.

Commentary

Nakamura Hajime is well known as an authority on Indian religion, thought, and philosophy. We have introduced one chapter, "Acceptance of Reality as Given," from *The Way of Thinking of the Japanese People* (*Nihonjin no Shii Hôhô*), one of the four volumes of his *Ways of Thinking of Eastern Peoples* (*Tôyôjin no Shii Hôhô*). The author discusses other characteristics of the Japanese way of thinking in chapters entitled "The Tendency to Emphasize Human Relationships" and "The Tendency Toward Irrationality."

The distinctive feature of Nakamura's discussion of the Japanese way of thinking is that he first elucidates the nature of the ancient Japanese, and then examines in careful detail how Buddhism and Confucianism were assimilated. In particular, he compares the development of Buddhist teachings in India and the configuration of beliefs of the Indian people with those of China and Japan, vividly delineating the Japanese way of thinking from a historical and a contemporary perspective.

Nakamura rejects the idea that the Japanese absorbed the essence of Eastern culture. He asserts that the Japanese markedly transformed both Buddhism and Confucianism in the process of assimilation. However, such transformation does not necessarily signify a loss of their original values but instead includes within it a potential for the germination of new values.

Tôyôjin no Shii Hôhô has been translated into English by Phillip P. Wiener as *Ways of Thinking of Eastern People: India, China, Tibet, Japan* (Honolulu: East-West Center Press, 1964).

15. ANATOMY OF THE JAPANESE CONSCIOUSNESS

Nihonjin no Ishiki Kôzô By Aida Yûji
Tokyo: Kôdansha, 1970.

When comparing Japanese and Western life, an interesting analogy can be made between human beings and honey bees. According to the entomologist Sakagami Shôichi, Japanese honey bees and Occidental honey bees are, for the most part, similar, but there are three situations to which they react in an exactly opposite manner.

When a hive made for and used by Japanese bees is presented to Occidental bees, they will quickly remodel it for use as their own; but if an Occidental beehive is presented to Japanese bees, they seem to consider it unclean, for they immediately set to work destroying it and building an entirely new hive of their own. (The Japanese people also consider articles that have come into direct contact with others unclean. Even eating utensils are considered very personal, and a Japanese will seldom use the chopsticks or teacup of another.)

If a few Occidental bees are introduced into a Japanese beehive, they are accepted without discrimination; but Occidental bees will immediately attack and kill new Japanese bees.

The third difference is in the stance taken against outside threat. Honey bees are very sensitive to humidity. As it rises the infant bees inside the hive are overcome and die. Adult bees will sometimes take up positions at the entrance and fan dry air inside with their wings. This instinctive action is common to both Occidental and Japanese bees, but they take opposite positions to perform the task. Occidental bees face outward and keep watch for danger as they fan, while Japanese bees face into the hive. While it could be argued that the Japanese bees have their stingers aimed at intruders, it must be admitted that they are far less vigilant.

One possible explanation for these differences is the natural environment. Japanese summers are long and give sufficient time for complete rebuilding, whereas European summers are short, making it necessary for bees to house themselves as best they can with the materials at hand. The variety and quantity of flowers in Japan is great enough to allow for prosperous communal living, whereas the comparative lack of nectar in Europe makes it difficult for closely related bees to put in sufficient stocks. Fewer natural enemies, finally, result in lessened vigilance.

Interesting parallels can be drawn between bees and human beings.

An American writer once said: "The Japanese are a strange race. They bend forward as they fight. A mother anywhere might reasonably draw her children to her and turn her back on an oncoming vehicle or an attacking animal. But in the case of the Japanese, this is the defensive posture taken by both sexes and all ages. It is the stance of the Japanese." This observation is quite accurate. One would be hard put to find a Japanese who would not so behave when trying to protect a child. On a visit to the United States, I asked several housewives what they would do to protect their children, if they were suddenly confronted by a speeding vehicle or a wild animal on the loose. They invariably answered that they would stand in front of their children, arms outstretched, facing the danger.

This seems to indicate a basic difference in the emotional and thought patterns of Japanese and Occidentals. The forward crouching stance, with the back toward the danger, is typical of the Japanese, whatever the situation.

The main flaw in the Japanese defensive position is his inability to look at the enemy clearly and assess his strength. All through the Pacific War, Japanese forces relied on the single strategy of circling to attack the enemy from behind, even though it had early proved ineffective. The concept became fixed, and failed because of an inability to analyze the enemy forces and assess their strength. This protective stance also suggests a Japanese tendency to turn thoughts inward, and make observations of the outside world extremely conceptual. There is also a strong tendency to compete with colleagues and not with outsiders. Competition within the Japanese economic world is due not only to crowding society. It derives from the whole anatomy of the Japanese consciousness.

Thus there is extreme timidity in the face of abrupt changes in personal or social relationships. Peace is seen as the status quo, and preserving peace as opposing change, whatever may happen in the outside world. To the Occidental, peace is something that must be built. He faces outward to build peace, and at the same time works for internal changes that will make peace more effective in the totality of things. He sees that a balance can be destroyed and the result will be war. In contrast to this Occidental "building" consciousness, the Japanese think of things "happening" or "becoming" of themselves. Even things that have been decided upon, are thought of as having "happened." Asked what he did, he is likely to say not "I did such and such," but "Things came out so and so."

The defensive turning of the back indicates the passivity. While the Japanese are not assertive and do not face an opponent as Occidentals do, they have the ability to communicate with their backs. If this "backside communication" is ignored, serious misunderstanding can ensue. When a Japanese woman receives a confession of love, she will immediately turn her back and say, "Oh, no." She may well be communicating happiness and affection through her back.

For the Japanese, intuition and sympathy are very important means of communication, while assertion and logical explanation are often considered detrimental to understanding. The assumption is that others will "sense" a purpose and intent without verbal explanation.

Let us take a look at an example of radical misunderstanding between a Japanese couple and an Occidental student.

The couple rented a room to a French exchange student. The rent was to include two meals a day, and the special menu demanded by the student came to almost the entire rental. The couple were happy to contribute what they could to Japanese-French relations, and they assumed that the student understood. He was happy to find such kind landlords. The mother of the husband, who lived with the couple, died suddenly. The wife did not have time to prepare a meal for the student, and assumed that he would understand and, without an explanation, take the meal elsewhere. The student came home and demanded his meal as usual. When he was told that there was nothing prepared for him, he accused the couple of breaking the contract. They became indignant, relations deteriorated, and he moved out, putting an end to a small experiment in international relations.

The view that words are unnecessary for understanding is very deeply rooted in the Japanese mind. Perhaps it can be attributed to the fact that when the Japanese language was taking shape life was supported by gathering and farming, with a total lack of experience in hunting. European races were meanwhile supporting themselves by hunting. Hunting requires careful explanation to one's fellows.

Agricultural peoples developed words for the exchange of such sentiments as sympathy, appreciation, and encouragement. The Japanese language has achieved a high level of development for the expression of complicated emotional nuances, but it is lacking in adequate means for the precise exchange of intents and purposes.

Commentary

Aida Yûji was originally a student of European history. Toward the end of the Pacific War, he was drafted into the army. After the surrender, he was taken prisoner by the British army in Burma, where he was put into a labor camp. He saw the "reasonable cruelty" of the British, and was made painfully aware of the shortcomings of the Japanese mentality. His *Arron Concentration Camp* has been a longtime best seller in Japan. It was published by Cresset Press, London, in 1966, as *Prisoner of the British; a Japanese Soldier's Experiences in Burma.*

His view of European culture is explained in *The Limits of European Humanity*, and he has written several books on the essence of Japanese culture, of which the present volume is typical. In it he compares Japanese and Occidental patterns of behavior.

16. INDIGENOUS THOUGHT OF JAPAN

Nihon no Dochaku Shisô By Ueyama Shunpei
Tokyo: Kôbundô, 1965.

The Japanese thinkers discussed in this book, while firmly grounded in the traditional thought of East Asian civilization, have also grappled directly with the philosophical problems generated by the modern Western civilization and have formulated their own distinctive systems of modern thought. These may seem to lack the vigor of the modern European systems, but their originality conceals an ever-maturing potential to become a driving force toward world community of humankind. The peoples of Asia have known despair and the depths of human folly. They have not stopped at that stage, however, but have staked their existence on the belief that man remains logical and that logic will eventually prevail.

The philosophy of Nishida Kitarô, for example, is influenced by Zen thought, which is held to have the Buddhist "logic of negation" – an attempt to break free from the biased system of Vedic philosophy – as its core, as well as elements of Taoist thought, itself an attempt to escape the Confucianism that constituted orthodox Chinese philosophy. Western philosophy from the time of ancient Greece, Indian philosophy from the age of the Vedas, Chinese philosophy from the time of the Spring and Autumn (770-403 B.C.) and Warring States (403-221 B.C.) periods of the Chou dynasty – each promoted the exchange of thought within its own sphere of influence. But today, when the need for the free exchange of thought on a global scale is growing, have these various currents not become instead systems of powerful prejudice, blocking exchange of thought? If so, the significance of Nishida's "logic of *mu*" ("emptiness" or "negation," in the Buddhist sense), based as it is on the thorough demolition of prejudice, must one day be acknowledged.

The Thought of Nishida Kitarô

With Japan's defeat in World War II, evaluation of Nishida's philosophy in this country made a complete about-face. Once held to be Japan's first truly original modern philosophy it became a foolish idealism. The downfall of Nishida's philosophy was due to his being labeled a war collaborator. Actually he advocated a kind of internationalism, asserting that each nation, "being both true to self and transcending self," should help shape the world.

At first Nishida was attracted by Nakae Chômin's materialism, which denied both God and soul. But he achieved a religious viewpoint through Zen practice, finding therein the ground for his thought. "Religious consciousness, being the basic fact of our lives, must be the foundation of both learning and morality," he asserted. *An Inquiry into Good* (*Zen no Kenkyû*) represents a scholarly expression of his religious convictions. The religious belief that permeates this work is expressed directly in the concept of "pure experience" (*junsui keiken*). Nishida held that true existence, including good, God, man's will, mind, and nature, is nothing other than a single pure experience. Pure experience, to Nishida, is the differentiated development of the universal and at the same time the basic mode that establishes existence. From it is derived his proposition that "the one is also many, the many are also one," the basic formula of existence.

Several years after the publication of *An Inquiry into Good,* Nishida's thought advanced from a psychological to a more logical mode of expression, and he developed the concepts known as the "logic of place" (*basho no ronri*) and the "logic of *mu*." These comprise a kind of epistemology; but whereas former epistemologies grew out of the opposition of subjectivity and objectivity, his grew out of the fact of self-awareness: that the true meaning of "knowing" is the reflection of the self within the self. His "logic of place" is a logic not of the realm of things nor of the realm of consciousness but of the realm of the transcendental self, the self of wisdom. This transcendental self is the logical expression of the "will of absolute freedom" (*zettai jiyû no ishi*) at which he ultimately arrived.

Nishida said: "Experience is not predicated on the individual; self is predicated on experience." The fundamental characteristic of his philosophy is a supraindividualistic (in the sense of transcending the individual while penetrating to the depths of the individual) blending of liberalism and intuitionalism. Through his confrontation with Western thought, Nishida Kitarô imparted new light to the traditions of the Zen and Taoist thought unique to East Asia.

*

Nishida Kitarô (1870-1945). After graduating from the University of Tokyo, he held a succession of teaching posts, and devoted himself to Zen practice. In 1911 he published *An Inquiry into Good,* based on his notes for high-school lectures. The same year he became a professor at Kyoto University, where he created what came to be called the Nishida philosophy, at the same time guiding a group of students known as the Kyoto School.

The Thought of Nakae Chômin

Nakae's thought, briefly, is a materialism that unequivocally advocates an objective and scientific world-view. As a young man he studied in France, and his thought includes many points in common with French materialism; but Nakae's brand of atheism is much more thoroughgoing. He denied not only God and the soul but also egocentrism and anthropocentrism. It is because man is narrowly preoccupied with his own concerns and does not take into consideration the standpoint of birds, beasts, insects, and fish, he said, that such nonsense as ideas of God and the soul are generated. Behind this conclusion lies Buddhist thought, with its wish that all sentient beings attain Buddhahood.

One drawback of all materialistic philosophies is the weak structure of their systems of ethics. Nakae, however, invoked Confucian ethical thought to construct such a system. As for the influence of Nakae's thought, it was one of the philosophies energizing the bourgeois revolutionary movement known as the democratic rights movement (*jiyû minken undô*). In that sense it has the same significance in Japanese history as English empiricism in the English Revolution or French materialism in the French Revolution.

*

Nakae Chômin (1847-1910) was born into a low-ranking samurai family of the Tosa feudal domain (now Kôchi Prefecture, Shikoku), from which many leaders of the Meiji Restoration sprang. In 1871 he went to Paris as a government-sponsored student and there studied philosophy, history, and literature. On returning to Japan he opened a school of French studies, inaugurating new fields of scholarship. As a journalist he attacked the autocratic politics of the government and earned fame as a critic. Though he later entered politics, his career was cut short by cancer, and he died leaving the works *The Last Year and a Half* (*Ichinen Yûhan*) and *The Last Year and a Half, Part Two* (*Zoku Ichinen Yûhan*) as statements of his thought.

The Labor-Farmer Faction

In the 1920s Japanese Marxists split into two opposed groups, the Labor-Farmer (*rônô*) faction and the Lecture Series (*kôza*) faction. The Lecture Series faction followed the Comintern line (the Third International), supported the Japan Communist Party, and leaned toward Leninism. The Labor-Farmer faction, on the other hand, advocated autonomous national movements, and favored Marx's *Das Kapital*.

The ideology of the Labor-Farmer faction had its beginnings in the ideas of Kôtoku Shûsui and Sakai Toshihiko and was given its established form by Yamakawa Hitoshi. These men all assimilated foreign socialistic ideology and fought against indigenous reactionary thought. Their thought is also called "indigenous," however, because it was generated from within and based upon autonomous study and investigation.

*

Kôtoku Shûsui (1871-1911) took part in the democratic rights movement as a youth and later studied Nakae Chômin's theory of materialism. He was active as a journalist. In 1901, with Sakai Toshihiko (1870-1933) and others, he founded the Social Democratic Party (Shakai Minshu-tô), which was banned the same day. As the Russo-Japanese War of 1904-5 approached, he and Sakai inaugurated a socialist antiwar movement. After returning from six months in the United States, Kôtoku became an anarchist, and in 1910 he was arrested and later executed on charges of having plotted to assassinate the emperor.

In 1906 Sakai and Yamakawa Hitoshi (1880-1958) took part in the founding of the Japan Socialist Party, and in 1919 the first issue of *Studies in Socialism* (*Shakaishugi Kenkyû*) was published. In 1922 they participated in the founding of the Japan Communist Party, but when it was forced to disband, they abandoned the Comintern line. In 1927 they launched the magazine *Labor and Farmer* (*Rônô*), and so one of the currents of the Japanese socialist movement took shape.

When the Comintern handed down its 1932 program, scholars supporting it published a *Lecture Series on the Development of Japanese Capitalism* (*Nihon Shihonshugi Hattatsu-shi Kôza*), which led to their being known as the Lecture Series faction. The Labor-Farmer faction attacked their position and a bitter controversy arose between the two groups. The Communist Party of today is descended from the Lecture Series faction and the Socialist Party from the Labor-Farmer faction.

The Thought of Imanishi Kinji

Imanishi's methodology and his world-view can be seen as the developed form of Nishida Kitarô's philosophy of life (*seimei tetsugaku*). Imanishi advocated not the "closed" nationalism of World War II but an "open" nationalism. He believes most strongly that Japanese daily life should not be directed toward the exclusive profit of the Japanese people but toward the welfare of all humankind.

Imanishi based his views on the principle of habitat segregation (*sumiwake*) he had discovered in his study of insect ecology, which led him to a different idea of evolution from Darwin's theory of natural selection. He has also led studies of the group life of higher mammals, culminating in his recent *Origins of the Human Family* (*Ningen Kazoku no Kigen*), which attempts to build a bridge between animal sociology and social anthropology. He urges the importance of abundant observation above all; his speculative thought is supported by a deep intuitive insight which does not depart from logic. His viewpoint can be summed up as follows: "Inanimate things and living beings, animals and plants, are derived from the same source."

*

Imanishi Kinji (b. 1902). After graduating from the Department of Agriculture of Kyoto University he engaged in scientific research in Mongolia, Ponape, the Karakoram mountains, and Africa. In addition to his activities as a biologist, he is known as an alpinist and explorer. After World War II, as a professor at Kyoto University, he was a pioneer in animal sociology. His thoroughgoing field work led to his theory of habitat segregation (*sumiwake*) and laid the groundwork for his research in primatology.

Commentary

While expecting much of the traditions of East Asian civilization, the author does not simply emphasize their originality but also attempts comparison with European counterparts on the basis of the comparative history of thought. Although European derives from Christianity and Japanese from Mahayana Buddhism, there are a number of common categories that lend themselves to analysis.

In this book, Ueyama Shunpei discusses Nishida Kitarô, Nakae Chômin, the leaders of the Labor-Farmer faction, and Imanishi Kinji as exemplars of the indigenous thought of Japan. The two themes of the book are the elucidation of the philosophical lineage extending from Nishida to Imanishi and the theoretical and political currents of the Labor-Farmer faction as represented by the line from Nakae to Kôtoku and the line from Sakai to Yamakawa.

When Nakae and Nishida are compared, Nakae is seen as dedicated to enlightenment and as anti-religious, basing his thought on materialism, and is linked to internationalism; Nishida is a romantic and is linked to nationalism. But Nakae's ethical thought is Japanese in its reliance on Confucian concepts. The anti-government stance and materialism of the Labor-Farmer faction belongs to Nakae's lineage, while Imanishi's use of intuitive understanding as a tool of scientific methodology ties him to the lineage of Nishida.

The author, thus establishing two major lines in Japan's indigenous thought, has restored to its rightful place the thought of Nishida, accused after the war of collaboration. In fact, the book devotes much more space to Nishida than to any other thinker. The author's own philosophical position recognizes some validity in the lineages of both idealism and materialism.

17. THE INTELLECTUAL TRADITION IN JAPAN

Nihon no Shisô By Maruyama Masao
Tokyo: Iwanami Shinsho #434, Iwanami Shoten, 1961.

The Intellectual Tradition in Japan

There is no comprehensive study in Japan of the nation's intellectual history, which fact in itself is indicative of the relatively minor historical significance that the Japanese assign to the subject. Put in another way, there is no single stream of thought that serves as a frame of reference in defining the mutual relationships among philosophies and ideas of all periods in Japanese history, and in assigning the relative place to all ideological points of view.

The pre-modern and the super-modern have come together in a curious manner in Japan to form the modern era. Aspects of Buddhism, Confucianism, shamanism, and Western thought all live under the same roof. Because "traditional" thought (i.e. the mainstream of a nation's intellectual heritage) in Japan has never really established itself as tradition, it is forever susceptible to outside influence. And because ideas and principles do not accumulate with time into a repository of traditional philosophy, a variety of heterogeneous alien and native philosophies coexist in a sort of timeless spectrum, regardless of when they were introduced, ready to be called forth whenever the occasion requires. The manner in which a Japanese identifies with the ideals of a certain period of his life or with the philosophy of a certain age in the nation's history may seem arbitrary to an outsider. But he does so in all seriousness and sincerity, because for him it is simply a matter of putting to use something that has been dormant in that timeless spectrum. He believes each time, moreover, that he is going back to his "true self."

The Japanese, then, have adopted new and heterogeneous ideas from the West without that necessary confrontation with their own tradition. They import Western philosophy and thought piecemeal and in rapid succession, with no relation whatsoever to their original context. Not infrequently, they will import what in Europe were rather desperate expressions of resistance only to find that these fit in quite well with their own common-sense views, and that sometimes the highly abstract theories, paradoxically, readily appeal to their traditional way of life.

To this very day, it is in the Japanese character to embrace without reservation all philosophy, religion, and learning. (It is symbolic in a way that Shinto, the indigenous Japanese faith that originated prior to the introduction of Confucianism and Buddhism, has no absolute being in its pantheon of deities, no founder, no sacred scriptures.) This tendency reveals itself in a general aversion to abstract ideologies, in a distrust of deductive reasoning and a dependence on intuition and direct, practical experience, and in a reliance on a critical method that seeks to undermine the credibility of an adversary by exposing his argumentative posturing or inconsistencies in his thought and behavior rather than by countering his arguments in any rigorously logical fashion.

Just past the middle of the nineteenth century, when Confucianism – the only traditional philosophy in Japan based on a system of natural law and the supporting creed of the Tokugawa shogunate – was going into a decline, as was the shogunate itself, the theory of natural evolution was introduced into Japan, followed by the theory of historical evolution and the Hegelian scheme of dialectics. Such a rapid influx of ideas worked against the establishment of any continuity in Japanese philosophical tradition. The notion of historical evolution, moreover, was introduced into a country that had no absolute, permanent standard against which to measure things. The Japanese therefore tended to conceive of it in terms of a rootless, flat transition, from one stage to the next – in a word, progress without process.

Evolution to early-Meiji Japan meant catching up with the advanced West, but the sense of inferiority that Japanese had toward the West and their preoccupation with progress were indelibly linked to the way in which they evaluated Western ideas. Rather than evaluate an alien philosophical system through an appreciation of its meaning for their own nation, the Japanese would arbitrarily determine its superiority by its place in the stream of Western thought, assuming from an evolutionary standpoint the more recent philosophy to be the better.

With the promulgation of the Meiji Constitution in 1889, Japan emerged as a modern state. Itô Hirobumi, then President of the Privy Council and perhaps the most influential statesman of the day, saw that traditional religions and philosophies could not serve as the central core of the state. The policy of opening the country to foreign intercourse had made it necessary to form a government along Western lines and to find a way to cope with the flood of Western ideas at a time when traditional values were in a state of flux. Itô tried to fill this vacuum by establishing as the political and spiritual core of the state the emperor himself.

This is how the pseudo-religion of "national polity" (*kokutai*), with the emperor as the locus of sovereignty, came to cast such a magical spell over the nation. A school principal lost his life in an attempt to save the imperial portrait from a fire that raged through his school; the entire population of a village, which happened to be the home of a criminal involved in *lèse majesté*, went into voluntary confinement in a mass gesture of penitence. These are isolated incidents that show how powerful the spell was. National polity was sustained by the unlimited responsibilities of the nation's subjects. And yet it resisted any attempts at clear-cut definition or analysis because of its all-embracing ideology and its inherent ambiguity. The embodiment of a confusedly heterogenous tradition, national polity served not as a guiding principle for giving any meaningful order to the clutter of ideologies and philosophies that existed in Japan, but only as a strong reactionary force rejecting as heretic ideas that could not be absorbed. National polity was thus destined to block decisively the establishment of personal identity, thinking and acting for itself.

When the pseudo-religion of national polity suddenly collapsed after World War II, the confused heterogeneity which had always existed in the Japanese mentality was painfully laid bare. The intellectual world was literally in a shambles. The problem today remains that a jumble of heterogenous philosophies coexist in the same intellectual space without truly mixing or blending. Before we can develop a new hybrid – something that requires a true blending – out of this confused multiplicity of thought, we must first develop a solid identity as people and as nation. That is just the problem of our "revolution."

Toward a New Intellectual Tradition

We can think of a society or cultural tradition as one of two types: that which resembles a tree, and has many branches growing out of a single trunk; and that which resembles a honey-comb, a collection of isolated cubicles.

Japan began to import wholesale modern Western science and philosophy in the second half of the nineteenth century, a time when the various branches of academia in Europe were growing more specialized and independent. These branches were nonetheless pluralistic manifestations of a single cultural continuum that extended from Greco-Roman to medieval to Renaissance times, a continuum which we might liken to a single tree trunk and root system out of which myriad branches grow. In their studies of Western science, Japanese scholars disregarded this long cultural tradition and dealt only with the branches. They were not concerned with effecting a transplant, but only with furnishing clippings, to be arranged at will. From the start scholars in each field worked in a vacuum, taking only what they felt was needed for their own academic pursuits and never venturing out of their self-sufficient cubicles. Even philosophy, that patriarch of all academic pursuits, is a cubicle. There is, moreover, a paucity of communication between these cubicles. Little information is exchanged between scholars in the various branches of the social sciences, for example, let alone between social scientists and natural scientists. Only scholars within a single field – that is to say, within a single cubicle – engage in any real dialogue.

Although modern institutions in the West – corporations, government bureaucracies, educational organizations, labor unions – have become pluralistic and more specialized over the years, they continue to be linked by groups which cut across institutional lines and to which members of different institutions are party. Church groups, clubs, and salons, for example, have been traditionally active as channels of communication. But such private, autonomous channels are virtually non-existent in Japan. With the influx of Western civilization in post-Restoration Japan, modern institutions have developed in the place of fraternities, assemblies, and other such traditional guilds that flourished in the feudal era. But even these modern institutions lead cellular existences, completely isolated from one another. Members of an institution, moreover, are so completely dominated by that institution that they are cut off from the outside world. Even in the world of journalism we find an isolationist esprit de corps. The only true communication is within a single cubicle. Even the mass media do not facilitate true intercommunication between the institutions. They cannot penetrate into the cubicles nor break the barriers between them.

Commentary

After World War II, the author's analysis of the political structure of the Japanese nation up until the end of the war and his treatises on Japanese intellectual thought have had considerable influence in Japan, particularly on the postwar generation of intellectuals. Political scientists under his influence belong to a group known as the "Maruyama School."

In the title chapter "The Intellectual Tradition in Japan" he attempts neither a survey of Japanese intellectual history nor an outline of Japanese intellectual thought. Rather, he attempts to demonstrate that Japan fostered no intellectual tradition which could serve as a frame of reference in assigning the relative place in history to all the miscellaneous philosophies and ideas that have existed in Japan; and that nearly all the thought and philosophical systems bequeathed by the world's most important thinkers during the past millennium are currently stocked in the repository of Japanese thought. His two main points are in reality two sides of the same coin. He attempts to correlate to as great a degree as possible the many issues in Japanese intellectual history that spring from these two points.

In Chapter Three "Toward a New Intellectual Tradition" the author divides societies and cultural traditions into two types – one resembling a tree and one resembling a honeycomb. In the original text, he argues the examples of the whisk (*sasara*) used in the tea ceremony and made by cutting very finely one end of a piece of bamboo, and an octopus pot (*takotsubo*), an urn-shaped trap which is similar to a lobster pot inasfar as both catch their prey without the use of a lid or snaring device. Japanese academicians entered into their own isolated cubicles when Western civilization was introduced into Japan. Maruyama argues that this tendency to import the cuttings without the roots is intensified by the sharp discrimination that Japanese make between "belongers" to a given group and outsiders, and that this practice has not only frustrated debate between academic groups but also hindered any creative academic growth through the medium of mutual criticism.

In the other two chapters, he deals with the so-called literary revival in the 1930s and the intellectual background against which a flurry of ideological controversies arose. He sheds light on some of the ideological themes in modern Japanese literature, exploring the scientific and political elements in the theories of proletarian literature and studying the relationship between politics, science, and literature. Finally, he discusses the virtues of social class and status versus those of merit. Social status in Japan derives from the Confucian ethic, which argues that one's position or class (as a wife, or as a samurai, for example) has in itself a certain value or worth that requires one to act appropriately to one's social position in relationships with others. Merit derives from the modern value system, which postulates that an individual's worth is determined not simply by his position in society, but by how well he functions in that position. A leader, for instance, is considered great not because he is a leader but because he is a person of commendable achievements and character. Maruyama suggests that the change in value systems, from one based on social class to one based on merit, has been an important factor behind Japan's remarkable development as a modern nation. Yet he also stresses that the class system (based on social and not economic status), far from being dead, is still firmly imbedded in Japanese society, which fact is a cause of perplexity and confusion when a Japanese deals with the outside world.

V
Social Relations

18. INTERPERSONAL RELATIONSHIPS IN A VERTICAL SOCIETY

Tateshakai no Ningen Kankei By Nakane Chie
Tokyo: Kôdansha Gendai Shinsho #105, Kôdansha, 1967.

Frame and Attribute

Japanese and Indian society are in extreme contrast. The group consciousness of the Japanese strongly emphasizes "frame" (*ba*), while that of the Indians stresses "attribute" (*shikaku*), of which caste is a symbolic manifestation. "Attribute" as used here has a much broader meaning than in common parlance. A qualitative standard distinguishing one individual from others, it includes lineage, gender, and occupation. "Frame," on the other hand, indicates an individual insofar as he constitutes part of a specific group within a particular framework, such as a locality or institution, without reference to any difference in attribute. For example, a man is identified in terms of attribute as a lathe operator and in terms of frame as an employee of P Company.

In any society an individual belongs to groups characterized by both attribute and frame. What is of interest here is that sometimes the function of either attribute or frame takes precedence, while sometimes both function equally. Their functions are intimately interrelated with value systems based on social understanding. Through them we can examine the structure of a society.

When the Japanese place themselves in a social position, they choose to give frame precedence over attribute. They identify themselves in terms of frame, as an employee of A Company or B Company, rather than in terms of individual attribute, as a journalist or an engineer. The group to which one belongs is seen not as an objective entity over against oneself but as a subjective entity: "my" or "our" group.

This particular form of group consciousness is typified by the traditional concept of *ie*, or household. The *ie* is a community in daily life. As in the case of farmers, this may be a managerial body; through its "household members," it constitutes a clear-cut social unit. In short, it is a social grouping within the framework of a residential or managerial body.

Interpersonal relationships within this household (*ie*) group are considered to take precedence over all other human relationships. Women marrying into a family thus have incomparably more importance than daughters or sisters who have married into other families. Even a brother who sets up a separate household considers himself then to belong to a different family. Sibling relationships in Japan thus differ dramatically from those in India, where the powerful function of the sibling relationship, based on the common attribute of having been born of the same parents, persists after marriage and even until death.

In Japan, problems between mother-in-law and daughter-in-law must be solved strictly within the framework of the family into which the daughter-in-law has married. In farming villages in India, however, a daughter-in-law can go home to stay with her consanguineous family for long periods, and her brothers and sisters constantly visit her and help out in one way and another. And when mother-in-law and daughter-in-law quarrel, the neighboring wives and mothers-in-law (of the same caste) flock round and lend their support to one side or the other. Here too we see that in India the social function of a common attribute (in this case that of daughter-in-law) operates in opposition to the framework of family; in Japan the opposite is true.

Japanese business enterprises, too, are characterized by "family-like" interpersonal relationships. As can be seen in the systems of company housing, recreational gatherings for employees, customs connected with marriage and birth, congratulatory bonuses, condolence money, and so on, the functions of the company extend even to employees' families. A business enterprise is not merely the agent with which one concludes a contractual relationship for the sake of work but constitutes an all-encompassing link between individuals. Even labor unions, which underwent dramatic growth following World War II, are organized on the basis of one union per enterprise and include white-collar and blue-collar workers alike, regardless of differences in attribute or type of work.

Employees of such enterprises, like it or not, stay on in the same group. Even should they wish to switch to another group, no route is provided. In other words, because there are no horizontal links with outside workers in the same field, such as are found in craft unions, they receive no outside information and cannot gain the support of other workers in the same field. Their problem closely resembles that of the Japanese bride, who must solve her problems within the confines of the family into which she has married.

Because attribute is a rational matter, emotions must be relied upon to transcend it. Both household and business enterprise emphasize the group consciousness of "us" against the outside, and within the group constant personal contacts are arranged. This frequently entails the possibility of group-centered interpersonal relationships invading all personal areas. It may even happen that the employee finds himself in a situation in which he can no longer tell where "private life" begins. While there are some who see in this a danger of violating the principle of respect for the individual, others feel security in a thoroughgoing sense of fellowship. What is significant is that the latter feeling is the stronger.

The sense of group solidarity emphasized, indeed compelled, by complete emotional participation in the group creates in itself a closed world and leads to isolation. This inevitably breeds what are known in Japan as "family ways" (*kafû*) and "company ways" (*shafû*). And these in turn are raised as slogans to support group solidarity, thereby further reinforcing the group. Distances among those within the framework who have different attributes continually shrinks, and the consciousness and functioning of groups based on common attributes is numbed. Consciousness of the difference between "our people" (*uchi no mono*) and "outsiders" (*yosomono*) becomes explicit.

Rank: Vertical Organization

Interpersonal relationships can be divided into the vertical and the horizontal. The former category includes such relationships as parent and child or superior and subordinate; over against this we have such horizontal relationships as siblings or colleagues. Depending on the society, one or the other functions more strongly or both function equally. In the case of Japan, the predominance of vertical relationships is seen to be common to all social groupings. In such organizations as business enterprises, vertical relationships (rank) are perceived much more strongly than horizontal ones (among persons doing the same sort of work on the same level).

Even lathe operators with the same qualifications (*shikaku*) and belonging to the same company are differentiated according to age and length of service. Again, professors of the same university are ranked according to the date of official appointment. Differences in rank are not just perceived as such by the members of the organization; they actually exist. In the case of company employees with the same educational background (graduation from university or high school), rank is normally determined on the basis of the year of entering the company. The ranking of senior (*senpai*) and junior (*kôhai*) is clearly established, and advancement generally follows this ranking. When one member of the same year-group is promoted over his fellows, all the others are inclined to say: "If it can happen to him, it should happen to us, too." There is great agitation when a junior (*kôhai*) is promoted over a senior (*senpai*). Personnel management based on merit thus operates under strong limitations. This is not to say that there are no attempts to introduce the merit system; but the seniority system always exercises an overwhelming weight.

The advantage of the seniority system as an institution is that once the employee relationship is established (and in Japan this is generally based on the premise of lifetime employment) no subsequent change or revision is necessary, and management can proceed systematically. The basic premise is that difference in individual ability be given minimal consideration, amounting at most to adjustments loosely based on differences in educational background.

Traditionally the Japanese pay attention to how hard people work, labeling them "hard workers" or "lazybones." At the same time, their sense of equality of ability – the feeling that "anyone can do it if he tries" – is extremely strongly rooted. To classify individuals by establishing some form of distinction among them is a necessary concomitant of organizing them. When it is not possible to make adequate use of differences in ability or attribute as indices the only thing left is distinction by rank. There is an obvious correlation between a sense of equality of ability on the one hand and an overemphasis on rank on the other.

This overemphasis on rank not only applies to the seniority system of organizations developed in modern society but permeates every aspect of daily life. Japanese cannot even seat themselves without a consciousness of relative rank, nor can they talk to each other. Even writers and actors, for whom success depends entirely on individual ability, are strongly rank-conscious. For example, a writer, on receiving a literary award, is known to have remarked, "For someone like me to receive this award ahead of my seniors . . ."

Commentary

This book is an inquiry into social structure, the basic principles inherent in a particular society, by a social anthropologist, and as such presents a yardstick by which to assess the structure of Japanese society. There are seven chapters, of which we have introduced the second and third. To note two or three of the major points we could not cover here, chapter five discusses the weaknesses and strengths of Japanese groups and considers the factionalism that inevitably arises. Chapter six, "The

Relationship Between Leader and Group," discusses how leadership is hemmed in by restrictions; the qualifications (*shikaku*) of a leader depend less upon outstanding ability than upon his being the kind of "boss" (*oyabun*) who can emotionally understand his underlings (*kobun*) and establish a close relationship with them. In chapter seven, "Relationships Between Individuals," the author points out that Japanese society has traditionally lacked the contractual way of thinking; the key to interpersonal relationships has been the effort to "maintain harmony" (*wa o tamotsu*), in which emotion takes precedence over logic.

The term "vertical society" (*tateshakai*) has now become thoroughly familiar to the general Japanese public, testifying to the acuteness and validity of the author's analysis. Her observations constitute one of the most talked-about theories for the study of Japanese society. Her English-language adaptation of this book has been published as *Japanese Society* (London: Weidenfeld and Nicolson, 1970; Berkeley and Los Angeles: University of California Press, 1972; Harmondsworth, England: Pelican Books, 1973).

19. THE STRUCTURE OF AMAE

Amae no Kôzô By Doi Takeo
Tokyo: Kôbundô, 1971.

The author's interest in that peculiar form of psychological dependence, with its corollary expectation of acceptance or indulgence, known in Japanese as *amae* was aroused by his own experiences of "culture shock" when studying psychiatry in the United States. A typical episode is the following encounter with someone introduced by a mutual acquaintance. Doi called on this friend of a friend, and after chatting a while his host said, "If you're hungry I have some ice cream." Doi replied automatically, "I'm not hungry, thank you," with the vague expectation of being urged again to have something to eat. But the other simply said, "Oh, I see," and dropped the subject, leaving Doi somehow disappointed and at a loss. This contretemps led Doi to reflect that had the other person been Japanese, he probably would not have asked someone he was meeting for the first time whether he was hungry but would have shown his hospitality by simply setting out something to eat. Such incidents led Doi to feel that the Americans, unlike the Japanese, generally do not consider or try to anticipate others' wishes and feelings. At about this time he read Ruth Benedict's *The Chrysanthemum and the Sword,* which piqued his intellectual curiosity as to why the psychology of Japanese and Americans should be so different.

Returning to Japan and seeing patients of his own, Doi continually mulled the question of how they differed from their American counterparts. He took great pains to record complaints and appeals in their exact Japanese. Thoughts concerning the special significance of the verb *amaeru* began to take form in his mind. The following episode reconfirmed for him the special meaning of the term. An Englishwoman who was fluent in Japanese was discussing the early childhood of her daughter, a patient of Doi's suffering from neurotic anxiety. The woman had been speaking in English, but suddenly switching to Japanese she said clearly, "*Kono ko wa amari amaemasen deshita*" – "She didn't show much *amae*." When Doi asked why she had spoken in Japanese, she said it was because there was no appropriate expression in English.

One day in 1959 Doi realized with both astonishment and delight that what Michael Balint seeks to describe by the term "passive object-love" in his *Primary Love and Psychoanalytic Technique* is nothing other than *amae*. Balint's comment that European languages are limited by their inability to distinguish between active and passive love led Doi to feel that he had received further endorsement for his idea that the very fact of the existence of the word *amae* in everyday Japanese to signify such passive love indicates that this phenomenon provides an index to Japanese society and culture. In short, he concluded, *amae* is a key concept for the understanding not only of the Japanese mental structure but of the structure of Japanese society.

Considered developmentally, the psychological prototype of *amae* is found in infant psychology in the mother-child relationship. But we do not speak of a newborn baby as exhibiting the kind of passive love and dependence known as *amae*. Usually we first use this word in reference to a baby's behavior after the first six months of life, when he has achieved some degree of self-awareness and has begun actively to seek the mother. In other words, *amae* arises only when the baby has to some extent developed mentally. It is after he has perceived that he and the mother are separate entities and has come to feel that the mother's existence is necessary to him. It is a psychological state predicated on an active wish to cling to the mother. We can thus define *amae* as a psychological device by which to deny the inexorable fact of separation and sublimate its pain. When the psychology of *amae* dominates a person, we can infer that it conceals feelings of conflict and anxiety over separation.

In principle, this phenomenon can be observed in all infants, East or West. However, the fact that the Japanese language has devised a special word for it, *amae,* is useful in allowing us to focus more closely on its psychology. Through the mediation of this concept the mother can understand the child's psychology and respond to his needs, and so mother and child can enjoy a harmonious sense of oneness.

Without *amae* the mother-child relationship does not develop, and without the development of this relationship the child cannot mature. Even after attaining adulthood, the psychology of *amae* always comes into play when new human relationships are formed, at least at the outset. In this sense, *amae* plays an indispensable role in maintaining mental health. Just as it is unrealistic to close one's eyes entirely to the fact of human separation, it is unrealistic to be so overwhelmed by the fact of separation that one despairs of the possibility of human relationships and so isolates oneself.

In comparison to peoples who have no specific word for the phenomenon of *amae,* the Japanese have developed the psychology of *amae* in every aspect of mental life. They have created many words expressing variations upon it, so much so that we can speak of Japanese society as "the world of *amae*." For example, the verb *higamu* means to have the delusion of being treated unfairly; but this feeling springs from the fact that the aim of one's impulse toward dependence (*amae*) has been, as it were, deflected. One feels betrayed or let down by someone on whom one thought to show the kind of dependence discussed above.

R.P. Dore in *City Life in Japan* singles out the verb *tanomu* for special attention. He explains its meaning as between "to ask" and "to rely on": to entrust a personal matter to another with the expectation of his acting in one's behalf. In other words, *tanomu* means that one wishes another to allow dependency (*amae*) on him.

The verb *sumanai* (or *sumimasen*), which the Japanese use often, has attracted the interest of foreigners because it is used to express both apology ("excuse me") and gratitude ("thank you"), contexts that appear at first to be quite different. Etymologically, this word is the negative form of the verb *sumu*: to end, conclude, finish. One excuses oneself (*sumanai*) for not having finished or completed (*sumanai*) something one should have done. The word strongly expresses a feeling of apology for having caused trouble or inconvenience to another. One says *sumanai* to acknowledge a kindness because one conjectures that performing the kindness must have put the other person to some degree of trouble – not because, as Ruth Benedict imagines, one is immediately aware of the obligation to return the kindness.

However, what is at issue here is why the Japanese are not content simply to express thanks but must also apologize for the inconvenience to which they imagine the other person to have been put. The reason is that they are afraid that if they do not apologize, the other person will take this as indicating ingratitude and so they will lose the other person's good will. Saying *sumanai* expresses the psychology of not wanting to lose another's good will in the future and of wishing to continue indefinitely to depend (*amae*) on him.

The following episode, related to the author by an American psychiatrist visiting Japan, shows how easily the Japanese can arrive at reconciliation through the simple apology *sumanai.* The psychiatrist was taken to task by an Immigration Bureau official for some deficiency in his documents. The doctor painstakingly explained that the lack was due to unavoidable circumstances, but he made no impression whatsoever on the official. At his wits' end, the doctor finally said, "I'm sorry" – whereupon suddenly the official's face cleared and the doctor's documents were approved without further ado. The psychiatrist's "I'm sorry" was not the same as the Japanese *sumanai,* but clearly the official so interpreted his words. When the psychiatrist related this incident to the author, he remarked that the Japanese really are an odd people. But of course if we consider the episode from the Japanese point of view, it suggests equally the oddness of Western psychology. While Benedict characterizes Westerners as belonging to a "guilt culture," ironically, they may dislike apologizing precisely because they belong to such a culture.

Commentary

This book, published in 1971, became a best seller in Japan because of its extremely original view of Japanese culture. It was greeted with a sense of refreshing surprise for its skilled application of the concept of *amae* to the character of Japanese society.

The first of the book's five chapters describes how the author arrived at *amae* as the key concept underlying the mental and social structure of the Japanese. In the second chapter, "The World of *Amae*," he attempts a reinterpretation in terms of his theory of *amae* of several concepts which have been discussed by a number of theorists and which have been thought to express peculiarly Japanese patterns, such as *giri* and *ninjô* ("duty" and "human feeling"), *uchi* and *soto* ("inside" and "outside"; "insider" and "outsider"), and *tsumi* and *haji* ("guilt" and "shame"). The author's criticism of Ruth Benedict, who was an early influence, is of particular interest.

In the third chapter, "The Logic of *Amae*," the author discusses how the Japanese themselves evaluate *amae*. He also examines why it is that although *amae*, a universal psychological phenomenon common to all people, is something of which any Japanese is aware, the West has not until recently been conscious of it.

The fourth chapter, "The Pathology of *Amae*," examines the significance of *amae* as manifested in pathological phenomena. Here the author is allowed fullest scope as a specialist. He also discusses Morita Masatake, known for his theory of neuroses peculiar to the Japanese and for his method of treating neurotic patients. Doi maintains that the central concept of Morita's theory, *toraware* – a word best translated perhaps by the slang expression "hung up" – is related to the psychology of *amae* and can indeed be understood as a variation thereof.

In the fifth and final chapter, "*Amae* and Contemporary Society," Doi argues that the universal rebelliousness of the young today grows out of a sense of dependence (*amae*) on the older generation, coupled with the older generation's loss of self-confidence. Contemporary society, he says, can be characterized as "the century of fatherless children."

Amae no Kôzô has been translated into English by John Bester as *Amae: The Anatomy of Dependence* (Tokyo: Kôdansha International, 1973).

VI
Literature

20. THE WORLD OF THE MANYÔSHÛ

Manyô no Sekai By Nakanishi Susumu
Tokyo: Chûkô Shinsho #341, Chûô Kôron-sha, 1973.

The *Manyôshû*, the oldest anthology of Japanese poetry, is the best known and loved of all anthologies in all Japanese classical literature. The "Manyô" tradition was a wellspring of unceasing inspiration for later Japanese poets, who looked to the *Manyôshû* to provide their own literary movements and styles with new ideas and fresh expression.

Yet the Manyô tradition, deeply and widely as it ran, never did become itself a main current in literature. One reason is that poets and their audiences in the Manyô era often differed from those in later eras. Classical Japanese poetry (*waka*) is essentially a court tradition; but the *Manyôshû* is redolent of everyday life, rich in poems by commoners as well as by courtiers. Another reason is that poems in the *Manyôshû* were not influenced by the artistic, religious, and social norms – the aestheticism of the Heian period, the Buddhism of the middle ages, the Confucianism of the pre-modern era – which were to color the literature of later ages. The freedom of poets from such potentially constricting conventions makes for rich and varied expression in the *Manyôshû*.

It is the poems of the humble and nameless, of the simple, common people, which give the *Manyôshû* its distinctive character. The tradition in Japan, maintained to this day, of poetry as a universal pastime has its roots in the *Manyôshû*. In this sense, at least, the anthology mirrors the Japanese character.

Japanese poetry seems to have its beginnings in ritual and incantation. In the earliest literary chronicles we find passages describing how the gods gave the world language and transformed the confusion of noise into an order of words. Primitive Japanese believed that the spoken word possessed magical powers, and that verse, with its special rhythms, was a particularly effective exorciser of evil spirits. Tradition says that one of the principal duties of the Kumebe, a clan who served not only as the guard to the Yamato court (300-645) but also as court chanters and poets, was to chant incantations at official ceremonies and in battle. The descendants of the Kumebe are said to be the Ôtomo, who carried on their professional duties as court poets. It is no coincidence, then, that the Ôtomo produced a wealth of contributors to, and an editor of, the *Manyôshû*.

The editors of the *Manyôshû* divided poems in the anthology into three major categories: *zôka, sômon,* and *banka. Zôka* are "miscellaneous poems," but the expression actually refers to the genre of official poems recited at court ceremonies. *Sômon* is a poetic exchange between two persons, one who presents a *waka* and the other who provides a response. *Banka* means elegy, but it actually had a wider use, to poems composed not only upon a death but also when paying homage to the gods, singing praises of imperial realm, and praying for long life. With time, however, *zôka* evolved into informal verse, *sômon* into love poems, and *banka* into laments.

Many of the earlier poems in the *Manyôshû* were occasional in nature, composed at court ceremonies, upon spring outings into the country to pick young shoots in the fields, and during banquets and parties. These poems all share a communal sensibility. The requiems, hymns, benedictions, and prayers of this period, moreover, contain an element of reverie.

While community and reverie are at the heart of the early *Manyôshû* poems, a few later court poets such as Yamabe no Akahito (d. 736?) and Ôtomo no Yakamochi (718-785), outstanding in their own right, digress from this sensibility to create in addition to conventional verse a more personal lyric, addressed to no specific audience. The appearance of this personal lyric tells of the appearance of a society – a kind of petite bourgeoisie? – whose members composed verse freely on any subject.

Although some poems in the *Manyôshû* were written as early as the fourth century, the hundred-year period from the middle of the seventh century to the middle of the eighth is the most richly represented. It can be further divided into four periods, and in each period poets have a role distinct from the others. In the first period court ladies wrote poems by proxy for the emperor, presented poems at official occasions, and recited impromptu verse in the style of *sômon*. In the second period the professional male court poet took over the duties of composition, writing informal verse, posing as others (the poet's wife, for example), as well as writing official, congratulatory verse.

In the first two periods, the court was apparently the only forum for poetry. Beginning with the third period, around the year 700, Chinese poetry came into vogue at court and was composed by male court poets on all public occasions. Courtiers continued to write *waka* privately, however, using as their forum the less formal setting of aristocratic residences. In the fourth period some poets continued to use such residences as literary salons and encouraged women (who had played a lesser role since the first period) to participate, which fact brought about a revival of women's poetry to a point that women became the principal caretakers of court *waka*. Simultaneously, the world of *waka* poets came to include common people, from villagers to nameless itinerants and female entertainers. The latter circumstance accounts for the fact that fully half the poems in the *Manyôshû* are anonymous.

The matter of authorship was of little concern in the days of the *Manyôshû*. A great many poems are virtually identical yet listed under different poets. A poet might be credited with the authorship of a certain poem by virtue of having recited some remembered old ditty in the presence of others. A poem was not thought of as reflecting an independent sensibility or containing emotions or modes of expression unique to the author. While it would be an overstatement to say that poets in the age of the *Manyôshû* had no individuality, theirs was an individualism by proxy, a characteristic central to the Manyô tradition.

The *sedôka* also sheds some light on the attitude toward authorship. *Sedôka* means "head-repeated poem" and normally comprises two three-lined stanzas that repeat a given theme. The form itself, however, seems to have been capable of accommodating any number of stanzas. As a two-stanza exchange between poets it had no refrain, but in its longer form, as a folk poem of two or more stanzas, each stanza was composed by a different poet and had a common refrain, or at least a similar concluding phrase. Thus the *sedôka* could either be the product of an individual poet or, like a folk song, have multiple authorship.

Another characteristic genre of *waka* in the *Manyôshû*, particularly conspicuous among later poems, is the banquet poem. Such poems were not thought of as independent verses; rather, like *renga* (linked verse), they were composed impromptu in a series by those present at a festivity, each person reciting a verse that carried the theme of the one preceding it. Old, familiar ditties would be interjected from time to time when appropriate.

The Japanese language in the age of the *Manyôshû* was more a spoken than a written language. Communication meant verbal communication, and took place only when both speaker and audience were present. It is important to consider the poems in this light. In fact, we can classify poems in the *Manyôshû* according to the relationship between poet and audience: one-to-one (e.g. love poems): one-to-many (banquet poems); many-to-many (folk songs); and one-to-none (personal lyrics). Only the fourth presumes no audience, and it is outside the mainstream of the Manyô tradition. The keynote of *Manyôshû* poems is the link between poet and audience, for it sets the tone of a poem.

While the personal lyric ostensibly has no audience, we can nonetheless think of poets who wrote such verse as imagining a specific audience. A court poet, for example, may appear to be delivering a soliloquy of sorts when in his mind's eye he is actually addressing another courtier. The tradition of the personal lyric, moreover, led to the appearance of such poets as Ôtomo no Yakamochi (one of the editors of and a most important contributor to the *Manyôshû*), whose verses are unique in that he considered them to be complete with their creation, not with their transmission to an audience. Poems in the *Manyôshû* thus include both verse of a communal sort, composed chiefly in the earlier period in a convivial setting and suggesting group authorship, and verse of a more personal sort, composed in the later period and having a quasi-modern, individualistic sensibility and an awareness of the poet's own existence as a solitary being.

Love poetry was in the main the property of lady poets. Just as the official poem is conspicuous in the middle of the *Manyôshû* period, when the professional male court poets were active, the love poem is conspicuous in the poetry of the earlier and especially the later periods, when female poets were active. In the later period, poetry written in Chinese had come into vogue among court gentlemen, who considered it more learned and dignified than poetry written in their native tongue. Yet although the *waka* no longer had a place in official court functions, it retained its vitality through the poetic activity of court ladies as well as the lower classes.

Commentary

No study of Japanese literature would be complete without a discussion of the *Manyôshû*. *Manyôshû* literally means "A Collection of Ten Thousand Leaves," suggesting that the anthology contains myriad poems and implying that it is an anthology for myriad generations.

The anthology in fact contains about forty-five hundred poems, from the fourth to the eighth centuries. It is believed to have been completed around the beginning of the Heian period, although it is not known exactly when. No fewer than two hundred sixty poets contributed to the anthology, but more than half the poems are anonymous. The poets in the *Manyôshû* represent every level of society and every walk of life, from emperors, members of the imperial family and courtiers in the capital to nameless soldiers and humble peasants in remote provinces. The only requirement for inclusion in the anthology was literary excellence. This is a distinctive feature of the *Manyôshû.*

In *Manyô no Sekai*, the author writes: "The *Manyôshû* is indeed a strange work. Although it has universal appeal among Japanese, it admits the reader only a certain distance into its world." Perhaps the author is saying that while there are few books in classical literature better known and loved by the Japanese, the modern reader's knowledge and level of appreciation are in reality limited and stereotyped.

The *Manyôshû* is like a rich yet mysterious cavern, the recesses of which are cloaked in darkness. The average reader sees only a little past the entrance, and yet is quick to proclaim the anthology a paragon of simplicity and genuineness of feeling, qualities which modern man has lost, and a kind of spiritual home. Expressing his dissatisfaction with such stereotyped interpretations, the author sheds new light on the anthology by inquiring into the relationships between the poems and the poets. He examines the function of poetry in early times as well as settings, subject matter, authors, and aesthetic purpose. He stresses – and here lies his main strength – that poems in the *Manyôshû*, particularly the earlier poems, cannot be thought of as individual creations in the modern sense, for they were communal in origin, incantations often with group authorship.

21. THE TALE OF GENJI

Genji Monogatari By Akiyama Ken
Tokyo: Iwanami Shinsho #667, Iwanami Shoten, 1968.

The Origin of the Image of the Shining Genji

The protagonist of the *Genji Monogatari,* or *Tale of Genji*, is the Shining Genji. The child of Emperor Kiritsubo and a concubine, he was of such radiant beauty that he was named Hikaru, "shining." He is described as a man of boundlessly tender and generous love and a paragon of learning and the arts. All the heroes of the ancient Japanese *monogatari*, or romantic narrative tales, were idealized by literary convention. The Shining Genji is no exception. But he is incomparably more perfect than any of the others. This is not so much because the author extended and idealized the traditional *monogatari* hero as because the context of *The Tale of Genji* itself demanded such a lofty hero-figure.

"In the reign of a certain emperor, among the many imperial ladies and concubines there was one who, though not of particularly high status, nevertheless took precedence over all in her lord's favor." These are the opening words of the first book of *The Tale of Genji*, "Kiritsubo." The narrative continues as follows. The imperial ladies of high birth considered the lady a shameless upstart with no sense of her proper place, and were consumed with jealous and scornful hatred. Her companions could not bear the thought that she had gone so far as to seize their lord's affections. The victim of such spite, the lady grew weak and sickly; a forlorn and pathetic figure, she wished to leave the court and return to her parental home, and so made the emperor feel all the more tenderly toward her. The reader here realizes that the emperor's overwhelming love clearly creates the conditions that instead drive her to misery.

The order of rank among the court ladies in waiting during the Fujiwara period (967-1068), when *The Tale of Genji* was written, paralleled the relative power of the families from which the ladies came. For the author to have such a character whose official guardian lacked power, enjoy the special favor of the emperor meant ignoring reality. We can interpret this state of affairs in the story as reflecting the author's protest against the established practice that forced love to yield to social status. But her resistance is fragile and short-lived. When the new prince, fine as a jewel, is born to the emperor and his lady, the emperor's love for mother and child only grows; but the author has no choice but to bring such a state of affairs to an end by having the lady die a miserable death. Through this expedient the author at the same time confronts Genji with the harshness of the way of the world. Not because of superiority to the conventions of the *monogatari* but because he was thus left alone and friendless in the court was it necessary that the hero be endowed with character and talents that would gain him support despite his circumstances.

At the age of seven Genji is reduced from royal status and given with the surname Genji or Minamoto. *The Tale of Genji* was not written as a fanciful tale of a nonexistent past. The author clearly took as her models the reign of Emperor Daigo (897-930) and Minamoto no Takaakira, an imperial prince who was reduced to the status of subject and given the surname Minamoto and presently became Minister of the Left, one of the most powerful government posts.

The system by which an imperial prince was reduced from royal status to establish a new family began in the early ninth century and served two purposes. Directly, it was a means to help an imperial family in reduced circumstances; but it was also a way for families proudly aware of being royal to counteract the powerful Fujiwara clan. Minamoto no Takaakira was banished as a result of a Fujiwara plot, but this only aroused popular sympathy. By giving her protagonist the name Genji, the author of *The Tale of Genji* secured the support of her readers.

Another point that should be noted is the divination of Genji's singular future. "He has the features of one who can rise to the topmost rank as emperor, but his future so read entails the danger of national upheaval. However, read as the face of one who will become regent and chancellor and thus counsel the emperor in affairs of state, it does not bear that cast." The soothsayer repeatedly cocks his head in puzzlement. On another occasion it is predicted of Genji that "the impossible, the unthinkable, will occur."

Through the device of these divinations the author predicts that while he will achieve the acme of success, the hero's immeasurably varied and magnanimous spirit will also cause him to suffer. It is precisely this contradiction and conflict that is the distinctive quality of Genji's life.

The Permutations of Karma

The plot unfolds as follows. After the death of Genji's mother, the emperor brings to court a woman named Fujitsubo, who closely resembles the dead lady. Genji, hearing of Fujitsubo's likeness to his mother, whom he lost when he was three years of age, is attracted to her. Imperceptibly this feeling grows into love for Fujitsubo as the embodiment of ideal womanhood.

Genji urges his suit on Fujitsubo, wishing that this brief, dreamlike, forbidden interlude might last forever. Fujitsubo trembles with fear lest their trysts become the target of gossip. She neither refuses him nor completely loses herself in love. She holds an extraordinary fascination for him. Pregnant as a result of her involvement with Genji, she feels ashamed to face the emperor and her anguish grows ever more intense. The emperor, knowing nothing of the affair, rejoices at the birth of the baby boy and plans to designate him crown prince. At the same time he promotes Genji to high post that he may become the little prince's future guardian.

At this time the most powerful lady in the palace is Kokiden, who has strong backing. Her son has already been named crown prince. The emperor abdicates and persuades Kokiden to recognize Fujitsubo's son as the next crown prince in return for raising her own son to the throne.

In this way he partially assuages his regret at not having been able to make Genji, his favorite son, crown prince. He also manages to strengthen the new crown prince's position through raising Genji to high rank.

In exchange for this exceptional honor, Genji and Fujitsubo both endure an ever-mounting sense of anxiety and guilt. The reader sees that thus is fulfilled the prophecy "the unthinkable will occur."

With the new reign, Genji's power suddenly wanes. As if to soothe his anger, he again importunes Fujitsubo, and even sees Oborozukiyo, one of the new emperor's ladies, in secret. Fujitsubo, anxious for her son's future, desperately repels his advances. But his tryst with Oborozukiyo, coming to Kokiden's attention, leads to his banishment to Suma (a part of Kobe). The device of his exile allows the author to describe his sorrow at leaving the capital and to extol eloquently his way of life as a man of taste and refinement. Because this description is based on the historical facts of men who were disgraced through the machinations of the Fujiwara, she draws sympathy to her hero and lays the groundwork for Genji's spectacular reinstatement.

The Shining Genji's Power and His Milieu

With the abdication of Emperor Suzaku and the simultaneous accession of the crown prince at the age of eleven circumstances change again, and Genji attains to heights of glory. Fujitsubo has died young, and the new emperor, Reizei, learns the secret of his birth, with the result that Genji's position is secured for life. In discussing Genji's power, the author depicts episodes showing not only his resourcefulness but also his mastery of learning and the arts, thus making the point that this indeed is the kind of person who should be at the helm of state.

In the autumn of his thirty-fourth year Genji builds a magnificent new mansion, the Rokujô-in, on a vast plot divided into four compounds, each designed for one of the four seasons. He installs an appropriate lady in each of the four. In her description of the Rokujô mansion is the very essence of *miyabi*, grace and opulence.

Murasaki Shikibu and *The Tale of Genji*

The author of *The Tale of Genji*, Murasaki Shikibu, is thought to have been born around 975. Her family belonged to the Fujiwara clan, but in comparison to Fujiwara no Michinaga, who was at the height of prosperity, her family was of relatively low status. It produced a number of poets and men of letters, however. Murasaki Shikibu showed intellectual brilliance at an early age, and her father lamented that she had not been born a boy. But the fact of her having been a woman is the great good fortune of Japanese literature, because the talents of brilliant men were all too often expended in utilitarian pursuits.

In her grief following her husband's death Murasaki Shikibu imagined the life of the Shining Genji and began to create her fictional world. At the beginning of the eleventh century she was appointed a lady-in-waiting to Michinaga's eldest daughter, Shôshi (or Akiko), who enjoyed great influence as consort of the Emperor Ichijô's. It is believed that a part of *The Tale of Genji* was already known at court and Murasaki Shikibu's talent recognized. For her family, here was an unattainable world to be gazed upon from afar. It is hard to believe that Murasaki Shikibu was eager to enter court service. While it is unclear how far the writing of *The Tale of Genji* had progressed at that time, it is thought that Genji's attainment of the pinnacle of power reflects Murasaki Shikibu's first-hand observation of the prosperity of Michinaga's family.

In the conventional thinking of the time, *monogatari* (what we today would call romances or novels) were idle amusement for women and children, so that it is difficult to believe that Michinaga would actually have read *The Tale of Genji* seriously. Emperor Ichijô, however, did recognize Murasaki Shikibu's exceptional brilliance. Through Genji she presents her own theory of the *monogatari*: that the *Nihongi* and other such chronicles record only one side of history. The *monogatari* does not narrate facts as such but describes human life as it really is, good and bad alike. Her insight into the true nature of the *monogatari* can be applied unchanged to the modern concept of the novel.

It is only natural, the author espousing such a concept of the *monogatari*, that *The Tale of Genji* should not end with Genji at heights of prosperity. His joyful progress already harbors the seeds of suffering. The full moon must wane. And in her tale Murasaki Shikibu proceeds to depict the fleeting nature of human life, an endless battle against loneliness and despair.

Commentary

It goes without saying that *The Tale of Genji* is the world's oldest novel and marks the high point in the history of Japanese literature. Because of the author's superb plotting and deep perception of human nature, this tale has been considered the model for the novel in Japan since ancient times. In the almost one thousand years since it was written it has never lacked for readers and has continued to influence later writers. An immense number of annotations, commentaries, and appreciations of *The Tale of Genji* have been produced. Even now, over a hundred books and papers concerning *The Tale of Genji* are published yearly in Japan.

Professor Akiyama's book, following in this tradition, is written for a general readership; while following the development of the plot of *The Tale of Genji*, it includes commentary and appreciation based on the author's own views. The book has two distinctive features: on the one hand, the discussion is based on the history of the period in which *The Tale of Genji* was written and the life and view of life of its author, Murasaki Shikibu, whose diary is extant; on the other hand, the skillful construction of *The Tale of Genji*, the author's penetrating insight into human nature, and the philosophy implicit in the work are presented in a well-balanced and easily understood style. Here we have introduced roughly the first half of the book.

22. JAPANESE LITERATURE AND THE SENSE OF IMPERMANENCE

Mujôkan no Bungaku By Kobayashi Tomoaki
Tokyo: Kôbundô, 1965.

The monk Dôgen (1200-53) once said that the act of contemplating the impermanence of life (*mujô*) was itself a form of religious awakening and a state of immanent Buddhahood. He was, of course explaining the mental preparation needed for the true practice of Buddhism. This fascination with the impermanence of life is also, however, an important element in much of Japanese literature.

The word *mujô* can be defined in three broad senses. First, it is the idea that everything is in a state of flux; blossoms fall, men die, friends here today are gone tomorrow, and there is a sense of emptiness in the contemplation of life. Impermanence, which nullifies human aspiration toward the eternal and immortal, is an inexorable reality, and yet this very fact evokes deep feelings of poignancy which in turn form a strong motive in artistic expression. The sense of evanescence that pervades Japanese literature is exclusively of this lyrical kind. Although close to the heart of Buddhist thought, it is also an expression of a universal human emotion.

Mujô is, secondly, the idea that man, who recognizes and judges everything to be mutable, is himself impermanent. It is the denial of all matter, physical sensation, concepts, will, reason and the self – again a tenet of Buddhism.

Thirdly there is the world of Nirvana where there exists neither transience nor permanence, a sphere of the absolute which transcends being and nonbeing. Of these three categories only the first is directly related to literature. The other two are already on a different plane, but they too must be appreciated before the first kind can be fully understood.

The aim of literature is nothing more or less than to depict man in all his folly. Buddhism on the other hand sets out to enlighten man in his folly. In essence, then, the concept of *mujô* is incompatible with literature; there is no place for literature in the face of an attitude toward the impermanence of life which insists that all truth is relative and that all ideas and judgments are irrelevancies bound up inextricably in the 'self'.

If common ground is to be found between the two, it is *mujô* that must change. It must become more humanistic, and when this shift occurs *mujô* loses its fundamental meaning and becomes an expression of feeling, an emotive shadow of its former self. Japanese literature thus represents a fusion of the principle of *mujô* with the idea of literature through pathos. Yet it also gave rise to the idea that literature is not merely an empty pastime, but a possible aid to enlightenment. This concept was most highly developed in court poetry (*waka*), which had a venerable tradition to vie with the authority of Buddhism itself. Here the marriage of poetry and religion was accepted with little hesitation. Thus the literature of *mujô* is based on a combination of a deeply rooted and very real consciousness of the self with a concept of the impermanence of life which aims to deny and destroy that consciousness.

When this concept of *mujô*, which sees all worldly beauty and pride as empty and meaningless, becomes objectified in a work of literary art, the result is the crystallization of an unusual kind of literary beauty: a world of gloom and darkness devoid of blossoms and bright maple leaves. In the middle ages there developed such aesthetic ideals as "dark and mysterious beauty," *yûgen*; "the beauty of simplicity," *wabi*; "the beauty of loneliness in tranquillity," *sabi*; "chill melancholy," *hie*; and "delicacy of feeling," *hosomi*. All somehow denied the validity of color. These concepts were valued because they were abstract and ran counter to the sentient world; because of their otherworldly tone they were eminently suited to a sense of *mujô*.

The poems in the *Manyôshû*, an eighth century anthology, are usually thought simple, direct and vigorous in style, and the poets themselves practical men who experienced life through the physical senses. It is worth noting, however, that in the shade of vigorous poems affirming reality there are already poems that express a sense of the impermanence of life and which deny the sentient world.

In the late tenth century, when the power of the Fujiwaras were at its peak, court literature was permeated with this sense of *mujô*, and the feeling grew stronger in the late Heian period, perhaps reflecting the collapse of the established political system and the insecurity which resulted. But the fact that references to the pathos of *mujô* became more and more frequent does not necessarily mean that the experience was more profound. On the contrary, worldly desires were stressed, and a Buddhism, which might have urged change, became man-centered. The sense of *mujô* might have become an incentive to take religious vows and renounce the world, but desires and ties with this world often proved too strong, and the conflict, hesitation and anguish which resulted is to be seen in all Heian writing.

The first appearance of a sense of *mujô* as an actual literary motif was in *The Tales of Yamato* (*Yamato Monogatari*)*, where, with the support of Buddhism, it is intermingled with the subjective emotionalism, *mono no aware*. The classic example of the expression of *mujô* in court literature is, of course, *The Tale of Genji*. It is no exaggeration to say that the whole work is permeated with Buddhist thought; on the one hand there unrolls a picture scroll of colorful Buddhist rituals and festivals, and on the other hand the transience and sadness of life is stressed, and a drive to transcend it. But the religion of Genji is less the result of an earnest personal search for truth than the result of more mundane ideas and realities, such as worldly failure, or a strong suspicion of worldly success. In that *The Tale of Genji* can be defined in these terms the influence of *mujô* is indeed strong, but one also gets a very powerful impression of human desires in all their uncertainty and pain, their joy and satisfaction; salvation lies elsewhere. The author never touches on the subject of salvation and only deals directly with such themes as the consciousness of transgression and the principle of impermanence. We are presented with a long procession of human beings who stand in fear and trembling before such a reality.

The poet-priest Saigyô, who lived in the twelfth century, wrote many poems on the subject of *mujô*, reflecting the uncertainty of his age. A sense of the lonely anguish of man underlies his austere poetry; and yet he found it impossible to discard his love of nature and his passion for poetry itself.

The middle ages was a long period of transition which saw the breakdown of the Heian polity and the emergence of the feudal system. Literature reflects the contradictions and confusion of the times. *Mujô* is always understood as sadness and pain and, it is worth noting, is closely tied to the Buddhist idea of rebirth in paradise. The battleground between this concept of rebirth in which all should rejoice and man's deep attachment to life is a most promising subject for literature.

In *The Tales of the Heike* (*Heike Monogatari*)*, the best example, historical reality is neither affirmed nor denied; such simple attitudes are transcended and reality is looked at for what it is, a reality full of sudden surprises and in a perpetual state of change. It is the sense of *mujô* which softens this realism with an element of pathos and sentiment. *The Tales of the Heike* vividly depicts a meteoric rise and decline, thrown into relief by a sense of gentle melancholy. Whereas the Buddhist attitude to *mujô* is one of spiritual awakening to the truth of reality, here we have an expression of sadness and loss; it is an "ethic of destruction" in that all things are destined to pass away.

In *An Account of My Hut* (*Hôjôki*)*, another classic in the same vein, a consciousness of the self stands side by side with a sense of *mujô*. The mundane and the otherworldly are inextricably mixed. In the turmoil of the age it was often recluses such as Kamo no Chômei, the author, who bore the burden of keeping civilization alive. They were Buddhist dilettantes, who had chosen to withdraw from life, but they were proud of their solitude.

To them it was life as it should be. They were interpreters of the classical literary tradition and contemporary intellectuals as well. Yoshida Kenkô, the author of *Essays in Idleness* (*Tsurezuregusa*)*, was not unlike Chômei, but in his work the sense of *mujô* is far more positive. At root Kenkô was a confirmed humanist, but when he looked at the world as a Buddhist he often expressed himself in terms very close to Buddhism.

The tradition of *mujô* is also found in Tokugawa literature, in the work of Bashô. The development of his *sabi* presents a difficult problem, but there is no doubt that the concept of *mujô* played a large part in it.

Nozarashi o/kokoro ni kaze no/shimu mi kana

A weather-exposed skeleton
Haunts my mind: how the wind
Penetrates my body! (Tr. Ueda Makoto, *Matsuo Bashô*)

Here *mujô* itself is seen as reality, and there is a claim that true reality lies beyond the empty vanities of this world.

Commentary

The term "literature of *mujô*" is used here in a special sense. *Mujô* is usually seen as characteristic of medieval writing, and it is often contrasted with the "elegance" of court literature, the "beauty of loneliness" (*sabi*) of Bashô, and the "savoir faire" (*iki*) of Saikaku in the Tokugawa period. At the same time, however, it may be said that this sense of the impermanence of life is an emotion basic to much of Japanese art. Kobayashi argues that the principle of *mujô*, a fundamental Buddhist belief, is rather different from the sense of *mujô* as objectified in literature, the latter being far more humanistic; and it is with the aid of this insight that he succeeds in illuminating the relation between the two.

Literature is, in the last analysis, wedded to reality. Buddhism is quite the opposite, and it is Kobayashi's thesis that they are fundamentally incompatible. The *mujô* of literature is very different from that of Buddhism, being often little more than a sense of pathos. Although there seems to have occurred a fusion of religion and literature in the middle ages, it is an illusion, for *mujô* changed fundamentally in the process. Kobayashi does not attribute to this sense of impermanence the power to vitalize a work of literature; such power comes from the attempt to fuse two incompatibles, of Buddhism and literature. The strength of such writing lies in the fact that the consciousness of the self is, in the end, an undying flame. Bashô would seem to lie at the end of this tradition, for in his work the idealized concepts of *sabi* and *wabi* create a world where not only death and parting but all natural phenomena, even man's pleasures and his love of splendor, evoke a sense of *mujô*, a second world where the sense of nature transcends immediate physical sensations.

[NOTES]

**Yamato Monogatari.* Compiled c. 951. Author unknown. Classified as a poem-tale. The first half describes the genesis of the poems. The latter half lays more emphasis on the prose narrative element and includes many tales and legends related to the poems.

**Heike Monogatari*. Compiled about the middle of the thirteenth century. A war tale which describes the rise and fall of the Heike clan. Twelve volumes. Recited to musical accompaniment by *biwa hôshi*. Widely known amongst all classes, it has exerted great influence on later writing.

**Hôjôki.* By Kamo no Chômei (1155-1216). A typical example of the genre known as occasional or discursive essays (*zuihitsu*).

**Tsurezuregusa.* By Yoshida Kenkô (c.1283-c.1353). Most famous medieval collection of essays. Often read today as an introduction to the classics.

23. OBLIGATION AND SENTIMENT

Giri to Ninjô By Minamoto Ryôen
Tokyo: Chûkô Shinsho #191, Chûô Kôron-sha, 1969.

To investigate "obligation" (*giri*) and "sentiment" (*ninjô*) as they appear in literature, it is necessary to differentiate between those cases in which the author has used an actual social situation and those which are fabrications of his imagination. It is important that the latter not be ignored, for it is very often an idealization of moral values which provides important clues to the heart and mind of the Japanese.

The works of Ihara Saikaku which deal with the problem of obligation make up a very small percentage of the total, but they are important in the history of the concept of obligation. Saikaku depicted obligation as it was found in the already outdated warrior code of the late Muromachi period. His warriors are masterless wanderers or hermits, and not the successful bureaucrats of his own day. Possibly Saikaku was praising old-fashioned ethics as a plea to the townsmen (who held the economic power but were forced to live under the political sway of the warrior class) to live like true townsmen and to the warriors to live like true warriors.

Most examples of obligation in Saikaku's *Tales of Warrior Obligation* (*Buke Giri Monogatari*) show situations of mutual trust and spiritual concord. They seem isolated and accidental, and not normative.

In one story, two young retainers of the same lord quarrel. Ôshiro Dennosuke, the older, is killed. When the father of Nanao Hachijûrô, the younger, hears of the incident, he sends Hachijûrô to Dennosuke's parents with a note giving them leave to do what they will by way of retribution. Dennosuke's mother seizes a halberd to kill Hachijûrô on the spot, but her husband adopts Hachijûrô into the family to carry on the family name. This is an example of "obligation in response to trust."

Another story tells of a warrior intellectual named Oguri who travels from Bizen (Okayama Prefecture) to Kyoto one snowy morning to visit Ishikawa Jôzan, a cultured recluse. On Oguri's departure for Bizen the previous month, Ishikawa extended the invitation. Oguri arrives on the appointed day, but Ishikawa has forgotten the invitation. Ishikawa prepares breakfast, which they take together, and Oguri immediately departs, saying that he will be in Bizen until spring. Here is an example of "obligation to fulfil a contract."

Thus we see the fulfilling of obligation as basically for the protection of one's own honor. To be considered untrustworthy was the most painful humiliation imaginable.

In another incident, a young warrior is ill and unable to participate in a battle. Three of his fellows sneer at his weakness. As soon as he is well enough, he challenges the three to a duel, kills them all, and commits suicide over their bodies. His suicide note is received with sympathy and approval.

To us the action taken by this young warrior may appear to be merely for personal honor, and lacking in a sense of duty toward his lord. But for Saikaku and his day, the man who did not protect his own honor was unworthy to carry out the orders of his lord.

Chikamatsu Monzaemon is often described as a playwright who treated of conflicts between obligation and sentiment. But his main preoccupation can better be described as the purity of love and the beauty of sentiment. In such early works as *Double Suicide at Sonezaki* (*Sonezaki Shinjû*), hindrances produce mounting passion which culminates in death. There is intense sadness evoked, but no sense of guilt. As Chikamatsu matured, the violence of the passions subsided and the espousal of love took on a melancholy air, and a concern for common social ethics came to the fore.

The lovers in his early suicide pieces are extremely young. In his later works, he chose such characters as Jihei, the father of two children (in *Suicide at Amijima*) and the thrice married O-chiyo (in *The Kôshin Suicides*), not models of unconditional passion. In his middle period, secondary characters who have undergone great trials lend human depth to his writing.

Chikamatsu develops the conflict between obligation and sentiment yet further in, for instance, *Murder in a Hell of Oil* (*Onna-Goroshi Abura-no-Jigoku*), in which a man and woman sacrifice themselves for a child. They thus seek to go beyond personal feelings.

In *Suicide at Amijima*, Jihei's wife O-san and the courtesan Koharu, rivals for the same man's love and of different social classes, go to great lengths in their kindness to each other. Each seeks to be worthy of the other's trust. Obligation is seen not in terms of traditional, formalized standards, but as feeling.

The hopeful world of Saikaku's townsman, in which success depended upon talent, had become for Chikamatsu a society in which such possibilities were severely limited. Business became almost impossible outside the commercial establishment. The ethics of obligation, which had been the exclusive property of the warrior class, permeated the world of the townsman.

Saikaku's warriors strove to fulfill themselves through fidelity to their obligations. Chikamatsu drew his characters as manifestations of the conflict between obligation and sentiment. The sense of obligation found in Chikamatsu is not simply an imposition of outside forces, as in later puppet plays. It is always felt in relation to another person. We do not find in his works direct confrontations between obligation and sentiment.

After Chikamatsu, plays about obligation and sentiment became more frequent. Obligation is always presented in terms of social pressure: "Obligation is the saddest aspect of life"; "Nothing is so painful as obligation"; "Obligation is the warrior's enemy." A hierarchy came into being in which great value was placed upon obligation to lord and family. This gave rise to a number of now-famous stories in which the sacrifice of a child is a demonstration of loyalty.

In the works of Takizawa Bakin, there is a strong element of Confucian morality. Sentiment is abandoned in favor of obligation to one's lord. This willingness to sacrifice personal sentiments and even life for higher authority was the nucleus of Tokugawa society.

It survived until the end of the Pacific War. After the Meiji Restoration, economic values undermined political priorities. Even the old warrior class, whose main aim had been the pursuit of rectitude, began now to join the old merchant class in the pursuit of profit. Utsumi Bunzô in Futabatei Shimei's *Floating Clouds* (*Ukigumo*) and Hazama Kanichi in Ozaki Kôyô's *Golden Demon* (*Konjiki Yasha*) find it impossible to cope with the dilemmas of such a world.

There were those who, dissatisfied with Philistine values, turned to the world of obligation and sentiment. The first writer to revolt against material values in favor of the old ethics was Ozaki Kôyô's student Izumi Kyôka. In *A Woman's Lineage* (*Onna Keizu*), Kyôka extols obligation to one's teacher as an absolute and at the same time urges the demands of pure love. Kyôka thought of the old-fashioned values as the only bulwark against Philistinism.

Commentary

Obligation as a key to an understanding of Japan is a popular theme. Minamoto claims that the concept of obligation can only be understood when obligation and sentiment are grasped as part of the same code of ethics. He maintains that the ethics of obligation were already at work in ancient farming villages, but that they were not explicit until the seventeenth century. He traces the concept of obligation from Saikaku to modern times.

The present book is in three parts. The first stresses the part played by sentiment in the psychology of the Japanese, and the close relationship between obligation and sentiment. The second gives Minamoto's own view of obligation and his criticism of such writers on the subject as Ruth Benedict. The third section is the real core of the book. Obligation and sentiment are examined in literature from the Edo period to the present. It is an excellent commentary on modern Japanese literature. We have discussed only this third section.

24. BASHÔ: HIS LIFE AND ART

Bashô = Sono Jinsei to Geijutsu By Imoto Nôichi
Tokyo: Kôdansha Gendai Shinsho #151, Kôdansha, 1968.

Bashô was born in Iga (Mie Prefecture) in 1644, the second son of a landed samurai. At the age of eighteen, he entered the service of a son of the powerful Tôdô family who was two years his elder and very fond of the *haikai* style of poetry. It is thought that poetry led to a very close relationship. Unfortunately his lord died when Bashô was only twenty-two, and so it became necessary for him to depend on his older brother for a living. He spent several years rather aimlessly. Shortly before he turned thirty, he made up his mind to dedicate his life to *haikai* poetry.

At the New Year of his twenty-eighth year, he dedicated his first collection of poetry to the Tenman Shrine at Ueno in Iga. It is the shrine of a god of culture to whom it had long been a custom to dedicate literary works.

Bashô had been trained in the popular Teimon School of *haikai*, which parodied classical poetry and delighted in word play. His first collection of poetry was very much in the Teimon style, revealing a ready wit, a bold use of slang, and a great deal of youthful ambition. It also contained a protest against the mannerisms into which *haikai* had fallen and Bashô's own frustrations.

Shortly afterward Bashô went to Edo, which was becoming not only a center of politics and economics, but of culture as well. There were few restrictions due to tradition or lineage. Bashô worked very hard to make a name for himself in the Edo literary world. The collection of poetry dedicated to the shrine in Ueno was published in Edo about a year after his arrival, but it evoked no response, and he found it necessary to make a living as a clerk for the city waterworks.

His name gradually became known in Edo, particularly when he joined a new group of reforming poets known as the Danrin School. He was recognized as an independent master at the age of thirty-five. A large group of students gathered around him, and his position in the world of haiku was clearly established as he and his students published successive volumes of poetry.

It was at this time of apparent success that Bashô found himself in need of change. The Danrin School of which he was a member had established itself in the name of freshness and freedom as opposed to the triteness of the Teimon School. This very striving after newness had become a boring mannerism. Bashô had been studying the philosophy and poetry of China, Chaung-tsu and Tu Fu and others, and he suddenly felt that his own poetry was by comparison nothing more than word play. Even his new eminence seemed tenuous and ephemeral. At the age of thirty-seven, he moved to the suburbs and went into retirement.

He gave up wealth and fame to pursue a simpler life and become a purer artist. In two or three years, he had begun to be uncomfortable with retirement, and in 1684, at the age of forty, he set out on a trip that lasted from summer through the following spring.

Knowing I may be
Left out on the plain to rot,
I face the cold wind.

This is the introduction to his travelogue. The idea that a man would set out on a journey expecting to die and be left to rot on the open plains seemed quite insane. And this was indeed his announcement that he had become a mad poet.

By the time he returned, his fame had spread throughout Edo. He was no longer simply a poet of talent, but the most refined of recluse poets. In the autumn of 1687, he once more set out on a journey, this time to the Kansai area. A gigantic farewell party was given for him, and haiku gatherings were held at each station along the Tôkaidô Highway. He spent the New Year holidays in his home town, made the rounds of the famous places in the Kansai area with his students, and returned to Edo the following autumn. During these two or three years, the Bashô style of haiku gained general popularity. He seems to have enjoyed his journeys and life in general. His poetry, however, began to show signs of stagnation.

He had numerous callers and he was inundated with invitations to haiku gatherings. Again he decided to give up the life of the great poet and set out on a journey to bring new life into his work. In 1689 he made the journey to the northern provinces that produced his most famous work, *The Narrow Road to the Deep North* (*Oku no Hosomichi*). He sold all his worldly possessions, including his house, and dissolved all relationships that were of a binding nature, putting everything into his life as an artist. In a letter to his disciple he stated that he was willing to lead a life of penury for the sake of his art.

During his northern journey, Bashô sought out famous places mentioned in classical poetry, hoping to use them toward his own artistic development. He believed that the best way to maintain and carry on traditions was to accept them unconditionally and use them as a basis for his own work.

As he left Edo, he expressed in verse the melancholy of the season and the sadness of parting:

In the fading spring
A bird crys and tears well up
In the eyes of fish.

He journeyed through the Tôhoku area as far as Hiraizumi, and thence through the Ôu Mountains to the Japan Sea. He came to feel that some traditions are unchangeable and others are not. He found ways to conform to tradition without being bound by tradition.

He saw that something unchanging flows through all good poetry and that from it derives all appreciation, and that good poetry must be unique, fresh, and of its times. He thereupon moved what he termed the "heaviness" of concepts and ideas to the "lightness" of ordinary incident.

After his northern trip, Bashô returned to his native Iga, and very soon set out once more to wander about the Ôtsu and Kyoto area for about two years. The Tôdô family offered to give him a home, but he was not interested. He returned to Edo, homeless and impoverished, but satisfied that dedication to art had allowed him to attain to the life of a beggar.

Bashô's *The Narrow Road to the Deep North* was actually completed and published about two years after all these journeys were over. Much has been said about discrepancies between this work and the actual facts of his journeys, which have been called fabrications. To Bashô, however, the "fabrications" contained the real truth. For him there was nothing but art, and just as the artistic life was the only true life, the facts of his journeys were of no importance. Only his artistic fabrications were true and important.

In 1694, at the age of fifty, Bashô returned to Iga. In October he suddenly fell ill on a short trip to Osaka. As he lay dying, he dictated his final verse to one of his students.

Ill on a journey.
All about the dreary fields
Fly my broken dreams.

Commentary

This is a book about the life and art of Bashô, written for easy reading by a Bashô authority. Imoto presents a biography of the poet followed by a description of the haiku world of his day, and goes on to analyze his style and his works in terms of the two changes in his life. These changes took place during Bashô's late thirties and his late forties, when he made a name for himself as an independent master in Edo, and when he gave up fame and fortune and set out on his journeys. Bashô loved to travel. He spent much of his life on journeys, and finally died on a journey. It is as though he considered life itself a journey in pursuit of art.

The author considers the following words of Bashô a summation of his way of thinking. "A man who looks at and thinks about flowers and the moon and centers all his thoughts on them is a human being. A man only becomes a human being when he buries his life in art."

Imoto rarely uses the words *wabi* and *sabi* that are so very popular with most scholars of Bashô. He centers his main argument upon the "lightness" that Bashô spoke of in his later years, the essence of which is found in the following verse.

Deep in autumn days
What do you think those neighbors
Of ours are up to?

The meaning of this verse is clear. We talk about the activities of our immediate neighbors. The poem is not an explanation of life. The opening phrase, says the author, gives the poem a loneliness that expresses the loneliness and isolation even of next-door neighbors.

A unique aspect of this book is that the author himself is a poet who has been close to the great poet Bashô through research into his life and works.

VII
Autobiography

25. THE AUTOBIOGRAPHY OF FUKUZAWA YUKICHI

Fukuô Jiden By Fukuzawa Yukichi
Tokyo: Iwanami Bunko, green series #22, Iwanami Shoten, 1954.

I was born in Osaka in 1835, the fifth of five children and second son of a lower samurai. My father died when I was still an infant. My mother took us children soon afterwards to our parents' native home in Nakatsu, in northern Kyushu. Compared to Osaka, a city of merchants, Nakatsu still had a deep-rooted feudal tradition that determined even the ranks of children we were allowed to associate with. The class structure and laws of inheritance were very strict: sons of chief retainers became chief retainers, and sons of foot-soldiers became foot-soldiers. My father, who was a samurai by birth but a scholar by inclination, wanted me to become a priest because the priesthood stood outside this class system and was the only road to advancement. I saw in my father a victim of the system, and I saw my own life as a mission to take revenge.

When I was about twelve I began studying Chinese history and philosophy. At nineteen I went to Nagasaki to learn Dutch. The main reason for going, however, was that I simply wanted to get away from Nakatsu and the claustrophobic way of life there. When I set out for Nagasaki, I spat on the ground and swore to myself that I would never return.

One year later I went to Osaka to study at Ogata Kôan's school of Dutch language and medicine, the most progressive in Japan. I was first taken in as a translator and given free room and board, but was eventually made a full-fledged student. Later I even became "head student" (*jukuchô*) and presided over the most advanced class.

The school had about fifty or sixty students. We were all poor. Our meals were simple, and since the floor of the dining room was covered with bare boards and no mats we ate standing up. Summers in Osaka are hot, and we walked about the dormitory in the nude and wore only a loose cotton robe in class and in the dining room. One hot summer night I had settled down in bed after a few drinks when I heard a woman call me from downstairs. Thinking it was the maid, I yelled out a reply and trotted downstairs to the hallway without a stitch on. It turned out to be not the maid, however, but the schoolmaster's wife. I was at a loss for words; yet I could not very well turn around and leave. It was she who finally turned and left. She had taken pity on me, I suppose. I could not bring myself to apologize the next morning for my misbehavior – in fact, I never did say a word about it. I still blush when I recall the incident.

We students would amuse ourselves by dissecting a bear or a pig and then eating it. When we went into town we made a show of fighting in the streets. Our student life was admittedly wild, but we would throw ourselves with the same zeal into our studies. Each student prepared his lessons on his own, relying only on his few texts in physics and medicine and the school dictionary.

Three years later, in 1858 – it was when I was twenty-three – I was called up to Edo by Nakatsu clan headquarters to teach Dutch to members of the clan and later to people from other clans as well. The following year I made a visit to the nearby port of Yokohama, which had just been formally opened for trade with foreign countries. To my chagrin, I found that I could not read a single store sign in the foreign quarter, nor could I understand a word the foreign merchants were saying. I felt that all the years and effort spent learning the Dutch language had been a waste. But the next day I shook off my disappointment and resolved to study English (for that is what I decided the strange language must be) on my own – there being no one who could teach it – relying on a Dutch-English dictionary. Once I began studying I was encouraged by the similarity of the two languages.

In January, 1860, I joined the first Tokugawa mission to the United States on the Japanese warship *Kanrin-maru*, serving as personal steward to the ship's captain. A mere seven years had passed since the Japanese first laid eyes on a steamship, but they did all the navigating on this voyage.

The ship was given a tremendous welcome when it landed in San Francisco. Everything we saw was new and different. I was not particularly impressed by any of the technology I saw in America, such as the telegraph system and the sugar refinery, for I had already studied the operations at Ogata's school; but when it came to social conventions and matters related to daily life, I was completely lost. I had no idea what a carriage was, and I was amazed to discover not only that the floors of our hotel were covered with luxurious carpeting but that people would actually walk on it – shoes and all! Once at a party I got out my pipe and had a smoke, but since I could not find anything that resembled a brazier or ash pot, I was at a loss what to do with the ashes. When I finished smoking I wrapped the ashes in tissue paper, carefully crushed them, and placed them in the sleeve of my robe. A little later I noticed smoke coming out of my sleeve – I had come within a hairbreadth of setting myself on fire! I was surprised at the high position of women in American society, and shocked by the fact that no one seemed to know what had become of the descendants of George Washington. Before I sailed home I bought a copy of Webster's dictionary, the very first to be imported into Japan.

When I returned to Japan in June, 1860, the government hired me as a translator. In January, 1862, I sailed from Nagasaki as a member of the Tokugawa embassy to Europe. We landed in France and went on to tour several other countries. The trip was a valuable experience, for we became acquainted with banking, postal, and governmental systems. While I was in Russia, incidentally one of the members of our reception committee urged me repeatedly to settle in that country. I declined, of course. What it seemed he was really after was my collaboration in diplomatic intrigue. Back in France, news reached us from Japan that an Englishman named Richardson had been cut down in Yokohama by a samurai from the Satsuma clan when he rode across the path of the Satsuma daimyo. When we returned to Japan the movement to "expel the foreigners" had reached its height. Foreign trading shops had all closed their doors, and anti-foreign violence by groups of extremist masterless samurai (*rônin*, mostly from the distant provinces) was directed against even us students of Western civilization. I avoided discussing politics with people I did not know and devoted myself strictly to writing and translating.

In February, 1863, a few months after the Richardson incident, the government called on me to help translate a letter from the British minister. It demanded payment of a one-hundred-thousand-pound indemnity and the execution of the samurai who killed Richardson. The French minister sent the government a letter shortly thereafter backing the British demands and threatening to assist the British fleet in bombarding Edo if they were not met. The government stalled for time, and I resigned myself to war and prepared to evacuate my home. Finally one of the senior government officials acted on his own authority and paid out the enormous sum; and thus open hostilities were avoided. A very tense period followed, in which the government advocated opening the country to foreign intercourse while nearly all the samurai favored a seclusionist policy. Assassinations occurred almost daily. I tried to make myself as inconspicuous as possible. I also resolved to sell all my swords to a dealer, seeing no more use in them. I lived a life of seclusion, and for years never ventured outdoors at night.

In 1867 I visited America a second time, again as a member of a Tokugawa mission. The purpose of the mission was to purchase a warship ordered several years previously. A regular mail service had just opened between Japan and the United States, and we took passage on the return trip of the steamer making the maiden voyage.

When I returned to Japan this time the political factions had polarized. The masterless samurai had gathered in Kyoto from all over Japan to rally around the emperor and were engaging in skirmishes with forces still loyal to the shogunate. I had personally grown disgusted with the seclusionist policies of the shogunate and the incompetence of its officials. But I knew also that the imperial forces were far more xenophobic in their outlook; and so I remained completely aloof from politics at both the national and clan level. When I received a ceremonial kimono from the daimyo of Nakatsu bearing his family crest – quite an honor, really – I immediately sold it.

In 1868, the year of the Meiji Restoration, I opened Keio Gijuku and taught students from the many textbooks I had purchased in America the year before with my generous government allowance. The texts that I had selected eventually came to be used nationwide, and thus American texts prevailed in the first years of the Meiji period.

The Meiji government asked me to serve in the government, but, direct association with politics being against my principles, I declined, pleading illness. During those first war-torn years of the Meiji period, the new regime was in no position to run the schools formerly supported by the Tokugawa shogunate. Keio Gijuku was for a while the only school in the entire country where any real instruction was taking place. In a speech to my students, I once said that Keio would not close its doors a single day no matter how the country was wracked by warfare, and that as long as the school existed Japan would remain a civilized nation.

In founding Keio I believed that education should be based on the laws of nature and the principles of science, and that man, as the highest order in creation, should acquire self-respect, independence, and character.

Commentary

Fukuzawa Yukichi (1835-1901) is the best known of the "enlightenment" (*keimô*) thinkers who flourished in the early Meiji period. His major work, *In Praise of Learning* (*Gakumon no Susume*), became an unprecedented best-seller, and its opening words, "Heaven created man to be the equal of all men" (*Ten wa hito no ue ni hito wo tsukurazu, hito no shita ni hito wo tsukurazu to ieri*), are known by every Japanese.

His autobiography, *Fukuô Jiden*, first appeared in serial form in 1897, when he was sixty-four, in the *Jiji Shinpô*, a newspaper Fukuzawa himself established in 1882.

It is the product of dictation to his secretary, later revised. In it Fukuzawa relates in detail the events of his life in a simple, colloquial style, and his independent philosophy emerges vividly against the historical backdrop of his age.

From his youth, Fukuzawa had a very practical mind with a mechanical bent. He had no use for superstition or the supernatural, or for the strict conventions of traditional Confucianist morality. He despised the feudal ways of his native province and saw in his father a man victimized by reactionary laws.

In Fukuzawa's autobiography the reader is treated to a vivid picture of student life during an age of transformation. Some of Fukuzawa's most animated descriptions are of his years at the Ogata school in Osaka and a reckless life given to blustering, swaggering and street fighting – as well as to furious studying – a life that was to typify future generations of university students.

Through the medium of "Dutch learning" (*rangaku*), Japanese studies of Western civilization had focused on science and technology. The study of social systems really began with Fukuzawa, when he visited America. He made his debut as an "enlightenment thinker" a few years later, following his tour of Europe, with the publication of *Things Western* (*Seiyô Jijô*), in which he describes the socioeconomic aspects of the nations he visited, from hospital administration to military conscription, from banking and postal systems to the parliamentary process.

With the establishment of the new Meiji regime, Fukuzawa not only opened his school of Western learning, Keio Gijuku, but also published two important works, *In Praise of Learning* and *An Outline Theory of Civilization* (*Bunmeiron no Gairyaku*). With these works he established himself as a leading thinker of the new age, denouncing the feudal ethic while advocating individual liberty and national independence, equality among nations, and a utilitarian society. The dominant intellectual trend of the times was expressed in the words "Japanese spirit, Western learning" (*wakon yôsai*), which advocated the grafting of Western science and technology onto the Confucian ethic. But Fukuzawa argued that the Japanese social fabric should undergo Westernization as well.

In short, there was no more avid a proponent of Western civilization than Fukuzawa, nor a more violent critic of feudalism and its supporting Confucianist ethic. He was therefore regarded as the standard-bearer of liberalism in Japan; but even more than that, he was a nationalist. Fukuzawa saw the development of Western civilization in Japan, the adoption of science (he invented his own word for "science" out of the Chinese characters for "numbers" and "reason"), and the nurturing of a spirit of independence as the only ways for his country to deal on equal terms with the powerful nations of the West.

During the tense early years of the Meiji period a growing antagonism developed between government leaders and leaders of the Human Rights Movement (*jiyû minken undô*), with the former advocating the creation of a rich country and a strong army (*fukoku kyôhei*) and a program of Westernization under bureaucratic leadership, and the latter pressing for individual freedom and equality and for the establishment of a republican form of government. But Fukuzawa and the other scholars of Western learning active in the Meirokusha (a popular education movement named after its founding date, the sixth year of Meiji) argued for *both* the strengthening of individual human rights *and* a national effort to realize Japan's independent status among nations, urging the people to leave to government the task of governing and to work in harmony with the State.

As a political realist, Fukuzawa approved on the whole of the absolutist rule that was the Meiji regime, but he remained to the last out of the government, preferring to serve his country from a position of complete autonomy. As an educator, too, he preached this spirit of independence. Keio Gijuku (Keio University) is today one of the nation's leading private institutions. Fiercely proud of its utilitarian and independent tradition, it rivals the finest public universities.

Fukuô Jiden has been translated by Kiyooka Eiichi as *The Autobiography of Fukuzawa Yukichi* (Tokyo: Hokuseidô, 1960).

26. HALF OF MY LIFE

Warawa no Han Seigai By Fukuda Hideko
Tokyo: Iwanami Bunko, white series #161, Iwanami Shoten, 1958.

In 1881 I was seventeen. It was an unforgettable year for me. The famous Miss Kishida Toshiko came to my home town, Okayama, to lecture. The audience filled the hall as clouds fill the sky. The eloquence of her plea for women's rights moved me to organize a women's social group. I was a pioneer in the work. We brought in polemicists, listened avidly to their views on rights, freedom, and equality, and labored for the abolishment of the traditional disabilities.

In the summer of the same year, a retreat was held by the Liberal Party on the Asahi River, in which our women's group participated. We boarded a boat, and as we floated down the river, we raised our voices in a song of freedom to the accompaniment of musical instruments. One of us stood up and made a speech. There was no government out here upon the water, we were told, and no one to interfere with our freedom, and all the while a policeman was listening from under the water. He suddenly came up through the waves like a sea monster, and ordered us to disband.

Although I was a woman, I resolved to set out for Tokyo to gain sympathizers toward combatting the misgovernment that permitted such incidents. I was waiting for an opportunity when one day an old friend called and invited me to a local festival. This would be my chance to run away. I asked my mother and older sister to go with me to visit the family graves. I prayed silently, speaking of my plans and asking their approval, taking great care to avoid any outward expression of my feelings. On the way home, my mother suddenly said that I should not rot away here in a village. She proposed that I go to the city and continue my education. How full of tender compassion were her words to me that day! She suggested that we discuss the idea further, but I did not respond. I felt certain that my father would refuse his approval.

I traveled to Osaka, where I was granted an audience with Count Itagaki Taisuke, who gave me words of sympathy and encouragement and presented me with introductions to influential persons in Tokyo. I finally reached Tokyo, where I studied hard, and founded Society for the Liberation of Women (Fujutsui Kaisha) with Miss Tomii Oto, through which we taught self-reliance. Reports of the opening of Sino-Japanese negotiations, upon the heels of the Korean uprising, filled me with deep indignation at suppression at home and treachery abroad. I felt even more strongly that I must do something to rouse people from their slumbers. Miss Tomii and I determined to assist Omoi and others in the Korean reformation movement. She set out for home to obtain funds from her brother, and we pawned our clothes for her travel expenses.

After our farewells, I set out by myself, and was barely able to eke out a living with such odd jobs as hairdressing and sewing. I continued working for the cause and was most successful in gaining trust and confidence.

One morning before daybreak, Miss Tomii suddenly appeared at my boarding house, dressed in a soiled cotton kimono. Her brother had threatened to report our activities to the police, and then had locked her up. She told me how she had broken out and left a note for her brother saying that she had decided to dedicate her life to Christianity and the work of the Lord. She had traveled all the way to Tokyo with but the one kimono. "I am no longer of the same mind as you and the others," she said. "Please forgive me." How pure the heart of this woman who would sacrifice herself to keep our secrets from her brother, who would change her whole purpose in life that she might serve her fellows at a time when able-bodied men were selling their integrity for a bit of gold!

In October, 1885, I set out for Korea with some companions carrying explosives, which would escape notice in my possession. When our bags were weighed at Kobe Station, I was viewed with suspicion, but I put on an unconcerned air, shook my bag, and complained that the rough train ride had broken some toys I had bought for my children. They nodded sympathetically and let me go on my way.

In December our activities were exposed. I was arrested at an inn in Nagasaki. The police treated me like a common thief, imprisoning me in a black cell. Sent to Osaka, I was treated as a political offender. I was able to spend my days reading and studying. I tried to study English for a time, but I am ashamed to report that I gave it up.

A public hearing was presently held for sixty-three suspects, including myself. I had already lost faith in our fellows. Haishi, whom I had respected as our leader and to whom I had become engaged, and even the family men were always finding excuses to enjoy themselves with prostitutes. There were even those like Isoyama who absconded with funds.

I suddenly began to receive passionate letters from Omoi. Feeling that his passion had to do with my being the only woman in the group, I refrained from answering. His persistence finally won me over, even though I had taken a vow of chastity after my cruel experience with Haishi.

I was sentenced to a year and a half more of imprisonment, and was sent from Osaka to Tsu (in Mie Prefecture). I was not forced to work, but I requested work all the same, and made it my custom to spend two of my free hours each day reading. The warden put two young girls into my care to whom I taught not only reading and writing and the use of the abacus, but also the principles of humanitarianism. They became very fond of me and competed for my affection.

After a year, I was released in the general amnesty in celebration of the Meiji Constitution. I met with a wildly enthusiastic reception when I got off the train at Osaka Station. In the crowds of strangers, my father, whom I had not seen in seven years, proclaimed joyfully and tearfully that all his anxieties in my behalf were over and that he could now die happily. My fame had spread throughout the countryside. I was much moved to find that even children of two and three knew my name.

After a month or two at home, I told my parents about Omoi. I went back to Tokyo. Late in July, 1889, I began to feel unwell. I had progressively worse morning sickness, and I began to vomit violently.

I now began to see the situation for what it really was. I told Omoi about my illness and expressed a desire to discuss it with my parents. He insisted that we not tell anyone for a time. So I found a quiet place where I might live like an ordinary housewife. My shock and surprise were great when I found that Omoi was prepared to treat me only as a mistress. Unpleasant days lengthened into unpleasant months. In March, 1890, I gave birth to a son, and found that Omoi had begun having an affair with my close friend Izumi Tomiko. I informed Omoi that I was leaving him for good and that I would take our child.

I founded a women's business school. My family supported me enthusiastically. Our classrooms were full to overflowing when I was once more reminded of the cruel transience of life. In the winter of 1893 my father took to bed with a cold. The cold brought about a heart condition that soon proved fatal. Before long, my aunt passed away. And in the following April, my dear brother died too. Three funerals in such a short space of time totally depleted our already precarious finances. I was bemoaning my circumstances and thinking that I should go abroad to forget them, when I found that the heavens had not forgotten me after all. I had the good fortune of a chance meeting with Fukuda Tomosaku, a man for whom I came to feel the greatest esteem.

He was most solicitous in comforting me, and even confided that he was considering going abroad permanently because of a disagreement with his parents. While I was greatly moved, I found it difficult to see why he should be so downhearted. He was the heir of a wealthy family, had graduated from the University of Michigan law school, and had just returned triumphantly to Japan. I described my own destitution and said that our two lives should not even be discussed on the same day. His eyes filled with tears. I was wrong to think that happiness was a matter of wealth, he said. The cupboard might be bare, but if a family had a good home, there could be no greater happiness in the world.

He announced to his parents that he wished to have his freedom. The family name and fortune should go to his younger brother. He asked only a small portion to set himself up in life, but he was denounced for irresponsibility and disowned. He returned to Tokyo penniless, but with great determination to make good on his own. Through the kind offices of a friend, he obtained a position on the *Manchôhô* newspaper, and there he received his first and only salary.

We were back on our feet, but only barely, since he had sold everything. I found pity for him leading to a deep affection. I discovered that riches of the heart pass boundaries of rank and class.

One day when we were discussing the future, he was offered a position as legal counselor for the Korean government. When his parents heard of it, they took him to court in a property suit, stripped him of everything he had, and made it impossible for him to go into government service. He demanded that his disinheritance be recognized by the entire family. I agreed with his decision. The family decided that our oldest son Tetsurô be reared as family heir by his grandparents.

Tomosaku came back to Tokyo determined to work for our happiness; but unfortunately his mind had become so disturbed by his sufferings, that despite rest and care, he fell into a coma at about the time our last son, Chiaki, was born, and died at the age of thirty-six.

I felt that it was my duty to rear strong and healthy citizens, in memory of the love Tomosaku had given me. After the year of mourning, I returned to the movement. I convinced my fellows that it was most important to provide business training for women. With their help, I opened the Tsunohazu Women's Technical School on the anniversary of my husband's death. For the maintenance of the school, I founded the Women's Real Property Society, through which I solicited volunteers to sell the products made by our students.

This work is still on its way toward fruition, and no one can say how it will proceed in the future in this ever changing world of ours. But I firmly believe that the carrying out of this plan is my true task and duty.

Commentary

In 1874, Itagaki Taisuke and his followers were defeated in their efforts to promote an attack on Korea. They resigned their official positions and went into the opposition. This began a radical civil rights movement that stirred the entire nation.

Fukuda Hideko, author of the book under discussion, was born in 1865, just prior to the Meiji Restoration. She grew up when the radical movement was sweeping across the country. In 1884, a party for the modernization of Korea executed a coup with the support of Japan and took over the government for a short time. Fifteen hundred Chinese troops finally defeated two hundred Japanese and brought back the old regime. Ôi Kentarô (Omoi in the text) led a group of young Japanese radicals to Korea where they sought to put the dissident party back in power. They sought Korean independence from China and revolution at home in Japan. Fukuda Hideko participated in the movement.

On the morning of the public hearing in May, 1887, the courtroom was packed. All wanted to see Fukuda Hideko "The Jeanne d'Arc of the Orient." She was given great notice by the press for her work in the movement and as a pioneer in the women's rights movement. In her later years, she became a believer in humanistic socialism.

The book under discussion is an autobiography that reflects back on her early life. It was first published in 1904 by Tokyodô. Fukuda Hideko (1865-1927) also wrote *"My Memories"* (*Warawa no Omoide*).

27. FLOWER OF THE MOORLANDS

Kôya no Hana By Ishimitsu Makiyo
Tokyo: Ryûseikaku, 1958.

In 1899 I was an army captain. In preparation for the Russo-Japanese war, I went to Russia to study under the assumed name of Kikuchi Shôzô. I traveled first to Blagoveshchensk, the Russian city from which Far East attacks were originated. I took lodging in the home of a Russian officer to perfect my knowledge of the language.

When I crossed the Amur River to Ai-hun, I learned that the innkeeper of a Chinese inn there was a Japanese woman. Out of curiosity I went to meet her. Her name was Mizuno Hana, and she was working for a Chinese named Sung Chi from Chichihaerh.

She told me that the inn was a front for a gold-dust business: the whole town was in business smuggling gold dust. On the surface it seemed very quiet, but behind the scenes there were murders, and mounted bandits even came to town once in a while.

With childlike curiosity, I asked O-hana to tell me all about these mounted bandits. She explained that they were fiercely loyal to each other, and that they made blood pacts. They were organized with two or three hundred to a thousand under one leader. The areas of their operations were clearly defined and they kept close contact with each other. All land outside of a one-hundred-kilometer radius around the fortresses was entirely under their control, and no one, not even military officers and government officials, could travel long distances without their protection.

On July 15, 1900, Chinese forces attacked Russia. In retaliation, the Russian army arrested three thousand resident Chinese and slaughtered them on the banks of the Amur River. Then on July 21, they invaded the opposite bank of the river, remainder of the citizenry, and entered northern Manchuria. I quickly gathered strategic information and broke through the closely watched cordon of the Russian army to return to Vladivostok. As soon as I arrived, I was ordered by the army to smuggle myself into Harbin.

Russia was converting this lonely town into a stronghold for the invasion of Manchuria. At the same time, the East China Railroad was under construction and the chaotic conditions along the line made it hopeless for a Japanese to travel in the area. I dressed in a soiled rubashka and farmer's boots and wandered around Khabarovsk searching for way to continue my journey.

I noticed that the Chinese inn in front of the station seemed to be the headquarters of the mounted bandit leader Tseng Shih-tse. I decided to make friends with the clerk of the inn. One day when I was wandering about the streets of the town, a Japanese woman named O-kimi approached me and led me to a general store that was operated by Tseng. O-kimi was Tseng's mistress. She invited me to join the bandits. Several days later Tseng himself appeared at the store and, after looking me over, asked me to be on his staff of advisers. He told me that Sung Chi was his senior among the bandits, that Sung Chi had been recently killed fighting the Russian army, and that Sung Chi's mistress O-hana of Ai-hun was missing. I advised Tseng that it would not be wise to oppose the Russian army. It would only give them an excuse for them to conquer China, and he would do better to prepare quietly for the future. Tseng decided to retire to the Iho Mountains. In gratitude, he got me a passport to Harbin.

I boarded a military ship bound for Harbin with one of Tseng's men, Chao, registered as a laundryman for the Russian army. As the ship proceeded up the Amur River, we decided to debark and travel by land. I felt that it was wiser to go visit the bandit leader Kao in Binchou. On the edge of a town along the way, we found three Japanese prostitutes who had been driven from town during an invasion and were dying of starvation. We gave them food and took them with us to Binchou. But while we were consulting with Kao, they were kidnapped by the coachman.

In Harbin a gigantic city planning project was underway. There was a great deal of activity around the East China Railroad station and the marshaling yards. Manchuria was about to be taken over and absorbed into Russia. I sat down on the stone steps of a recently constructed cathedral and was looking the town over when suddenly a Korean named Choi appeared out of the crowds. He was a Russian army spy with whom I had become acquainted on board ship. He was easily taken by flattery, so I did my best to praise and please him. When I explained my problems to him, he immediately obtained permission for me to set up shop as a laundryman for the Russian army and even provided me with assistants. The shop was unexpectedly successful, and the Russian army liked our work. Thus I was able to establish my first base of operations in Harbin.

Before long a young Chinese with a queue came to call on me. He turned out to be none other than O-hana in disguise. When the Russian army attacked Ai-hun, she had mingled with the evacuees to get out of town. She had saved the lives of three daughters of a wealthy man and taken them with her to wait for Sung Chi in a woodcutter's hut in the Hsing-an-ling Mountains. When Sung Chi did not appear, she saw the girls home and set out for Harbin to find me. I had her maintain her male disguise, gave her the name Ichirô, and hired her as chief clerk for my shop. Her bearing was so convincing in her male attire that she had been successful in evading all the unruly elements. But every day, when my assistants had gone home for the night, she took off her disguise and became the gentlest housewife imaginable.

About a month after I opened shop, the forces that had been stationed in Harbin left on an expedition and our business fell off. I made up my mind to follow the army and see what was going on. While I was being detained at the front lines by the Cossacks, there was an attack by Chinese forces. I was captured and thrown in prison at Lalin. It seemed that they intended to starve me to death. I grew thinner by the day, and so weak that I could not think clearly. I lost track of time. One day I was staring out of the window of the prison. Suddenly I saw one of the prostitutes I had rescued.

"O-yone! It's me!," I shouted. "It's Kikuchi!"

Since we had lost track of each other in Binchou, O-yone had wandered through the countryside, and was now the mistress of Sung, the bandit leader. I was brought once more to a realization of the strange workings of fate.

O-yone nursed me back to health and introduced me to Sung. When I announced myself as staff advisor to Tseng Shih-tse, Sung immediately knelt down on one knee in front of me, begged my forgiveness, and pleaded that I have O-yone sent back to Japan. I had been wanting to return to Vladivostok for further orders anyway, and so I set out with

O-yone. Along the way, we heard from an old couple at a roadside inn that Tseng Shih-tse had been captured by the Cossacks and executed. My eyes filled with tears.

As we continued our trip, we found it necessary to go over a mountain pass on foot that even trucks could not cross. It was thirty degrees below zero and the ground was frozen solid. O-yone was so exhausted that she urged me to leave her behind and go on alone. But I gave her words of encouragement, took her in my arms, and staggered on. When we were setting up camp in a thick forest, and I was out collecting fire wood, O-yone disappeared. When the long night was over, I searched the surrounding area and called out for her time and again, but she was nowhere to be found.

When I reached Vladivostok, I discussed my future movements with the intelligence people. Numerous Japanese, private citizens as well as military men, had come to Siberia and Manchuria with a strong sense of patriotism, to watch the movements of the Russian forces. There were also large numbers of Japanese working as laborers on the East China Railroad. One of them said that they were working in anticipation of the day when the railroad would become the property of Japan. They often showed their fellow feeling for us by assisting us in our activities.

It was decided that we would set up the center of our intelligence network in Harbin. We further decided to take advantage of the Russian love of photographs by setting up a photo studio as our front. I was chosen to manage the shop. To avoid suspicion, I made up my mind to resign from military service. Headquarters in Tokyo agreed to sponsor our plan by providing three thousand yen as initial capital with the stipulation that no further support of any kind would be forthcoming.

The Kikuchi Photo Studio opened in Harbin and did a booming business from the start. It consisted of not only individual portraits. We were appointed the official service for the military and the railroad as well. There were very strict regulations stipulating that all negatives be turned over to the military, but we intentionally made what we called "defective prints" whenever the subject matter was of strategic interest, and these we sent off to our home office. Once more with O-hana's assistance, I succeeded in getting into the Ch'ang-ch'ui and Shen-yang areas for reconnaissance. As soon as our work was going smoothly, I gave O-hana all the money from the laundry shop and sent her back to Japan. As we stood on the pier at Vladivostok, O-hana wept. "Make yourself a happy home," I said. "When you have yourself settled, write me one letter. I won't answer it, and we'll never meet again."

Early in 1904, Russo-Japanese relations were on the verge of rupture.

I secretly visited the leaders of the mounted bandits and urged them to revolt. I was determined to go with them against the rearguard of the Russian army, but they refused to make a move. Then at dawn on February 3, my fellow workers and I were ordered by the Russian military police to leave the country immediately. We burned all our letters, film, and photographic paper, and returned home to Japan, leaving all our worldly possessions behind.

Commentary

Ishimitsu Makiyo was born in Kumamoto in 1868, the son of a samurai family. He fought in the Sino-Japanese War. He became an avid student of Russian culture toward gathering intelligence in anticipation of Russian incursions to the south. This book relates his adventures as a spy. He worked as a laundryman, joined forces with the mounted bandits, and became the owner of a photo studio, always on highly dangerous missions. After his return to Japan, he once more went into the military service. When the war was over, he returned to Manchuria as a private citizen. He failed in venture after venture, and finally became a pirate. It was toward the end of the Meiji period that he came back to Tokyo penniless, to the wife and children whom he had left behind.

Beginning immediately after the Sino-French War in 1883, Japan set up an intelligence center in China from which agents were sent out all over the Asian Continent. Due to the nature of their work, little is known about them by the general public. This volume is one of three edited by Mahito, son of Ishimitsu Makiyo, from his father's notes and diaries left behind. The other two books are titled *Man of a Castle Town* (*Jôka no Hito*) and *Song of Home* (*Bôkyô no Uta*). They present fascinating information about one of the thousands of nameless Japanese who gave their lives to Imperial Japan.

28. MY SHANGHAI PERIOD

Shanhai Jidai By Matsumoto Shigeharu

Tokyo: Chûkô Shinsho #374, 380, 391, Chûô Kôron-sha, 1974-75.

The six years during which I worked in Shanghai were the high point of my life. They were also a period in which the direction that I was later to follow was to a large degree determined.

Graduating from the University of Tokyo in the spring of 1923, I went on to graduate school. In the following September, however, my house, my library, and the special research facilities at the university were all destroyed in the Great Tokyo Earthquake, and since this made it difficult for me to accomplish anything in Tokyo, I decided to go to the United States to study. While there, I not only developed the urge to become an international journalist, but even contributed a number of articles to *The Nation* and other periodicals. On my father's advice, I also did the best I could to become friends with Chinese students in America – an activity that led to heightened interest on my part in the affairs of China. I was influenced at this time by the teachings of Charles A. Beard, whose thesis was that the central problem in Japanese-American relations was a conflict of interests in the China market.

After a time in America, I went on to Europe to continue my studies. I was there in 1927, when my family was badly hit by an economic panic at home and it became necessary for me to return to Tokyo. I came back almost immediately, bringing with me my cousin and fiancée Hanako, who was then in London. Back in Japan, I assisted Professor Takagi Yasaka with his "Lectures on America" series and participated in the Pacific Conference in Kyoto and Shanghai. During the course of the conference, I formed lifelong friendships with a number of Chinese and Englishmen.

Anti-Japanese sentiment in the United States was so strong that the quota for immigration from Japan had been reduced to zero. In face of this, a number of internationally minded Japanese conceived a plan to send a lecturer to the University of California as an unofficial goodwill ambassador. I was selected for the post, but it proved impossible to work out the necessary arrangements with the university, and the project was dropped. At about the same time, an executive of the Shinbun Rengô-sha (Newspaper League; later to become the Dômei News Agency) asked me to become head of his company's Shanghai branch, and I decided to accept.

By this time, Japan had already occupied Manchuria, and Shanghai was a hotbed of anti-Japanese sentiment. I had the feeling that I was giving up one unfriendly country for another. Before leaving, I went to pay my respects at the home office and had the opportunity while there to talk with a veteran correspondent, Furuno Inosuke, whom I asked for some pointers. He told me, in substance: "In the first place, remember that covering the news is a give-and-take proposition. If you want information from someone, you must be prepared to give him information in return. In the second place, always keep in mind that it is of prime importance for a reporter to keep faith with his sources. No matter how badly you want to file a story, if your source says no, you must not file. In the third place, a reporter must create news. Make it your business to know important people, and arrange for them to get together from time to time. You will thus be making your own news." Furuno's three principles made a deep impression on me.

I left Tokyo in December, 1932, and crossed from Nagasaki to Shanghai by ship. Upon arriving, I found that competition among reporters was fierce. My way of outdoing the others was to make as many friends as I could among the Chinese and the members of the foreign community in Shanghai. Whenever possible, I exchanged opinions with them on Sino-Japanese relations. While giving them as much information as I could from Tokyo, I attempted to form personal ties with them that went beyond the usual relationship between reporter and sources.

In the fall of the following year, a Chinese friend brought me a big story. According to him, plans were afoot in Fukien Province to establish a new popular government, which would be anti-Japanese on the surface, but which was aimed primarily against Chiang Kai-shek. Fukien, said my informant, would be declared independent, and the new government would proclaim its opposition to totalitarianism. I cabled it off as a scoop and rushed our radioman to Fukien with transmitting equipment. My company continued to remain in the lead with news of the uprising, but after only two months Chiang Kai-shek sent in an army of two hundred thousand and put down the insurrection. The overall result was a strengthening of the coalition between Chiang Kai-shek and Wang Ching-wei.

In May, 1935, the Japanese ministry in China was raised to the status of an embassy. The diplomatic line adopted by the Japanese foreign minister, Hirota Kôki, and the ambassador to China, Ariyoshi Akira, was aimed at a closer cooperation between Japan and China. To the extent that I, as a reporter, could advance this cause, I did so. Unfortunately, however, the Japanese military, and particularly the medium-grade officers of the Kwantung Army, were not only opposed to a policy of conciliation, but downright contemptuous of it. Their aim was to force the Chinese to recognize the independence of Manchukuo and, having done this, to further weaken the Nanking government by carrying out a number of aggressive moves in both north and south China.

At one point I got wind of a plan by Tanaka Ryûkichi of the Kwantung Army staff to take control of Inner Mongolia and went to question him about it. He replied, "You're trying to treat the Chinese as though they were human beings, but I see them as pigs. We should do whatever we please. I have no intention of discussing my plans with anyone whose ideas are so different from my own." My retort was, "Never mind. You are quite right in saying that I consider the Chinese to be human beings. Just keep your plans to yourself. I don't want to hear about them." How sad for Japan, I thought, that irresponsible ruffians like this were in charge of the Kwantung Army! Their view of China was so warped that they could not conceivably have understood Chinese nationalism or the possibilities of working with Chiang Kai-shek. Herein lay Japan's tragedy.

It was clear that Chiang, who controlled both the government and the army, was doing everything he could through associates familiar with Japan to bring about a peaceful settlement of differences. Ambassador Ariyoshi said to me, "I can tell you this. The Chinese are quite prepared to reach a diplomatic agreement, but the Japanese side is badly split. I cannot think of anything sadder. But you must not cable what I have told you." The ambassador's orders from Tokyo revealed that the Foreign Office was unable to restrain the military hotheads. After refusing two or three directives, Ariyoshi was called back to Tokyo. His successor Kawagoe Shigeru also worked hard to preserve peace, but his efforts at negotiation were hampered by the Japanese army's insatiable demands on north China. Presently, because of the latter, a wave of anti-Japanese terrorism swept over the country.

In December, 1936, when Chiang Kai-shek was in Sian, I was startled by a report that telephone connections between Nanking and Sian had been cut off. I called one Chinese friend after another and finally discovered that Chang Hsüeh-liang was holding Chiang prisoner until he agreed to a truce in the civil war and to a cooperative front against Japan. I managed a scoop on this story, which made news around the world. As a result of the Sian incident, Chiang Kai-shek was forced to abandon his campaign against the Chinese Communists, but he continued to keep the door open for a diplomatic settlement with Japan, despite the increasingly anti-Japanese feelings of the Chinese public.

The Marco Polo Bridge Incident took place in July of the following year. In spite of efforts of the Japanese chief-of-staff in Tientsin and other military men opposed to war, the Japanese government and the Kwantung Army pressed ahead. Within the Chinese army, determination to resist was already too strong to be curbed by the more temperate mood of the high command. Chiang Kai-shek was no longer at liberty to proceed at his own pace. The situation had moved in the direction favored by the Communist opposition.

In August, a Japanese fleet advanced to Shanghai, and full-scale war broke out. On the evening before the fall of Shanghai, Mr. Temperley of the *Manchester Guardian* called on me suddenly and told me of an idea being advanced by a Catholic missionary who had been in China for twenty years. The priest's suggestion was that if the Chinese and Japanese forces could be persuaded to recognize a part of south Shanghai as a haven for refugees, the lives of two or three hundred thousand Chinese would be spared. I immediately relayed this proposal to a Japanese consular official whom I trusted, and the plan was accepted by the army commanders. As a result, though the fighting came right up to the boundary of the refugee zone, not one single Japanese shell fell within it. Chinese soldiers fleeing to the area were disarmed by a committee, and Japanese troops were prevented by their own military police from entering. A quarter of a million Chinese were spared, along with thousands of houses.

The war front was expanding, but I managed somehow to maintain friendly relations with a number of Chinese. From about March, 1938, I was in touch with both my friend Kao Tsung-wu, who was one of Chiang Kai-shek's advisors, and Colonel Kagesa Sadaaki of the Japanese war ministry. With their support, I talked with Prime Minister Konoe Fumimaro and attempted to create an opening for peace. Our group met from time to time in Hong Kong, and some members made secret trips to Japan, where they talked with important officials, including army leaders. Even though Japan and China were at war, they remained linked by inseparable ties.

The basic condition for peace was that Japan promise by a fixed date to withdraw its forces to an area north of the Great Wall and agree to revert to the status that had prevailed before the Marco Polo Bridge Incident. This would make it possible for Wang Ching-wei and other members of the Chinese peace faction to launch a movement for ending the war.

In September, while this plan was being explored, I contracted typhoid fever, which forced me to remain hospitalized for three months. Upon leaving the hospital in early December, I was dismayed to hear that Wang Ching-wei had broken with Chiang Kai-shek, but that Prime Minister Konoe's pronouncement on this occasion contained no reference to the withdrawal of Japanese troops. I realized that this boded ill for the future of the peace movement. It seemed clear to me that I could accomplish no more, and, with deep regret, I concluded that I should give first consideration to my own health, for I still needed a few more months of rest and recuperation. With Hanako at my side, I sailed back to Japan, thus ending my Shanghai period.

Commentary

This book contains the recollections of a man who worked as a reporter in Shanghai from late 1932 until late 1938. Equipped with a liberal philosophy and outstanding personal integrity, he made many foreign friends, particularly among the Chinese, and spent much time discussing the important issues of the time with them. He furnishes the reader with little-known information concerning movements in China and Japan in the thirties, together with vivid insights into the thinking of numerous leaders in both countries.

Matsumoto strongly maintains that the most important cause of the Sino-Japanese conflict was the inability or unwillingness of most Japanese to consider the feelings of the Chinese. In his opinion, if Japan had not persisted in making cruel and humiliating demands upon China, the Chinese government would have tacitly recognized Japanese dominance over Manchuria and agreed to the principle of peaceful coexistence. War could thus have been avoided.

Caught between the militant anti-Japanese faction in China and the aggressive faction in Japan, a number of persons on both sides labored during the thirties to achieve peace and cooperation between China and Japan. Matsumoto himself participated directly in one of several maneuvers aimed at avoiding war. His book is therefore not only a lively journalistic account of an exciting period, but also a mine of behind-the-scenes information concerning Sino-Japanese relations.

VIII
History

29. MOUNTED NOMADIC PEOPLES

Kiba Minzoku Kokka By Egami Namio
Tokyo: Chûkô Shinsho #147, Chûô Kôron-sha, 1967.

An inevitable and fundamental question facing historians is how to reconstruct history. This is an attempt to assemble all patterns of Eurasian farming peoples and of Eurasian mounted nomadic peoples and to make hypothetical historical generalizations about both groups.

In early Japanese history, including the Yayoi period (from the second century B.C. to the third century of the Christian Era) and the earlier tumulus period (fourth and fifth centuries), the agricultural pattern fits well. In the latter part of the tumulus period, on the other hand, the pattern of the mounted nomadic peoples – especially that of the conquering dynasties – fits extremely well. A theory of the conquest of Japan by nomadic peoples is here proposed.

From the fourth century into the fifth, continental mounted nomads from the north moved south along the Korean Peninsula and crossed the sea to Japan, where, owing to the superior military strength provided by their expert horsemanship, they conquered the Wajin (indigenous Japanese population) to become the rulers of Japan. At this time there were Wajin in the southern part of Korea. The imperial clan and other mounted peoples of southern Korea crossed to northern Kyushu in the first half of the fourth century. There they mobilized forces with the aim of taking the Yamato region, the base of operations of the Wajin. It took about one century to accomplish the conquest and to establish the Yamato dynasty. After this, in 663, when the imperial clan had lost supremacy in Korea, it began to insist upon its sovereignty over Japan since ancient times.

The first reason for averring a conquest of Japan by mounted nomads is the striking difference between the cultures of the early and later phases of the tumulus period. It is difficult to think that the agricultural Wajin adopted a foreign culture and altered their own traditional culture so radically. The culture of the later tumulus period was monarchical, aristocratic, and similar to that of mounted nomadic peoples. Probably it was spread by conquest and control. To verify this explanation, it is necessary to make a general survey of the representative mounted nomadic peoples who lived and were active in the arid regions of inner Eurasia.

In character and form, the culture created by the Scythians, a nomadic mounted people who lived on the steppes of southern Russia for several hundred years after the eighth century B.C., differs entirely from the culture of agricultural peoples. The Scythians concentrated on the limited field of personal ornaments, the weapons and the trappings of their horses that were their trade tools, and the equipment used in the wagons that were their homes. For their weapons, horse trappings, and personal adornments; they evolved a gold craft demanding delicate workmanship and employing distinctive animal motifs.

At pinnacle of the governing hierarchy of the Huns, a nomadic people active in the Mongolian highlands and surrounding areas from the third century B.C. to the first century of the Christian Era, was the khan. He was recognized as different from other human beings and divinely authorized to hold his position. The order of succession to the khanate was not fixed. Since the khan had many consorts, selecting one from among their many children to serve as legitimate successor was not easy. The popularity of the various princes was important. So were the wishes of the former khan; but the matter was finally decided in a tribal council of elders, sometimes in opposition to the last wishes of the former khan. Often disputes over the succession to the khanate reached such extremes that large-scale disturbances divided the Hun nation. Nonetheless, the linear descent of the rulers was preserved; and no one who was not of the Luan-ti clan ever attained the khanate.

The cultural complex of the mounted nomads examined here can be seen in the culture of the founders of the Yamato dynasty, who unified ancient Japan. It is thus possible to deduce the existence of an ancient Japanese state similar to those of mounted Asian nomads.

The ancient burial mounds, or tumuli, and the objects excavated from them must be examined first. The ordinary coffin in the early tumulus period was made of wood in the shape of cylinder and was placed in a pitlike stone chamber. In the later tumulus period, assembled wooden coffins and rectangular chestlike stone coffins, which may be considered continental or Chinese in origin, were prominent. Later still, the clearly continental side-entrance stone chamber appears in Japanese tombs. Most of the weapons, horse trappings, and ornaments buried in such tombs are almost very similar to those of the mounted nomadic peoples of northeastern Asia.

Second, in the Yamato court, under the imperial clan, there were aristocrats who served important functions and who bore such titles as *omi* and *muraji*. People whose names included the *omi* title usually employed local place names in their personal names. Their distribution is marked by strong regionality, and it is supposed that they were the regional aristocracy. In contrast, people with the *muraji* title generally derived their names from occupations. They were distributed throughout the country. At court, they formed craft guilds. Their role was especially great in military affairs and in economic affairs generally.

Such a duality is characteristic of the mounted nomadic peoples. The Scythians were divided into two groups: the nomads, like the Scythians themselves; and the agricultural people, like the Chinese. The former were governed according to a tribal system and the latter under a system of states and provinces. This overlapping of a conquering dynasty and a subject people closely resembles the governing structure of the Yamato court.

The third point is the resemblance between the rules of succession of the Yamato court and those of the mounted nomadic peoples. In the Yamato court, retainers gathered to deliberate on the succession. They then requested their choice to accept the position. After Ôjin, who is thought to have been a historical figure (according to the *Kojiki*, he was the fifteenth emperor and reigned from the end of the fourth to the early part of the fifth century), the rule of succession to the imperial throne in the Yamato court was no longer by descent to the eldest son of the principal wife. The throne first passed to the eldest son of a former emperor (who was called the *ôe*). His brothers succeeded him. After the brothers came the eldest son of the *ôe*. This was the principle of succession, though in many cases power and marriage relations prevented its application. Often bloody disputes occurred over the designation of the heir. But the important point to notice is this: in spite of frequent succession disputes, candidates always came from the imperial clan. The line of succession is similar to that which operated among the mounted nomads of the Asian Continent. In such agricultural nations as China and ancient Egypt, the dynastic system is not found.

The culture of Japan in the later part of the tumulus period has much in common with those of the mounted nomads of northern Asia and of the Korean Peninsula. It cannot be said that this complex was introduced into Japan only partly or on a selective basis. The cultural complex of the northern mounted nomads was brought intact and entire into Japan by some unknown people.

Commentary

In 1947, shortly after the end of World War II, four Japanese scholars held a symposium on the sources of the Japanese people and their culture. Egami Namio presented his theory of conquest of Japan by mounted nomadic people. Theories prevalent at the time explained the formation of a national state as the outcome of a process of development within the Japanese archipelago. Almost no one was interested in the idea of ethnic movements or of invaders from the Asian Continent. Linking the fortunes of East Asian peoples with Japanese history and concluding that a conquest of Japan had been achieved by mounted nomads seemed to go against historical common sense. The boldness of the idea produced strong reactions. In 1958, *Origins of the Japanese People* (*Nihon Minzoku no Kigen*) by Ishida Eiichirô, Okada Masao, Egami Namio, and Yawata Ichirô, published by Heibonsha, offered a record of debates on the subject and criticisms of the criticisms that had been leveled against the theory. It brought the theory of mounted nomads to a wider general audience.

Kiba Minzoku Kokka, the book summarized here, was published in 1967. The author had devoted nineteen years of study to the subject. The theory of mounted nomads had gained a following in the scholarly world. Egami here reveals his research methods and attempts to prove his theory in detail.

As an archaeologist, he has had much experience in the methods of historical reconstruction. He has adopted a system used in restoring ceramics. The corpus of ceramics of a related region and time is more useful in reconstructions than structural theories or principles of formal development. It is difficult in the case of historical reconstructions to make immediately understandable charts of concrete facts. Egami takes the attitude that corpus charts and hypothetical overall images are useful in historical reconstructions. He insists that this method is possible and necessary.

The composition of this book is based on the method. The first part contains hypothetical total images of the mounted nomadic tribes produced from concrete explanations of the ways of life, military organizations, national states, origins and development of such peoples as the Scythians, Huns, Tungus, Hsien-pei Tartars, and Wu-huan Mongolians. In the second part of the book, the author discusses the Yamato court on the basis of objects excavated from burial mounds, legends, traditions, and Chinese chronicles. From many vantage points, he clarifies the nature of the court as something created by a conquering dynasty of mounted nomads. To arguments that he has presented in the past, he adds results of broader comparative studies on such topics as duality in social composition, imperial succession, and matrimonial systems. The excerpts presented here are only a small part of these materials.

No generally accepted conclusion has been reached on Egami's theory of mounted nomadic conquerors. It is convincing, not as an arbitrary comparison of cultural elements, but as an attempt to clarify early relations between the Asian Continent and Japan by comparison of total cultural complexes.

30. THE ASUKA AND NARA PERIODS

Asuka to Nara *Nihon no Rekishi* vol.2
Tokyo: The Yomiuri Shinbun-sha, 1968.

In 593, the second year of the reign of his aunt Empress Suiko (592-628), Prince Shôtoku – familiar to all Japanese, if only because his face appears on two denominations of paper currency – became crown prince and regent. He thereafter achieved a status that enabled him to exert an influence on politics rivaled only by that of the great minister Soga no Umako (?-626). Until then, the politics of the Yamato court (which derives its name from the province where numbers of rulers had their capitals) had been largely controlled by powerful clan aristocrats. Prince Shôtoku was the first crown prince to assume an important role in Japanese politics, and his success signals an important historical change.

Earlier, governmental and court affairs had been based on clan titles (*shisei*); but the system reached an impasse when the aristocratic clans who had cooperated to rule in the name of the imperial house began to quarrel among themselves. The clan that emerged most successful was the relatively new Soga.

While recognizing the special privileges of the older clan ranks, Prince Shôtoku hoped to create a government of ministers appointed by the emperor. In 603 he took the revolutionary step of instituting a system of twelve court ranks. Still another of his important acts was the issuance of what has come to be called the Seventeen-article Constitution. It was a preparatory step toward direct imperial rule over all lands and the whole of the population. Not a basic national law, like modern constitutions, it is a set of precepts for the governing class. But its statement to the effect that the emperor is the sole lord of all lands and people under heaven deserves special notice.

In international affairs, Prince Shôtoku failed when he sent troops to the Korean Peninsula to attempt to protect the Japanese sphere of influence there against the Korean kingdom of Silla. He was more successful in elevating the international position of Japan by opening relations with the Sui dynasty (581-618), which had succeeded in unifying China. One result was the deliberate importation of cultural elements from the continent.

The prosperity of Buddhism in Japan is an achievement of Prince Shôtoku that must not be overlooked. Although the religion had been introduced into Japan earlier (traditionally, though perhaps not accurately, the date is given as 552), it was to a large extent because of his efforts that Buddhism took root in Japan.

The Asuka region, which gives its name to the historical period between 552 and 646, lies in the Yamato basin among three mountains – Unebi, Kagu, and Miminashi – famous in Japanese mythology. A heartland for the ancient culture, it saw the first Japanese flowering of Buddhism. It is believed that the first true Japanese temple was the Asuka-dera (also known as the Hôkô-ji), constructed by Soga no Umako in 588. Somewhat later, Prince Shôtoku built the Ikaruga-dera adjacent to his own residence. This temple is of major importance as the predecessor of the Hôryû-ji which includes the oldest wooden buildings in the world.

It seems possible that Prince Shôtoku turned increasingly to Buddhism for spiritual sustenance in his later years because he was growing aware of his own lack of political power. He had many ideas for a new political order, but he found his way blocked by the immense power of the Soga. After the death of Prince Shôtoku, who had been extremely popular, the Soga chose to ignore this popularity, brought about the downfall and death of his son Prince Yamashiro-no-ôe, and then assumed tyrannical powers exceeding those of the emperor himself.

But Prince Naka-no-ôe (who ruled as Emperor Tenchi from 661 to 671) and Nakatomi no Kamatari toppled the Soga from power and established the imperial house as the central authority. In 645, they engineered the murder of Soga no Iruka in the palace and forced Iruka's father to commit suicide. After this coup d'état, Empress Kôgyoku abdicated, and a prince assumed the throne as Emperor Kôtoku (645-654), with Naka-no-ôe as heir presumptive. In 645, for the first time, the Japanese adopted the Chinese practice of using era names. Symbolic of change, the age of Naka-no-ôe and Nakatomi no Kamatari was known as Taika, or Great Reform.

In 646, the famous Taika Reform Edict (*Kaishin no Mikotonori*) was promulgated during New Year's celebrations at court. The edict includes four articles. In the first it is stated that all lands and people belong to and are under the direct control of the state. In the second article, it is said that, to ensure such control, rural areas were to be divided into provinces (*kuni*) and districts (*gun*), governed by provincial administrators (*kokushi*) and district administrators (*gunji*). The remaining two articles provide for population registers and for a new system of taxation. Although the district administrators were appointed to control rural areas, the old aristocrats did not lose all of their authority, for they were given positions within a power structure that centered on the emperor. There were conscripted laborers at the service of the aristocracy.

In spite of these concessions, however, dissatisfaction with the new system continued to smolder among aristocrats who found it impossible to break with tradition. The great aim of bringing all land directly under state and imperial control was not achieved overnight.

The reformers encountered difficulties overseas when, in 660, the combined forces of the kingdom of Silla and the Chinese T'ang dynasty (618-907) marched on the kingdom of Paekche, a Japanese ally. Japan sent a large contingent to the aid of Paekche, which was so badly defeated at a place near the mouth of the Kum River – a place called Hakusukinoe in Japanese – that Japan lost all foothold on the continent. The defeat put the reform party in danger, which was aggravated by the disfavor with which much of the court viewed their political policies. A struggle known as the Jinshin* disturbances broke out in 672 over the succession to the throne.

The background of the struggle is intimately linked with the fate of the prince Naka-no-ôe, who had championed the cause of reform. At the accession to the throne of Emperor Kôtoku in 645, Naka-no-ôe became heir presumptive. In 661, he became Emperor Tenchi and moved the capital to the province of Ômi (Shiga Prefecture). Tenchi's younger brother Ôama became the crown prince. When Tenchi determined to replace Ôama with his own beloved son, Prince Ôtomo, relations between the two brothers deteriorated. Upon learning of the emperor's wishes, Ôama retired to the seclusion of the mountains of Yoshino. At the death of Emperor Tenchi, Prince Ôama got word that Prince Ôtomo and his court at Ômi were marshaling forces against him. Ôama resolved to act at once. After a month of warring, the forces of Prince Ôama, who numbered the aristocrats of the eastern provinces and of Yamato among his allies, were victorious. Ôama ascended the throne at Asuka to become Emperor Tenmu.

At about the same time, he promoted Princess Uno to consort; this lady was later to reign as Empress Jitô (690-697). During the reigns of Tenmu and Jitô, central control became firmly established. The aims of the Taika Reform Edict were largely realized. Tenmu complied with the wishes of the provincial aristocrats by opening the door to places of rank at court. In addition, he bestowed rank upon those aristocrats who had been his allies in the succession struggle. He made other promotions and brought the central governmental agencies to full strength. Moreover, he took the important steps of instituting the basic national legal code (*ritsuryô*) and of commissioning the compilation of a national history. The autocracy with which Tenmu ruled has very few parallels in Japanese history.

Emperor Monmu (697-707) succeeded Empress Jitô. In the first year of the Taihô era (701), the Taihô Legal Code (*Taihô Ritsuryô*), the culmination of nearly fifty years of struggle to make the imperial house the center of all authority, was promulgated and put into effect. The code consists of penal laws (*ritsu*) and of administrative laws (*ryô*), which deal with central and provincial officials and with land and tax systems. Its promulgation means that already, as early as the eighth century, Japan had a firm legal system.

Presently the court began to feel cramped in Asuka. In 708, in the reign of Emperor Genmei (707-715), construction began on a new capital at what was to become known as Nara (earlier the name of the city was Citadel of Peace). Modeled on the T'ang capital, Ch'ang-an, Nara was roughly 4.2 kilometers east and west and 4.8 kilometers north and south and was laid out in a regular checkerboard pattern with broad streets. Concerned about the beauty of the new city and about population concentration, the government had many of the temples that had stood in Asuka moved to the new capital. The people of Nara sang the praises of the beauty of bluish tile roofs and vermilion-painted posts in the great halls and towers of palace and temple. The most monumental of the many beautiful buildings was the Hall of the Great Buddha (*Daibutsu-den*) of the Tôdai-ji. In spite of the magnificence of such buildings, the capital yet had a rural flavor because of the fields with which it was dotted.

A daily market from noon until sunset under the supervision of an official known as the *ichi-no-tsukasa* or "market chief" conducted trade in such necessaries as food, clothing, farm implements, and writing materials. Horses, cows, and slaves were sold as well. To prevent corruption, even people of authority were forbidden to have goods delivered from the shops.

Taxes fell into three categories. The *so* was a land tax paid in rice;

the *yô* was a labor tax payable in produce; and the *chô* was a produce tax paid in such commodities as cloth and thread. In addition to these taxes, the common people were subjected to various kinds of corvée labor on court construction projects and on ponds and dikes. Peasants were called to the capital for such corvée work at slack seasons on the farms. They received food and wages. Since the *chô* and *yô* taxes had to be paid between October and December, the capital was then filled with country people. In the *Sequel Chronicle of Japan* (*Shoku Nihongi*), compiled in 759, it is said that, in the three winter months, there were many hungry people in the capital. They were farmers who had brought cloth, rice, and thread to the city in payment of taxes. Many of them fell ill, and others starved or froze.

Commentary

This book covers the history of Japan from the sixth to the eighth century, a time when the nation moved from a system of government by groups of aristocratic clan leaders to government by a powerful bureaucracy centered on the emperor. Japanese history during the period in question is characterized by three important developments.

First, the Japanese nation first became aware of Japan – or Yamato – as a national entity.

The second important development was the completion of a system in which the central government, with the emperor at its head, extended direct control to the lands and people of almost the entire country. This development was of especially great significance to later Japanese history. Although private ownership gained prevalence during the Heian period (794-1185) and in the middle ages, in principle, the idea of total state control – and latent legal support for it – persisted. The nature of the Japanese emperor had its initial definition in the Taika Reform Edict of 645.

The third important development was the importation of Buddhist culture through China. During the sixth, seventh, and eighth centuries, Buddhism entered Japan. Without serious conflicts with Shinto, the indigenous religion, Buddhism inspired a culture characterized by magnificent temple architecture. The foundation was laid for the Buddhism that is still an integral part of the Japanese personality.

This book is volume two of the fourteen-volume (the fourteenth is an appendix) *Nihon no Rekishi* (*History of Japan*), published by the Yomiuri Shinbun-sha. A committee of over thirty editors worked on the compilation. At the beginning of each volume is a list of historians who participated in its production. The history is a popular and useful work.

[NOTES]

* Jinshin is the Japanese reading of the ancient Chinese cyclical calender designation for the year 672.

31. HEIAN NOBILITY

Heian Kizoku *Nihon no Rekishi* vol.3
Tokyo: The Yomiuri Shinbun-sha, 1968.

During the reign of Emperor Kanmu (781-806), active governmental policies were pursued. Three important military expeditions were sent to quell the rebellious Ezo tribes in the northeast, with the result that Japanese rule was extended farther north than ever before. In the administrative sphere, a number of reforms were undertaken, of which the most important were the abolition of many superfluous bureaus and the institution of an auditing system to ensure that local government resources were properly passed on from one governor to the next.

In 784, the emperor transferred his palace from Nara to Nagaoka, in the province of Yamashiro (Kyoto Prefecture), and an official named Fujiwara no Tanetsugu was placed in charge of constructing a new capital there. When, in the following year, Tanetsugu was assassinated, the blame fell on members of the ancient Ôtomo and Saeki clans, who as a result suffered a great loss of political influence. A younger brother of the emperor, alleged to have been involved in the murder, was removed from the status of crown prince and banished. Partly because of this untoward incident, Nagaoka was abandoned in 794 and the capital moved to what is now Kyoto. Plans for building the new metropolis were impeded by a scarcity of funds (caused partly by the military campaigns mentioned above), and full-scale construction did not get under way until around 810, after the accession of Emperor Saga.

Heian-kyô, as the new city was named, was, like Nara, laid out on a rectangular grid plan, with great avenues running at fixed intervals from north to south and from east to west. Measuring 4.4 kilometers on the east-west axis and 5.2 on the north-south axis, the new capital was somewhat larger than Nara. Its northern half contained the imperial palace and chief governmental offices, along with the residences of high courtiers. Kyoto remained the capital of Japan until Emperor Meiji moved the government to Edo, more than a thousand years later.

After the downfall of the Ôtomo and the Saeki, there was no political group capable of competing with the Fujiwara clan for political control, but for some decades the strength of the Fujiwaras was blunted by internal rivalries. Then, upon the death in 842 of the abdicated Emperor Saga, who was nevertheless politically powerful, Fujiwara no Yoshifusa, aided by the deceased ex-sovereign's widow, succeeded in deposing the heir apparent and having his own nephew appointed crown prince. This young man came to the throne as Emperor Montoku and was succeeded some years later by his nine-year-old son, a grandson of Yoshifusa. Under this new ruler, whose name was Seiwa, Yoshifusa became the first grand chancellor (*dajô daijin*; two men had earlier held this title, but were presently discredited).

After Yoshifusa's death, political control passed to the hands of his adopted son, Mototsune, who became not only grand chancellor, but also *kanpaku*. In this latter capacity, he was charged with receiving all communications directed to the emperor and with transmitting all imperial commands. The Fujiwara family thus achieved unquestioned political primacy.

This clan was descended from Fujiwara no Kamatari, who had played an important role in carrying out the Taika Reform of 645. During the two centuries following, Fujiwara leaders had gradually strengthened their position at court, and in the latter half of the tenth century, they succeeded in monopolizing the highest positions in the government. In 1018, Fujiwara no Michinaga, then the head of the clan, composed a poem:

> This world around us
> I know to be my own world.
> Minded am I of
> The full moon floating on high,
> Flawless, perfect in all ways.

Throughout the duration of Fujiwara hegemony, the emperor remained, as in the past, the ultimate source of authority, for the Fujiwaras chose not to overthrow the imperial institution, but rather to utilize it. They supported the old legal system, which was centered upon the emperor, but at the same time assumed hereditary occupancy of all the high administrative offices, thus making the law their own. Simultaneously, they made it a practice to marry their daughters to emperors and choose crown princes from among the sons of Fujiwara consorts. As a rule, therefore, Heian emperors had Fujiwaras as grandfathers, uncles, cousins, and mentors.

The imperial court was concerned far more with the appointment of officials than with the practical business of running the country. Bureaucratic procedures were simplified or disregarded, and important matters were decided by the *kanpaku*. It is often called an age of government by aristocrats, but it should be kept in mind that most of the aristocrats were Fujiwaras.

Under Fujiwara rule, the social structure of the nation underwent great changes. In the Nara period (710-794), the government, to make up for a shortage of state-owned farmlands, had carried out large-scale development projects, and had recognized private ownership as an incentive toward farmlands development. As a result, the nobility, along with the great shrines and temples, had acquired great private estates called *shôen*, which were for the most part farmed by tenants. In the early Heian period, land held privately by the imperial family expanded greatly, and government offices undertook to manage estates directly. The legal principle that all land was to be owned by the state and allotted on an equal basis to the people thus ceased to have much practical meaning. Consequently, tax assessment, originally dependent on the number of heads engaged in cultivation, came to be based on produce. The farming populace was divided into new classes, and the more successful farmers, though situated inside the great estates, succeeded in gaining recognition of their rights to the land they cultivated. These name-holders (*myôshu*), as they were called, alongside the owners of small estates, made a practice of formally deeding their lands to great noblemen or powerful religious institutions in return for their protection, which meant, in effect, partial or total exemption from taxes. The great proprietors, for their part, invented all sorts of ingenious arguments for persuading the government not to tax their holdings or send officials to survey them.

In the early tenth century, the Fujiwaras, as high government officials, attempted strenuously to bolster the legal system, but in the latter part of the same century, after they had acquired effective control of the bureaucracy, they openly accepted, even encouraged, contributions of land from provincial owners. By this means, they accumulated vast tax-free estates, which served as the economic foundation for their power and glory.

The culture of the Heian court was distinctly elegant. While considering it an admirable accomplishment to be familiar with the Chinese and Japanese classics, they were not on the whole fond of vigorous scholarship.

Their tastes ran instead toward Chinese and Japanese poetry, lyrical letters, and flute and the Japanese koto. At the court it was considered a mark of breeding to be letter-perfect in the planning and carrying out of ceremonies.

The development during this age of a Japanese syllabary (*kana*), with which the language could be written phonetically, was of inestimable importance in the history of Japanese culture as a whole, for it freed Japanese writers from the constraints of written Chinese. The spread of the new script was closely related to the high status enjoyed by women.

The Fujiwaras, because of their strategy of marrying into the imperial family, rejoiced over the birth of daughters and sought out talented women of lower court rank to raise and educate their daughters as consorts for an emperor. Lesser noblewomen, too, devoted much effort to acquiring a reputation for wit and grace and eventually being singled out for service at the court. There consequently came into being a numerous contingent of court women who had not only a good education, but also the leisure needed to develop their ability as writers. Thanks largely to their activities, there developed a new literature in which *kana* and Chinese characters were both employed. The most outstanding of the women writers were Murasaki Shikibu, who wrote *The Tale of Genji*, and Sei Shônagon, the author of a collection of essays known as *The Pillow Book*. Both lived in the period when, under Michinaga, the fortunes of the Fujiwaras were at their peak.

During the tenth century, Japanese art was enriched by the development of the *Yamato-e*, a distinctively native style that was more colorful and congenial to Japanese tastes than the Chinese modes introduced in earlier centuries. The use of paintings as illustrations for picture-book scrolls furnished a great impetus to the growth and spread of this new art.

Court ceremonies, festivals, and parties occupied much of the Heian nobility's time. At a typical soirée of the age, the emperor and select noblemen might gather at one of the emperor's detached palaces to view the cherry blossoms in spring and compose poems on strips of exquisite colored paper. When the poems had been collected, one guest would be chosen to read them, and everyone would intone the emperor's poem in unison. The poetry session was frequently followed by a musicale, in which each guest performed on the instrument of his choice. If the emperor selected the free-reed mouth organ, the *kanpaku* or some other great dignitary might well play along on the Japanese koto. Or the emperor might order court musicians to play a series of requests. All the while there would be eating and drinking, and often the guests would stay all night, whether the emperor went to bed or not. In the morning, the group might decide to take a boat ride on the garden pond or play a game of kickball. Sometimes the parties went on for days.

The Heian aristocrats were on the whole a highly superstitious lot. Even in the imperial bureaucracy there was a department of divination charged with determining, by means of the *ying-yang* theories that had come from China, what was propitious and what was not. Taboos decreed by calendar experts were strictly observed, and soothsayers were consulted over every unusual occurrence or puzzling dream. The fortune-teller's verdict could well lead a courtier to shut himself off from the world for a given period.

The noblemen of the time were not as a rule attracted by the deeper teachings of the various Buddhist sects. It sufficed for them that their religion relieve their various anxieties and make their lives more secure. Accordingly, there was a great vogue for Esoteric Buddhist ceremonies aimed at realizing one worldly goal or another. Often the rituals were so elaborate and so beautifully staged that they served also as aesthetic diversions.

Toward the end of the Heian period, the nobility was attracted to the Pure Land Sect of Buddhism, which taught that everyone could, after death, be born in the magnificent western paradise of the Buddha Amida. Not a few courtiers died with their hands folded prayerfully and an invocation to Amida on their lips. Fujiwara no Michinaga, no less, is said to have died while gazing at a statue of Amida and listening to the chanting of sutras, serene in his confidence that he would be transported to Amida's paradise.

The weak political control of the Heian government was first shaken by the common people of Kyoto, who included, along with merchants and artisans, a sizable number of impoverished peasants from the surrounding farmlands. In the eleventh and twelfth centuries, many a prince or nobleman saw his mansion burned or his possessions stolen by urban thieves or vagrants. The central administration was also weakened by rebellions in the provinces. As early as the tenth century, Taira no Masakado led a major revolt in the east at almost the same time as Fujiwara no Sumitomo rebelled in the west. By the eleventh century, the central government was no longer able to put down local uprisings without the aid of the military class, which was eventually to gain enough momentum of its own to create a new historical epoch.

Commentary

The Heian period is usually held to encompass the four hundred years between the transfer of the capital to Heian-kyô in 794 and the establishment of a military government in Kamakura by Minamoto no Yoritomo in the late twelfth century. In the early years, the bureaucratic government centered around the emperor functioned fairly effectively, but as time went on, power passed into the hands of the Fujiwara clan. Toward the end of the period, the imperial family attempted to recover its authority, but by this time leagues of warriors were in sporadic revolt all over the country, and the general trend toward military domination was established.

The most outstanding feature of the Heian period was the coming of age of a new Japanese culture, centered around the elegant and highly mannered activities of the Fujiwara-dominated imperial court. The culture that had been imported from China underwent a process of fermentation and became something uniquely Japanese. With the development of the *kana* syllabary, there appeared a rich new native literature, comprising such works as *Collection of Ancient and Modern Poems* (*Kokinshû*) and *The Tale of Genji*, which are still regarded as models of good writing. Independent Japanese styles also appeared in painting, sculpture, and the crafts.

32. KAMAKURA SHOGUNATE

Kamakura Bakufu By Ishii Susumu
Nihon no Rekishi vol.7
Tokyo: Chûô Kôron-sha, 1965.

In the tenth and eleventh centuries, the Chinese-style legal system that had been adopted in the Asuka and Nara periods disintegrated, and a new class of warriors assumed control over much of the country. Living in farming villages, in houses surrounded by moats, these men trained soldiers to serve in their armies, accumulated grain and weapons, and asserted their authority over the farmers living around them. They did not hesitate to go to war to protect or expand the areas that they dominated, and as a rule they engaged in active efforts to bring new land under cultivation by clearing woods and digging ditches for irrigation. For this work, they often employed farmers who had fled from government-owned land because of burdensome taxes. The farmers in various provincial areas were, in effect, organized into large development teams, managed by military overlords with the aid of their retainers and vassals. This phenomenon was particularly prominent in the Kantô region during the latter part of the twelfth century. The more successful leaders of the military class also held the chief offices in the local governments and constabularies.

As the legal system of the earlier age collapsed, the revenues from state-owned land came to be allotted directly to courtiers in the capital, who sent deputies to represent them in the provinces. Simultaneously, large tracts of newly cultivated land were incorporated into personal estates belonging to the imperial family, the nobility, or the great shrines and temples of the central region, all of whom succeeded in remaining more or less immune to taxation. Tax-free estates were expanded by the widespread practice of commendation, whereby weaker landholders put their property in the names of great seigneurs. As this process continued, the interests of local magnates, who were of the warrior class, came into conflict with those of the deputies and proprietors, and the smaller provincial warriors banded together under more powerful warlords, who were able to resist the demands of the government, as well as those of the privileged courtiers who controlled it.

Typical of these regional leaders was Minamoto no Yoshitomo, head of the Genji clan (another name for the Minamoto clan), which was of imperial descent, and which had been known during the preceding two centuries for its military prowess. Basing himself in Kamakura, in the eastern province of Sagami (Kanagawa Prefecture), Yoshitomo built strongholds throughout the southern Kantô region and was regarded by the people of that area as their protector and benefactor. Though for a time he was probably the most influential warrior in the entire country, in 1159 he was slain in the Heiji War, a month-long conflict fought in Kyoto between partisans of rival factions in the imperial court. The victor in this confrontation was Taira no Kiyomori, who, with the backing of military organizations in western Japan, established himself as the chief power behind the imperial throne.

In 1180, Yoshitomo's son, Minamoto no Yoritomo, who after the Heiji War had been banished to the province of Izu, mobilized troops and attacked the Taira deputy in Izu. Yoritomo was acting on the secret appeal of an imperial prince, and though he was defeated in his first battle, he not only survived, but soon succeeded in organizing the more powerful military groups in the Kantô region into a powerful anti-Taira force.

The Taira-dominated court, regarding Yoritomo as a rebel, dispatched an army to subdue him, but as the forces faced each other on opposite sides of the Fujikawa, the Taira men, suddenly frightened by the sound of waterbirds, fled without fighting. Yoritomo's consequent victory lent encouragement to other factions opposed to the Taira, and the uprising spread throughout the country. Minamoto no Yoshinaka, from the province of Shinano (Nagano Prefecture), led his army westward and carried out a successful attack on Kyoto. The defeated Taira fled toward western Honshu, taking the seven-year-old Emperor Antoku with them. In the capital, the politically wily ex-Emperor Go-Shirakawa ordered Yoshinaka to go in pursuit of them and at the same time invited Yoritomo to enter the capital in Yoshinaka's stead. Driving an astute bargain with the ex-emperor, Yoritomo first obtained the court's recognition of his authority over the eastern region, and then dispatched his younger brother Yoshitsune to the capital. Yoshinaka hurriedly returned to Kyoto and set up a dictatorship, but he was attacked and killed by Yoshitsune's army, which then pursued the Taira to the western end of the Inland Sea and, in 1185, defeated them decisively at Dannoura.

During this time Yoritomo remained in Kamakura and devoted himself to consolidating his authority. One of his wisest moves was to include in his staff a number of intellectuals and lower-ranking bureaucrats from Kyoto. Among these, the most important and influential was Ôe no Hiromoto, a nobleman who was spoken of in his own time as a "bag of wisdom." Largely through the efforts of Ôe and his colleagues, there developed in Kamakura an organized military government, centered around the Office of Public Documents (*kumonjo*, an administrative organ), the Office of Investigation (*monchûsho*, a tribunal and investigatory body), and the Office of Samurai (*samuraidokoro*, a supervisory body in charge of the shogun's direct vassals). Simultaneously, Yoritomo defeated one by one a number of military leaders whom he regarded as potential rivals and thereby acquired dictatorial powers extending throughout the nation. After the defeat of the Taira, he turned against Yoshitsune and confiscated his territorial holdings.

When Yoshitsune, with the connivance of the ex-Emperor Go-Shirakawa, rose in resistance, Yoritomo intimidated the ex-emperor into compliance and sent out orders for Yoshitsune's arrest. Yoshitsune was driven into hiding, and Yoritomo's primacy was complete. For a time Yoshitsune was given asylum by the Fujiwara of the northeast region, but with their destruction by Yoritomo in 1189, the ten-year period of civil strife came to an end.

Yoritomo thus succeeded in unifying the country under the military government in Kamakura. In 1192 he was appointed shogun – short for *seii-taishôgun*, or "barbarian-subduing general" – and his government is consequently known as the shogunate. Because of its origins as a military command post, it is also called the *bakufu*, or "tent government."

The Genji were not long to retain family control, for true power was soon usurped by the Hôjô family, to which Yoritomo's remarkable wife Masako belonged. This came about in the following way.

Yoritomo died in 1199 and was succeeded as shogun by his eldest son, Yoriie. When Yoriie was seized by a sudden illness, Masako's father, Hôjô Tokimasa, had him confined at a temple in Izu and replaced him with his twelve-year-old brother, Minamoto no Sanetomo. Tokimasa, who assumed the office of regent, then plotted to do away with Sanetomo and have the husband of his own daughter by his second wife appointed shogun. At this point, however, Masako and her younger brother, Yoshitoki, succeeded in purging Tokimasa from the government, and Yoshitoki replaced him as regent. While using the shogun and Masako as fronts, Yoshitoki obtained the support of the higher officials in the shogunate, which enabled them to establish the hegemony of the Hôjô family. A few years later, Yoshitoki's supremacy was challenged by Wada Yoshimori, a powerful warrior who had been an important official in the shogunate since the beginning, but after 1213, when Yoshitoki attacked and defeated Wada, the Hôjô's position of leadership was secure. In 1219, Sanetomo was assassinated as he was making a ceremonial pilgrimage to the Tsurugaoka Hachiman Shrine in Kamakura, and a two-year-old son of the noble Fujiwara family in Kyoto was selected to succeed him. Henceforward until the end of the Kamakura period in 1333, the shogun was invariably a powerless minor dominated by a Hôjô regent.

In 1221, the ex-Emperor Go-Toba and some of his advisors, vexed by the growing power of the shogunate, conspired to overthrow it by force. When informed of this threat, Masako summoned a great number of warriors to the shogun's residence in Kamakura and delivered a celebrated speech in which she tearfully warned them that the overthrow of the shogunate would place them under the control of the nobility again. An army was assembled and dispatched to Kyoto, where it scored a shattering victory over the ex-emperor's forces. Go-Toba and other members of the imperial family were banished to distant islands, a new emperor was installed, and the court was reorganized around noblemen friendly to the shogunate. This incident, known as the Shôkyû Disturbance (from the name of the era in which it occurred), made it clear to most people that the shogunate, rather than the emperor, held the true reins of power.

In 1224, Hôjô Yoshitoki died suddenly, to be followed in the next year by Masako and Ôe no Hiromoto. The removal of these guiding spirits from the scene threw the shogunate into a crisis, which the succeeding regent, Hôjô Yasutoki, Yoshitoki's eldest son, overcame by devising a system of government by committee. Yasutoki's uncle, Tokifusa, was appointed "cosigner" and given responsibility virtually equal to that of the regent. At the same time, a deliberative council (*hyôjôshû*) with eleven members was set up to advise the regent and cosigner. This oligarchy of thirteen became the highest organ of government. Under its aegis, a new legal code in fifty-one articles was enacted in 1232. Known as the *Jôei Shikimoku*, this set of basic regulations differed from the ancient legal code in that it was based largely on common law prevailing among the military and agricultural classes. Its adoption was legal confirmation of the rights of the military class. With minor adjustments, the *Jôei Shikimoku* remained the fundamental law of the land throughout the Kamakura period (1180-1333) and the succeeding Muromachi period (1336-1573).

Buddhism in the Kamakura Period

As political stability declined in the late Heian period, the great religious organization on Mount Hiei, which not only functioned as the central force in Japanese Buddhism, but also exercised great influence over the imperial court in a variety of ways, became increasingly secularized and more deeply involved in political affairs. Ugly conflicts arose over the appointment of the abbot (the leader of the organization), and theological studies declined. Sincere priests became so outraged at this situation that they abandoned the mountain and devoted themselves to teaching Buddhism among the common people. One of these was Hônen, who in the spring of 1175, at the age of forty-three, arrived at the philosophical conclusion that the only requisite for being reborn in paradise was to pronounce the name of Amida Buddha. In the early years of the Kamakura period, Hônen's teachings, along with his personal integrity, gained him a multitude of followers. His success was of vast historical importance, for it signified not only the popularization of a creed that had hitherto belonged largely to the aristocracy, but also the transformation of Buddhism from a scholastic religion dedicated to the protection of the state into a popular faith centered upon personal salvation.

Another leading priest of the period was Shinran, who, having studied for a time at Mount Hiei, became a faithful follower of Hônen and cooperated in his missionary work among the common people. Both Hônen and Shinran were banished from Kyoto. Shinran, who to an even greater extent than his teacher stressed that salvation was possible only by faith in Amida, then spread his message among the people of the eastern provinces, where he completed the popularization of the faith. It was his practice not merely to preach to his followers, but also to hold question-and-answer sessions with them, in which everyone sought, by discussion, to achieve spiritual rewards. One of Shinran's disciples, Yuien, recorded some of his sayings in *Collection Inspired by Concern over Heresy* (*Tannishô*), which is still widely read and may be regarded as one of the most important religious writings of its time.

Another important figure in Kamakura Buddhism was the Zen priest Dôgen, who, having studied for a time in China, returned and preached that the perfection of human character through self-discipline was the essence of Buddhist teaching. By self-discipline, he meant, specifically, sitting in meditation (*zazen*), which he considered to be not simply a means of enlightenment, but enlightenment itself. This view is expounded in his 95-volume *Treasury of Knowledge of the True Law* (*Shôbôgenzô*).

Commentary

This book is a general history of the age in which a new medieval society created the Kamakura shogunate to replace the crumbling legal system imported from China.

The transition from the ancient to the medieval period in Japan was an internal development, showing no trace of foreign influence. The name "samurai," by which Japanese warriors of the past are most popularly known today, originally signified "one who serves," for the early samurai were employed as bodyguards and house troops by the Kyoto nobility. In the provinces, however, the warriors established a position for themselves as independent, self-protecting masters of large tracts of farmlands, as well as of the farmers on them. The military men used their status as local officials to expand and strengthen their territories and to accumulate economic and military strength. As time went on, they formed hierarchical organizations among themselves, which were able to resist the control of the central authorities; but the latter managed for a long time, partly by playing the warriors off against one another, to retain their traditional right to appoint officials and to levy taxes.

Control by the aristocracy in Kyoto came to an effective end with the establishment of a military hegemony by Minamoto no Yoritomo, the strongest of the warrior chieftains.

It is significant that this historical transformation was accomplished in Japan without destroying the established governmental institutions. Though the system that had prevailed became almost meaningless from the everyday, practical viewpoint, it was preserved in form. Specifically, the emperor and the court remained the fountainhead of honor and glory;

even after the Hôjô regency took over actual control, the office of shogun was retained because it enjoyed imperial sanction. Furthermore, the *Jôei Shikimoku*, which was the shogunate's basic law, preserved traditional laws except when they conflicted with the rights of the military class.

This book is volume seven of the twenty-six-volume *Nihon no Rekishi* (*History of Japan*), published by Chûô Kôron-sha. Each volume is written by a different authority. The writer of this volume, Ishii Susumu, is a staff member of the Institute of Historiography at the University of Tokyo.

33-a. THE AGE OF GEKOKUJÔ

Gekokujô no Jidai By Nagahara Keiji
Nihon no Rekishi Vol. 10
Tokyo: Chûô Kôron-sha, 1965.

33-b. THE PERIOD OF CIVIL WAR

Sengoku no Dôran By Nagahara Keiji
Nihon no Rekishi Vol. 14
Tokyo: Shôgakkan, 1975.

Preface

After the fall of the Kamakura shogunate in 1333, Emperor Go-Daigo tried to reestablish direct imperial rule over the nation, but was thwarted by the defection of Ashikaga Takauji, with whose aid the shogunate had been overthrown. Takauji placed a new emperor, Kômyô, on the throne, but Go-Daigo, insisting that he himself was still the legitimate ruler, fled south to Yoshino and established a rival court. For the next fifty-odd years there were two imperial governments, northern and southern, engaged in more or less constant warfare. The new shogunate established by Takauji in 1338 managed, despite a number of internal conflicts, to consolidate its control over the nation. Takauji was succeeded as shogun by his son Yoshiakira, who was followed in due course by his son Yoshimitsu.

The shogunate appointed constables (*shugo*) to control the provinces. Theoretically, these military governors were representatives of the central authority, but in fact they became increasingly independent. Organizing the local warriors (*jizamurai*) and farmers into armies under their direct command, they participated in the wars between the two courts and gradually built up feudal domains of their own, which the shogunate was unable to dominate.

*

The year 1428 was one of pronounced social unrest. Crops were poor because of a spell of bad weather since the previous year, and on top of widespread food shortages there occurred an outbreak of pestilence. In the eighth month of the year, there was an uprising among the teamsters of Ômi Province (Shiga Prefecture), not far from the capital, and shortly afterward similar disturbances occurred in the cities of Kyoto and Nara, where mobs attacked the premises of pawnbrokers and sake brewers. In the first month of the following year, a large revolt broke out in Harima Province (Hyôgo Prefecture), where the local gentry (warriors) collaborated with the peasants in an effort to oust the constable's forces. This was both an agrarian uprising and a resistance movement on the part of the regional samurai against the constable. Farmer-samurai also took the lead in a series of uprisings in 1441, when rioters seized control of the entrances to the city of Kyoto, attacked pawnbrokers as well as shrines and temples engaged in moneylending, burned loan documents, stole goods, and even dared resist the troops sent by the shogunate to restore order.

A majority of the peasant revolts started in the area around Kyoto, which was on the one hand the last toehold of the proprietors of the old estates and on the other the most economically advanced region in the country. A number of uprisings had their origin in fortified villages surrounded by moats and embankments. So long as the power of the estate proprietors had remained effective, the village had been merely a place of residence for the peasants, but as the owners grew weaker, it came to function as the rallying point for community action. The fortifications erected around the villages were both barriers against intrusion from without and symbols of internal unity.

Many villages acquired a degree of autonomy that enabled them not only to ignore the administrative and judicial authority of the owners, but also to manage affairs having to do with daily life and production on their own. Village self-government was promoted by communal management of irrigation facilities and communal exploitation of nearby mountain land. In turn, local autonomy led to more efficient use of available land, to intensive farming, and to increased stability in agricultural production.

The growth of agriculture brought about greater activity in the fields of commerce and hand manufacture. In Kyoto and Nara, merchants and artisans organized themselves into guilds (*za*), through whose efforts numerous commercial products flowed back into the farming village where the raw materials had been produced. Periodic markets were held at convenient points within the farming districts, and some of the marketplaces gradually developed into towns.

Since the middle of the Kamakura period, Japanese pirates, called *wakô*, had been engaging in forays on the Korean Peninsula, where they had not only stolen large quantities of rice, but also carried away Koreans to be sold as slaves. To a large extent, the *wakô* were the private armies of rich families in western Japan, and in a sense they were traders. In the latter part of the fourteenth century, they expanded their activities to include the coastline of China as well as Korea, but with the appearance of the Yi dynasty in Korea and the Ming dynasty in China, their depredations were to some extent curtailed. One result was that legitimate trade increased significantly. Owing to the expansion of commerce, cotton cloth came to be imported from Korea in sufficient quantity to cause a revolutionary change in Japanese clothing habits. Simultaneously, a large influx of copper coins from China facilitated the development of a commercial economy within Japan.

After the middle of the fifteenth century, the power of the shogunate declined drastically. This was to some extent a result of a series of natural disasters. In the single year 1459, for example, there was no rain at all in the Kyoto region during the third month, but in the ninth month the area was attacked by a typhoon that brought on serious floods. Many were drowned, and the flow of rice into the city came to a complete halt, with the result that the price of the grain rose sharply and there were numerous deaths from starvation. In the following year, a drought that lasted from spring to early summer and seriously hampered the transplanting of the annual rice crop was followed in the sixth month by heavy rains and unseasonable cold. Irrigation dikes broke; bridges were washed away; again there was an attack of pestilence. In the fall, the farmlands were ravaged by both typhoon and locusts, and the food shortage that had begun in the previous year was exacerbated. In the resultant famine, which did not reach a peak until the second month of 1461, many persons fled to Kyoto or outlying regions, but many more starved to death on the land they had inherited from their ancestors. It is said that more than eighty thousand persons died in Kyoto alone.

This disaster exposed the incompetence and lassitude of those in authority, who in the broader sense included not only the shogun and his government, but also the daimyo and the great religious institutions. The leaders of the Kamakura shogunate, who themselves had been owners of large agricultural domains, had had some knowledge of farm management, and their attitude toward the peasantry had been paternalistic. In the Tokugawa period, which followed the Ashikaga, the shogunate was guided by Confucian principles of government, which discouraged gross maltreatment of the peasants. In 1459, however, the shogun was a warrior-turned-aristocrat named Ashikaga Yoshimasa, who possessed neither the common sense of the Kamakura leaders nor the Confucian background of the Tokugawa rulers. His personal conduct, as well as that of the people around him, aggravated the effects of the natural disasters.

Yoshimasa, who at the age of thirty still had no male heir, selected as his successor a younger brother named Yoshimi, who had gone into the Buddhist priesthood but was now recalled to secular life. Only a year after this step was taken, Yoshimasa's wife gave birth to a boy named Yoshihisa, and there ensued a dispute over the shogunal succession. Simultaneously, succession quarrels came to a head in the Hatakeyama and Shiba families, who were among the leading mainstays of the Ashikaga government. As if this were not enough, a rivalry for actual control over the shogunate had been going on for some time between Yamana Mochitoyo and Hosokawa Katsumoto, the two key political figures of their time. Eventually all these conflicts culminated in a great civil war, which divided the shogunate and the nation in two.

Fighting began in Kyoto in the fifth month of 1467. The Eastern Army, under Hosokawa Katsumoto, numbered 160,000; the Western Army, under Yamana Mochitoyo, 116,000. Yoshimasa at first ordered the two forces to conclude a truce, but in the second month of the war he sided with the Eastern Army, which with his moral support and its own superior numbers appeared to be on the verge of winning. In the seventh and eighth months, however, the Western Army was bolstered by reinforcements, and the tide turned in its favor. The Eastern Army countered by coercing the emperor to endorse its cause, thus enabling it to pose as a government force attempting to subdue rebels.

As the battle moved back and forth across Kyoto, much of the city was laid waste. The war quickly spread to the provinces, where the important struggle was not, as it seemed, between daimyo and daimyo, but between local military leaders and the agricultural populace (farmer-samurai included). Many provincial barons succeeded in establishing virtually absolute personal control over the districts they inhabited. One, Asakura Takakage, even managed by sheer force to have himself made constable. This was the beginning of an age in which military strength and cunning were to count for much more than lineage or status – an age in which the established authorities were to be overturned by newcomers. This phenomenon was soon given the name *gekokujô*, "the low overcoming the high."

By 1471, the fighting in the Kyoto area had reached a stalemate. Two years later, both Hosokawa Katsumoto and Yamana Mochitoyo died. Peace was negotiated, but the war dragged on for another four years as various generals maneuvered for advantage. Finally, in 1477, the last of the Western forces withdrew from Kyoto, and the struggle ended.

During this lengthy conflict, known as the Ônin War, the opposing sides vied with each other to obtain the endorsement of the emperor or the shogun, but neither the head of state nor his deputy possessed enough power to act independently. Yoshimasa was increasingly inclined to shun reality and seek solace in aesthetic pursuits. Eventually, he retired into elegant seclusion, building for himself a villa in the foothills of Higashiyama – the string of low mountains on the eastern side of Kyoto – where he indulged in tea parties, performances of Noh plays, and art collecting. It was symbolic of his passive attitude that the central feature of his establishment at Higashiyama was a naturalistic garden, around which the various parts of the mansion were placed in such a way as to melt unobtrusively into their surroundings. The spiritual ideal Yoshimasa espoused is called *wabi*, an elusive term that has connotations of simplicity, rusticity, closeness to nature, and remoteness from the cares of this world. *Wabi* has elements associated with Zen Buddhism, but it is also related to the ideas of paradise in Pure Land Buddhism.

Yoshimasa played an important role as a patron of the arts: Around him there grew up a whole new cultural complex, known today as Higashiyama Culture, which encompassed such diverse fields as garden design, the Noh drama, ikebana, the tea ceremony, landscape painting, and poetry.

In these times of social upheaval, the common people created new cultural forms of their own, to be observed in popular festivals, in the dance, in the comical theatrical medium known as *kyôgen*, and in a new literature of unsophisticated storybooks and historical ballads. In general, the tendency of the popular arts was toward secularization, but religion nevertheless provided relief from the stress and uncertainty of the times.

The priest Rennyo, who became abbot of the Hongan-ji in 1457, is credited with carrying out a great revival of the True Sect of Pure Land Buddhism (*Jôdo-shin-shû*). This he accomplished by going among the masses and drumming into them the simple and appealing message that all needed for salvation is to call on the name of Amida Buddha. One of

Rennyo's most effective methods for spreading his faith was to organize meetings at which the believers discussed their religious experience. Typically, these were held monthly in an atmosphere of informality, and priests participated on terms of equality with the ordinary members. Rennyo made a special effort to attract community leaders and priests from other sects into the fold. He was not a great religious innovator like Shinran, the founder of the sect, but rather an organizer who understood the common man's need to identify himself with a group. His followers became a coherent nationwide force, willing to die on behalf of their beliefs and capable when provoked of taking military action. Although Rennyo himself urged obedience to temporal authority, the congregations often refused to pay their annual tax tribute or actually rose in rebellion against local rulers. In Kaga Province (Ishikawa Prefecture), where they were particularly strong, they even attacked and killed the constable.

By the middle of the Muromachi period various "pressure groups" – village farmers, religious partisans, farmer-samurai, urban rioters, and so on – had come to play a formative role in history. With the intertwining interests of these various classes as a background, the country entered a period of nearly constant internal warfare that continued from the end of the fifteenth century through most of the sixteenth. This was not merely an age of upheaval and destruction, but one in which the Japanese people were repudiating the system that had prevailed in the middle ages and groping for a more modern social framework. The period corresponded to that of the great European voyages of discovery.

During the first half of the sixteenth century, most of the nation fell into the hands of a new breed of military leaders known as civil-war daimyo. Among the earliest to gain prominence were Hôjô Sôun, who carved out a private domain for himself in the provinces of Izu and Sagami (Shizuoka and Kanagawa Prefectures), and Saitô Dôsan, who did likewise in Mino Province (Gifu Prefecture). Such warlords rejected the authority of the shogunate and governed as autocrats within their territories, which to all intents and purposes became independent principalities. Many of the civil-war daimyo were talented upstarts who had begun life without lineage or status; others were constables who refused to be dominated by the shogunate; the most numerous were either deputy-constables who had replaced their principals or local farmer-samurai who had first organized their fellows into leagues and then seized control of the leagues. The emergence of this new class of local rulers illustrates the social mobility and the hardy individualism of the period. It was an age when people sought to make the most of their abilities and in some cases succeeded with brilliance.

The European musket was first introduced to Japan in 1543 by Portuguese sailors whose ship drifted ashore on the island of Tanegashima, south of Kyushu. Though guns of Chinese provenance, introduced earlier, had not spread widely, within ten years of the appearance of the European firearm, imitations were being manufactured in Kyushu and the provinces around Kyoto for use in actual combat. One of the first Japanese leaders to recognize the value of the musket was Oda Nobunaga, who later came close to unifying the nation.

As suggested earlier, an important innovation of the age was cotton, which was used to make clothing for soldiers, sails for ships, and fuses for firearms. During the sixteenth century, Japan became self-sufficient in cotton production.

A new relationship was formed between the daimyo and the people under them. Retainers who served as army officers in times of war became civil administrators in times of peace, and their intermediate authority over the ordinary populace was given legal codification. To ensure stable revenues, the daimyo undertook surveys of the land under their control and systematized the assessment and collection of taxes. This had the effect of binding the peasantry more tightly to the soil.

It was important to the civil-war daimyo to have at their disposal the services of numerous craftsmen, for the manufacture of military supplies was the key to success on the battlefield. Smooth distribution of goods was also a requisite, and most of the new territorial rulers were at pains to attract merchants to the towns that grew up around their castles. Most of them took steps to stimulate markets, to facilitate transportation, and in other ways to transform their domains into flourishing economic units. They were particularly concerned with the development of gold and silver mines, the output from which was both large in monetary value and immediately usable for purchasing weapons or other military necessities. The demand for guns led to intensive exploitation of sand-iron resources in areas that possessed them.

In the second half of the sixteenth century, the wars ceased to be merely regional conflicts and became part of a struggle for supremacy over the whole nation. The first man to make notable progress in this direction was, as intimated earlier, Oda Nobunaga, a relatively obscure daimyo in Owari Province (Aichi Prefecture). In 1560, Nobunaga defeated a powerful neighbor, Imagawa Yoshimoto of Suruga Province (Shizuoka Prefecture), and set out on a campaign to bring the whole region around Kyoto under his control. Having defeated the Saitô family of Mino and concluded an alliance with the lord of Ômi Province, Nobunaga entered Kyoto in 1568 and installed Ashikaga Yoshiaki as the fifteenth Ashikaga shogun. Yoshiaki was the younger brother of the thirteenth shogun in the line, Yoshiteru, who had been murdered in 1565. Nobunaga then seized control of Kawachi Province (the Osaka area) and the city of Sakai, which was both a center of musket production and an important port for foreign trade.

There still remained many enemies for Nobunaga to face. None was more stubborn or dangerous than the Ishiyama Hongan-ji, which was now the leading monastery of the True Sect of Pure Land Buddhism. On more than one occasion Nobunaga, like other feudal lords before him, had difficulty quelling uprisings by Hongan-ji followers. One such instance occurred in 1570, when the sectarians rebelled at Nagashima, in Ise Province (Mie Prefecture), and killed Nobunaga's brother. Having unsuccessfully attacked the insurgents twice, in 1571 Nobunaga dispatched a large land and naval force to lay siege to their stronghold, and severe fighting continued at Nagashima for some time. About half the Buddhists died of starvation, and when the remainder tried to abandon their stand, Nobunaga had them slaughtered. About twenty thousand partisans are said to have perished.

Nobunaga clearly felt that if he showed compassion for the Buddhists, his own future would be in jeopardy. His ruthlessness in this case can be interpreted both as a determination to crush the authority of the medieval church and as a recognition of the principle that unification would have to be carried out by dictatorial means, if it was to be carried out at all.

Commentary

In these two volumes, the author presents a general history of the fifteenth and most of the sixteenth centuries, during which the inchoate feudalism of the medieval age collapsed and the way was laid for the establishment of the organized feudalism of the Tokugawa period. As a rule, the earlier part of this era is thought of as the Muromachi period, and the later part as the period of civil wars, though there is no clear division between the two.

The author has at least two primary aims. The first is to show that *gekokujô* occurred not merely in the power struggles of the dominant samurai class, but also in the efforts of the common people to challenge the authority of the rulers. The second, closely related to the first, is to demonstrate that, far from being exhausted by the wars, the populace displayed great energy and enterprise, which resulted both in increased production and in the appearance of new cultural patterns.

In 1573, Oda Nobunaga overthrew Ashikaga Yoshiaki, whom he

himself had made shogun, and during the next few years he succeeded in defeating nearly all opposition to him, including the vexatious Hongan-ji. He was on the verge of achieving hegemony over the entire nation when, in 1582, he was assassinated by a rebellious lieutenant named Akechi Mitsuhide. Immediately after this incident, Hashiba (Toyotomi) Hideyoshi, another of Nobunaga's aides, defeated Mitsuhide and set himself up as Nobunaga's successor. Hideyoshi not only brought the whole country under his rule, but also attempted twice to conquer Korea. Both campaigns failed, but Hideyoshi was still in power when he died in 1598.

By way of consolidating his position, Hideyoshi in the meantime carried out a complete survey of the nation's farmlands and effectively disarmed the agricultural populace by means of a famous swordhunt. The results were, first, the establishment of a new system of tax tribute based on actual production, and, second, the division of farmers and warriors into two distinct classes. In the process, the masses lost most of the rights they had gained during the period of internal strife, and a foundation was laid for the establishment of a rigid feudal social structure in the early seventeenth century.

34. THE TOKUGAWA PERIOD

Edo Jidai By Kitajima Masamoto
Tokyo: Iwanami Shinsho #332, Iwanami Shoten, 1958.

In 1590, after his successful unification of Japan, Toyotomi Hideyoshi ordered his vassal Tokugawa Ieyasu to give up the territories he had so painstakingly secured for himself in the region of Shizuoka and to move into the Kantô Plain. Ieyasu complied and for his new base of operations selected the site of Edo (Tokyo), then a small village. The Kantô region was vast in area and economically backward. These conditions, however, were not necessarily disadvantageous to Ieyasu. It is often said that the power of a feudal lord depended above all upon the number of his retainers and the size of his cadastral holdings. Ieyasu distributed his retainers strategically throughout his new domain so that he could extract ample taxes from the peasantry. He also brought the commerce and industry in the region under his control and set about building a number of castle towns.

Upon Hideyoshi's death in 1598, the struggle for power among the daimyo grew more intense, culminating in 1600 in the Battle of Sekigahara which saw the country split between two rival factions. Victory went to Ieyasu, the leader of one of the factions, and in 1603 he consolidated the hegemony of the Tokugawa family by assuming the title of shogun and establishing the Tokugawa shogunate in Edo.

The shogunate gradually strengthened its capacity to govern, although not without temporary resistance. For example, the Shimabara Revolt, which erupted in 1637 as an outgrowth of the ban on Christianity, was in fact a major rebellion by peasants and disgruntled samurai against increased exploitation. Although during Ieyasu's reign some daimyo became Christians out of a desire for the profits of trade with the West, they now repudiated the foreign faith and started persecuting the Christian converts in their domains. The popular Christian movement thus changed into a movement opposed to the shogunate, and as a direct consequence of this conflict, Japan withdrew almost totally from contact with the outside world. The shogunate adopted a policy of national seclusion (*sakoku*) out of fear that the Catholic countries of the West, under the guise of proselytizing, would seek territorial gains in Japan. But a seclusion policy was viable by this time because the shogunate and its feudatories had thoroughly established their power to extract taxes in rice from the peasantry, and no longer needed to rely upon the profits of foreign trade. In fact, it was the establishment of this control over the peasantry which was the basis of the Tokugawa feudal system.

The philosophical foundations underlying and supporting the Tokugawa feudal system were provided by Confucianism. Historically, Japanese Confucianism had played a secondary role to Buddhism, being of interest only to the aristocracy and the Buddhist clergy. Under Tokugawa rule, however, it rose to prominence as the basis of political and administrative theory. Although in Chinese society Confucianism had stressed loyalty to one's parents (*kô*) rather than loyalty to one's lord (*chû*), in Japan loyalty to one's lord was emphasized in order to strengthen the authority of the shogunate and feudatories. The long-established Japanese traditions of self-sacrifice and devotion, with their strong overtone of filial piety, were expanded under Confucianism into a rigidly defined code of social conduct.

Among the different schools of Confucian thought, the shogunate chose as its official orthodoxy the Neo-Confucianism founded by the Chinese philosopher Chu Hsi. The aim was to eradicate all thought of insurrection by lower-ranking warriors against their lords, a tendency which had been pronounced during the preceding centuries of internecine strife, and to link the warrior spirit of devotion with Confucian virtues. Another aim was to counter the otherworldliness of Buddhism and the teachings of Christianity. Neo-Confucianism, with its leanings toward realism and rationality, contributed greatly to the strengthening of the Tokugawa system. Under the influence of the Confucian concept of enlightened rule by moral suasion, and with peace and stability, the severe punishments imposed on farmers who did not submit their annual rice taxes were reduced. Nevertheless, the lot of the peasantry remained a hard one, for the shogunate and its feudatories followed a policy of extracting taxes in kind, allowing the peasantry to retain only a minimum subsistance. This policy was exemplified by a statement attributed to Ieyasu: "Give the peasants neither life nor death." The peasantry thus became no more than a tool for producing tax revenues.

Until the middle of the seventeenth century, the peasantry, forced to give up a large share of its crops as taxes, had no opportunity to market its produce. This situation changed greatly in the latter half of the century. To meet the growing demands of castle towns and other urban settlements, rice production was expanded rapidly, the need arose for specialization and commercialization of dry-field crops, and the shogunate and feudatories began encouraging the cultivation of agricultural produce for market. The castle towns developed as a natural consequence of the need to separate the warrior class from the peasantry. A lord would settle his retainers around his castle, and artisans and merchants were encouraged to settle nearby in order to supply the warriors with goods and services. Thus castle towns developed as the political and economic centers of the feudal domains. The population of the castle towns was generally between ten and twenty thousand, but Edo, which developed into a great consuming center, had a population of one million in the eighteenth century, making it the world's largest city. Osaka, meanwhile, functioning as a marketplace for goods brought by ship from all over the country, developed into a major commercial center, its merchants supplying the needs of Edo and other towns. The rise of a prosperous new class of wholesalers, middlemen, money lenders, and other townspeople provided impetus for the creation of a commercially oriented culture.

The prosperity of the countryside and the rapid development of cities during the latter half of the seventeenth century stimulated the flowering of a distinct culture in the Genroku age (1688-1705). Catering to the tastes of the new middle and upper urban classes, and the wealthy farming class near cities, Ihara Saikaku produced novels portraying the quest for love and money, and Chikamatsu Monzaemon plays for the puppet theatre depicting the conflict between duty (*giri*) and emotion (*ninjô*). The wandering poet Matsuo Bashô established haiku poetry as a new popular genre. Although the official Neo-Confucian orthodoxy gradually lost its vitality, new schools of thought, such as the "ancient learning" (*kogaku*), textual analysis of Chinese classics and "national learning" (*kokugaku*), emerged in response to a popular spirit of rationalism and positivism.

The school of "national learning" was elaborated and crystallized by Motoori Norinaga in the eighteenth century. Already in the time of Motoori's teacher, Kamo no Mabuchi, the main thrust of the movement had shifted from Kyoto and Osaka to the political center of Edo, and had come to exert a large influence on Edo society. And as the Tokugawa system, unable to adjust to changes in the economic structure, became increasingly rocked by contradictions and unrest on all sides, the "national learning" school gained favor with a growing number of influential supporters, laying the foundations for new scholarship and thought. In terms of class consciousness, Motoori Norinaga was unable to go beyond the bias of the upper class, the landlords and wealthy merchants who prospered most in the feudal system. In contrast, the philosophy of Andô Shôeki is noteworthy for its clearly anti-feudal perspective. Andô advocated that, above all else, men should live by tilling the soil. He strongly opposed the Tokugawa system, envisaging a society without classes, exploitation, and war, in which all men are equal.

Study of the West, or "Dutch learning" (*rangaku*), meanwhile, made great progress during the eighteenth century because of an increased demand for empirical knowledge brought on by the expansion of commerce. Japanese began to study medicine, geography, mathematics and the natural sciences, and to take an avid interest in Western products. In time, exposure to Western knowledge produced men critical of the feudal hierarchy. In literature, moreover, there emerged a trend toward extreme vulgarization and derision of authority, and toward social satire in such poetry as *senryû* and *kyôka*, published secretly, to avoid official censorship. The power and prestige of the shogunate began to dwindle rapidly.

The shogunate attempted from time to time to restore its faltering position by undertaking temporary "reforms," chiefly prohibitions against luxury and at exhortations to frugality and hard work. Most notable were the "Kyôhô Reforms" implemented in 1716 by the eighth shogun, Yoshimune, and the "Kansei Reforms" implemented in 1789 by Matsudaira Sadanobu. But the repeated failure of such reforms merely exacerbated social contradictions. By the early nineteenth century, the progressive farming villages around Osaka had become desperately impoverished by successive years of bad crops, a decline in cotton production, and a drop in the demand for rapeseed. In some cases, farmers abandoned their villages en masse. To make matters worse, a major famine broke out in 1833, and widespread deprivation and chaos threatened to upset the feudal system. Ôshio Heihachirô (a samurai deeply moved by the plight of the peasantry) was even prompted to rise in rebellion against the government.

Peasant uprisings and urban riots began to occur with increasing frequency throughout the country. However, the most important weapon of resistance possessed by the common people at the time was their ability to read and write. It was the ruling class which had actively encouraged the people to acquire such practical skills as reading, writing, and use of the abacus. When the ruling class found itself no longer capable of ruling by force alone, it attempted to offset the practical skills it had given the people by instilling in them Confucian ethics, and thereby to make them into docile producers of tax revenue. Ironically, the results were quite different. The general rise in the level of education, moreover, caused the mainstream of cultural creativity to shift from the upper urban class to the middle and lower urban classes. And education, in stimulating the development of a rich and varied culture not only in cities such as Edo and Osaka, but also in towns and villages, prepared for the coming new age.

Commentary

This book covers roughly the two and a half centuries of history from 1590, when Tokugawa Ieyasu entered Kantô, marking the first real step in his rise to power, to the 1840s, when, with the authority of the Tokugawa shogunate greatly weakened, the feudal system began to collapse. The book follows a generally chronological organization, with chapters entitled, "The Road to Hegemony," "Daimyo and Rônin," "Confucianism and Bushido," "Life in the Villages and Towns," "The Genroku Age," "The Age of the Rice Shogun (Yoshimune)," "The Age of Tanuma Okitsugu," "Edo Culture and the Kansei Reforms," and "The Period of the Tenpô Reforms."

Viewed in a comprehensive context, the Tokugawa period (or Edo period, as it is sometimes called) can be distinguished by the following three characteristics. First, the Tokugawa shogunate implemented a policy of withdrawing the samurai class from the countryside, and many samurai, without employment, began to lead a life of idleness, subsisting off fixed stipends. Some samurai, however, subsequently became bureaucrats and played an important role in administering the country and the feudal domains, thereby providing for two and a half centuries of peace. During the Genroku period the effectiveness of this administration by the warrior class was most apparent, and social stability and prosperity reached its peak. Second, the shogunate and its feudatories relied on taxes extracted from the peasantry as the economic basis for their authority, and consequently, with the development of a commercial economy, wealth became concentrated in the hands of merchants and other townspeople. Furthermore, the peasantry became impoverished, and there were for the shogunate periodic financial crises. (Utilizing its monopoly over coinage, the shogunate attempted to ride out these crises by deliberately debasing the currency.) And the warrior class was urged to endure a state of chronic poverty by adherence to the ideals of self-sacrifice and spiritual cultivation. Third, lacking knowledge of capitalist economics, the Tokugawa shogunate implemented reforms, based on Confucian ideology, which consisted of various prohibitions and exhortations designed to encourage hard work and frugality. These "reforms," however, continually failed in the face of economic realities. With the passage of time, therefore, the contradictions in the socioeconomic system became more pronounced, resulting eventually in the collapse of the system from within.

The author summarizes the major trends and features of the Tokugawa period. His analysis covers all aspects of Tokugawa history, from politics and economics to society and culture. Moreover, he maintains a balanced perspective by considering both the ruling class and the daily life of the common people, the peasants and townsmen.

35. MODERN JAPANESE POLITICAL HISTORY, Vol. 1

Kindai Nihon Seiji-shi By Oka Yoshitake
Tokyo: Sôbunsha, 1967.

Enforced Opening of the Nation

The defeat of China at the hands of the British in the Opium War of 1840 was a great shock to the Japanese. The Japanese had traditionally regarded China with deep respect as a great and culturally advanced nation. They now came to feel increasing wariness and fear of the military power of the Western nations, one of which had brought mighty China low. In 1853 the Tokugawa shogunate found itself confronted with Commodore Matthew C. Perry and his steam frigates off the shore of Uraga in Edo Bay. The primary motive of the Americans in sending ships to Japan was to insure coaling facilities for trade with China, but ultimately this visit became the key to opening Japan to relations with other foreign nations.

In 1854, a treaty of friendship was signed between the United States and Japan; four years later, a trade treaty was signed. Other trade treaties were concluded with Russia, Great Britain, France, and Holland. Most noteworthy in the treaties were two points of inequity. Japan was forced to recognize extraterritorial privileges for citizens of the five nations. During the period for which the treaties were in effect, Japan was unable to alter import and export customs duties. Throughout the Meiji period, Japan suffered under international pressures that took advantage of these inequitable agreements, and also from the attacks of domestic public opinion; and all of the policies of the new government were oriented toward revision of the treaties.

Problems and Policies of the Meiji Government

External pressure on the Tokugawa shogunate in its last years gave rise to extremely complicated political reactions within Japan. In addition to creating popular opposition and a popular awareness of crisis, it polarized the elements struggling for political power into supporters of the imperial court and supporters of the shogunate. As contacts with Western nations increased in frequency and depth, both parties became aware of the pressing need to unify and strengthen the nation. About ten years of violent debate and actual fighting were to pass before the imperial court became the main axis of national policy.

The political reforms that took place in the interests of national sovereignty may be regarded as revolutionary. The major problem of the Meiji government was furthering the revolution. In the following paragraphs certain concrete measures are discussed.

The government made clear what was meant by a policy of openness and friendliness. Japan was open to the world but would attempt to increase in wealth and power so as to emulate the nations of the West and ultimately overpower them. In the last years of the Tokugawa shogunate, advocates of opening the nation deliberately stirred popular resistance. The Meiji policy of openness and friendliness derives from their policies.

Second, the Meiji government turned its attention to revision of the treaties. Extraterritorial privileges amounted to an invasion of national sovereignty. Lack of customs autonomy placed serious obstacles in the way of capital growth and economic development. For a Japan that had only recently opened its doors to the world and must now face Western capitalist nations that had already gone through the Industrial Revolution, this was an extremely serious matter. In 1871, as a first step toward solving the problem, the government sent Iwakura Tomomi to Europe and the United States as a special ambassador plenipotentiary. While attempting to prepare the way for revision of the unequal treaties, Iwakura and his fellows were to observe conditions in the nations they visited. Although treaty negotiations got no farther than exchanges of opinion, Iwakura and other people important in the Japanese government were able to observe Western culture at first hand. What they saw had great influence on later policies.

The Japanese were worried about the actions of America and the European nations in Asia. In 1871, articles of amity were concluded between Japan and China. They stipulated that the two nations should recognize the other's judiciary rights and that they should have conventional tariff systems. The two nations agreed to cooperate against Western incursions.

On the domestic front, the government concentrated on modernization. For the sake of maintaining its international position, it was imperative that the country be modernized, or Westernized. Among the many measures taken to this end, three deserve special notice: agricultural reforms, strengthening of the military, and education.

To strengthen national finances, the system of land taxation was overhauled. All was assessed on the basis of fertility and transportation facilities. Land prices were based on this assessment, and 3 percent of the price was established as the land tariff. The system of paying taxes in kind was abandoned, and money payment required. Landowners and owner-farmers were granted deeds.

The government's first step toward strengthening the military forces was the seizure of all facilities for the manufacture of arms and their use for war industry. With the opening of the first railways in 1872, plans were laid for expansion. The shipbuilding and sea-transport industries were put under government protection.

But expansion of military facilities and war industries was not enough for military strength. General industrial development was indispensable. Vital industries were put under governmental control until they were securely established and then allowed them to pass into the private hands for the accumulation of private capital. This policy had the double effect of stimulating industrialization and helping build an independent national economy. The Ministry of Home Affairs, established in 1873, set up a number of model enterprises using modern Western industrial equipment and technology. They were first tested run and then put into full-scale operation. The government lavishly subsidized persons who were willing to undertake modern industrial enterprises. Private capital accumulation was small, and the absolute amount of commercial capital available for conversion into industrial capital was insufficient. It was necessary to advance capitalization on the strength of national capital.

But two difficulties stood in the way. Because the Japanese lacked customs autonomy, conventional tariffs were low. This made it impossible for private Japanese industry to make gains in the face of the Western competition. This in turn limited growth. Second, the government rigidly opposed the introduction of foreign capital. Reliance on foreign capital was thought to compromise national independence.

The government took positive measures to inform and educate the masses. In 1872, a system of public education was established, and appropriate statutes promulgated. The new system replaced the Confucian obligations and rejection of commercial gain with Western utilitarianism.

Great importance was placed on the role of newspapers. Extremely low rates were set for postal deliveries of newspapers and there was no charge for the delivery of manuscripts to newspaper offices.

The Movement for Democratic Rights

Along with other aspects of Western culture, modern democratic ideas were introduced into Japan and disseminated through the political movement known as the movement for democratic rights. For about ten years after the establishment of the new Meiji government, members of the old samurai class created disturbances in many parts of the nation. They presently came to see that armed force could not topple the government. They then decided to bring about major political reforms on a platform of democratic rights. Commoners began to take part in the movement from about 1880.

It was argued that a government responsive to public opinion would serve the cause of strengthening the nation, a position which may be described as national liberalism. It may thus be said that the attainment of national independence was the ardent desire of the whole populace.

The immediate aim of the movement was the convening of a national assembly. Feeling that the masses were yet too immature to be entrusted with control of the country, the government controlled political meetings and the formation of political organizations. In 1881, however, when public pressure had become irresistible, 1890 was set as the date for opening such an assembly. Internal pressure alone did not force the government to make this concession. The desire to bring treaty revisions by showing that Japan was becoming a democratic nation played a part in the decision. When the time for the opening of the national assembly was set, the leaders of the movement for democratic rights turned to organizing political parties.

Commentary

In the middle of the nineteenth century, Japan was shaken by great domestic and international forces. On the one hand, the long period of feudal control under the Tokugawa shogunate had brought grave crises. On the other hand, the West, which had already been through the Industrial Revolution and was in the imperialistic phase of its history was making alarming inroads in Asia. In 1867 the Tokugawa shogunate finally collapsed, and the emperor was restored to the head of the governing structure. Japan started on a path to modernization under a new political system. Many hardships lay along the way. This book is a lucid political interpretation of the period.

The text is divided into two chapters. The first is called "The Edo Feudal System and Its Collapse"; and the second, "Transition to a Modern Nation." In the first, the author presents a well-organized explanation of the internal and external elements leading to the collapse of the feudal system and the process by which the breakdown occurred. In the second, he calls on abundant historical materials to show Japan on the way to becoming modern nation and describes the official policies and the opposition activities.

Though the restoration of the emperor to the top of the political structure is commonly known as the "Meiji Restoration," the author does not interpret it as the replacement of one ruling class with another. Instead, he sees it as a revolution for the sake of national independence. He gives clear pictures of the crises Japan underwent and the direction the nation followed to modernization.

IX
The Arts

36. CHARACTERISTICS OF JAPANESE ART

Nihon Bijutsu no Tokushitsu By Yashiro Yukio
Tokyo: Iwanami Shoten, 1965.

Preface

In attempting a comparative study of the arts of Japan and those of other nations, two important problems must be considered: the East in relation to the West and Japan in relation to China. In Japan there exists an immature interpretation of the relation between the East and the West to the effect that Western culture is materialistic, Eastern culture is spiritual, and that people from the West cannot be expected to understand the East. The Japanese must revise this opinion and make careful comparative studies of the true nature of both cultures. It is important to correct still another prejudiced view to the effect that, because it is less ancient, Japanese culture is inferior to, or no more than a copy of, the culture of China. Scholars, especially orientalists in the West, confuse historical and archaeological research with judgments on aesthetic values to the extent that they are unable to develop a true aesthetic criticism. The following text tries to enable an understanding of the sources of the Japanese artistic disposition and talents and so to provide a basis for reflection and self-awareness toward appreciation of Japanese art throughout the world.

Impressionistic Nature of Japanese Art

All art is an attempt to copy nature. The intuitive attitude of a people toward nature and the ways they react emotionally to the natural world are the starting point from which develop the characteristics of that people's art. There are two opposite ways to understand and react to nature. The artist can efface himself in an attempt to copy the objective truths of nature; or he can attempt to extract his own subjective impressions of nature. Art is basically no more than the expression of images reflected on the mind. But whether the process of effecting such expression is subjective or objective greatly alters attitudes toward artistic production and gives birth to stylistic differences. Comparisons of the arts of the East and the West reveal contrasting approaches to this process. Western art has striven for objective representation; Eastern art has relied on subjective expression. Among the arts of the Orient, Japanese art has reached the extreme of bold and thorough impressionistic portrayal.

The way in which the famous wood-block artist Kitagawa Utamaro (1753-1806) treats the scene of a woman resting illustrates my point. For his purposes, it is sufficient to give straightforward expression to the woman's abundant black hair, her long, narrow eyes, her red lips, and her white skin, and to the bold ivy pattern in indigo on her white summer kimono. Had the picture been executed in accordance with the rules of Western realism, the physical presence of the human body would have been apparent. But the mind of the viewer might not have received the still more important impression of a beautiful woman.

Until the second half of the nineteenth century, Western painting concentrated on objective portrayal. The introduction to Western artists – especially in France – of the Japanese *ukiyoe* print proved to be an important stimulus and contributed to the beginnings of the Impressionist movement. The effect of these prints suggests something basic about the difference between Oriental and Occidental art.

If it has its merits, the thoroughgoing subjective impressionism of Japanese art is not without its defects. It can easily lack objectivity of the kind possible when realism has a sound theoretical basis. It is sometimes wanting in the kind of composure and dignity that results from attempts to capture the truths of nature.

Decorative Nature of Japanese Art

Two traits are the basis for the impressionistic nature of Japanese art. The Japanese have a keen sensitivity enabling them to grasp the colors and forms of natural phenomena readily; and they have a lively ability to give artistic expression to stimuli supplied by outward objects. These traits, or sensitivities, are manifested in a decorative style.

The Japanese countryside itself tends to favor this sensibility. Japan is in the temperate and subtropical zones, conducive to healthy and energetic living. Abundant sunlight and beneficial rains enrich the senses. The landscape is richly endowed with decorative elements. Mere copying results in decorative art.

Japanese painters add aesthetic and decorative elements to the phenomena of nature. Sometimes natural objects, the flowers and plants that embroider mountains and fields with the changing colors of the seasons, are employed in beautiful patterns for pictures, clothing, furniture, and handicrafts. The distinctive Japanese way of treating the patterns of flowing water and waves reaches its apex in the pair of screens called *Red and White Plums* by Ogata Kôrin (1658-1716). The overlapping, swirling lines of the water below beside the plum trees seem to transport the eyes and mind of the viewer to a distant, unchanging place.

A similarly decorative interpretation of natural objects occurs in bold, stylized renditions of the human form and face. In its most extreme applications, it results in faces that have no more than dashes for eyes and small hooks for noses. Such renditions are used in the scroll paintings of *The Tale of Genji*, from the Heian period. In no other art tradition is the decorative element as pervasive as in the art of Japan.

Symbolic Nature of Japanese Art

The impressionistic and decorative natures discussed in the preceding sections can be interpreted as manifestations of profound spiritual meaning in the formative arts. This spiritual meaning deserves the most intense examination as a unifying force in Japanese art.

Modern aesthetic theories argue that spiritual motifs are incompatible with art. But such an attitude has significance only as a historical reaction against the traditional emphasis on motif, as opposed to form. Aesthetic theories that ignore the need for the formative arts, as part of the greater artistic culture, to encompass the whole of the human spirit and give it inspiration are basically unsound.

Japanese painting has developed under a strong need to illustrate texts. In all ages, the popularity of the *waka* lyric has had a powerful influence on graphic art. The unification of text and illustrations achieved in the paintings of the *Yamato-e* tradition, which originated in about the ninth century and developed into a distinctly national style, is probably without parallel in the art of any other nation. A similar close relationship between text and painting is evident in picture scrolls.

But the pinnacle of expressionistic art was reached after painting had advanced beyond illustration and when its spiritual content had broken with fixed literary forms. This high point is to be found in the spiritual symbolism of Zen art.

Zen Buddhism urges that the senses be controlled. Zen artists used only monochrome ink and resort to maximum simplification of subject matter and extremely abbreviated brushwork. They insisted that it is impossible to express the free, untrammeled spirit in a world restricted by material phenomena. It was their aim to use a compressed style in which a few strokes of the brush reveal eternal spiritual values and boundless thought. Their point was not that abstraction is in itself aesthetically valuable, but that abstraction can be sublimated into sign, or symbol, inspiring spiritual activity.

An example is the *Bamboo and Sparrow* of Kaô Ninga (fourteenth century), one sparrow looking upward into the sky and a few lightly painted branches of bamboo. In spite of its simplicity, the painting produces a strong impression of vastness. A single sparrow becomes the limitless expanse of the heavens.

Emotion and Sentiment in Japanese Art

The spiritual content that Japanese art attempts to express is too complicated to permit general explanations. But I think it is possible to specify emotionalism as one of its most prominent characteristics. In about the Nara period, Japanese culture came under the influence of the culture of T'ang China and produced monumental sculpture in the T'ang style. In the Heian period, however, a Japan isolated from cultural exchange with the continent entered what might be called a period of nationalism. The elegant and gentle sadness of the court aristocracy came to the fore. I do not mean to imply that sentiment represents the whole of Japanese spiritual life, but it is possible to say that the sentimental tendency appears to a remarkable degree in Japanese art and that it often manifests itself in works of great excellence.

Feminine sentimentality governed even the religious faith of the Heian period and produced a Buddhist art that is extremely decorative. An interesting example is the decorated sutra picture, in which paintings in heavy pigments are executed on paper and sutra texts are superimposed on the paintings. The pictures portray genre scenes of the times, including representations of frolicking children and of love scenes. Though the copying of the sutra texts was probably done in a spirit of penitence, the underpainted decorations reveal amazing beauty and boldness of design. These pictures are a classic example of the way in which a feminine sensibility can serve to unify religious faith and beauty in Japanese art.

Commentary

Characteristics of Japanese Art (*Nihon Bijutsu no Tokushitsu*) is the sole inclusive explanation and critique of Japanese art. It was first published in 1943 and was reissued with revisions and additions in 1965. It is in two volumes. The first contains 737 pages of text, and the second 228 pages of illustrations. It covers all of the noteworthy works and phenomena in Japanese art and makes comparisons between the art of Japan and the arts of the West and China.

Under the heading "The Basic Formative Conditions of Japanese Art," the author first gives a general explanation of the natural environment, religion, and the Japanese character. The same chapter includes discussions of artistic materials and techniques. It is followed by a detailed treatment of the characteristics of Japanese art under four headings: impressionism, decoration, symbolism, and emotionalism or sentiment.

No attempt is made to study the history of Japanese art. Instead, the basic constituents of Japanese art are explained. It is, however, difficult to evaluate the expressive aims of a large number of works of art in terms of no more than the four concentrated characteristics the author sets forth. At the expense of a slight sacrificing of theoretical neatness, the author discusses various aspects of Japanese art on the basis of the available facts. At the same time, he calls upon his extensive knowledge of the arts of the West and China to formulate principles about Japanese art. The book is an outstanding guide to Japanese art.

Yashiro Yukio (1890-1975) graduated from the department of English literature of Tokyo University, and taught at the Tokyo Academy of Fine Arts (present: the Fine Arts Department of Tokyo University of Arts). He conducted study and research on the arts of the East and the West during frequent and extended trips to Europe, the United States, and China. Until 1970 he served as director of the Yamato Bunkakan in Nara. After World War II, at the instigation of Sir George B. Sansom, he was invited to Stanford University as guest lecturer. Plans for an English translation of the first edition stimulated him to devote six years to its revision and amplification. Unfortunately, the book was never translated. He published a number of books on Oriental and Occidental art.

37. THE JAPANESE RURAL DWELLING

Nihon no Minka By Kon Wajirô
Tokyo: Sagami Shobô, 1954.

In cities, ordinarily, residences are built apart from places of work and social contacts. It is sufficient to make the house a convenient and comfortable place for the family. But this is not true of houses in rural areas, where it is impossible to obtain good materials readily and where the builder must make do with materials at hand. Folk architecture must always take into consideration the climatic and topographical peculiarities of the region.

Rural dwellings do not come under international influences as do urban houses. Nor do they change as rapidly. Once something has been built in the country, it becomes part of the local scene and remains unaltered for a very long time. It is true that various local styles exist. They are the products and accretions of an old cultural tradition. In rural dwellings it is possible to find clear remnants of the culture of the Edo period, of course, and of Muromachi as well. Rural dwellings are useful for the study of the past, since they are closer to ordinary life than are temples and shrines.

In general, the Japanese do not use stone or brick masonry in constructing houses. They do not excavate earth or stone for their dwellings or construct mud buildings. Instead, they erect wooden frame structures; use clay walls; and roof with grass thatch, wooden shingles, or tiles. One reason is the abundance of wood in Japan; another is high humidity. It is not necessarily lack of sophistication that moves an architecture to employ wood with many openings and sliding panels (*shôji*). Indeed the Japanese rural house is in many respects more highly developed than the mud or brick folk dwellings of other countries.

It is generally characterized of the kind of settlement in which it is built: plains, mountains, or seashore.

Houses built on plains are found in two kinds of agricultural communities: those in which cultivation is in wet paddies and of dry-field cultivation. Generally, houses for farmers engaged in wet-rice cultivation are built in groups. Small clusters of houses dot the plains. Since they are surrounded by the water of the paddies, they are built on natural or artificial rises. There is generally a windbreak of trees on the side of the prevailing winds. Among groups of houses stands the grove of the local Shinto deity. Roofing is generally thatch, though sometimes tiles are used. The compact, convenient houses have well-developed sanitation facilities. Straw artifacts and weaving provide added income. There are also small vegetable gardens near the houses. It is a concentrated, compact living environment. The busiest times are planting in the spring and harvest in the fall. People from neighboring communities sometimes help at the work.

In areas where water is unavailable for wet paddies, dry-field cultivation is inevitable. Wet-field cultivation is more profitable, and dry-field agriculture involves much more labor. Dry-field farmers are at the mercy of the hard ground. The very field of vision from dry fields is limited. The earth, the crops, the forest, and the sky strike the eye one by one. The houses of dry-field farmers are usually built separately; two or three stand at the edge of the forest, facing south to get as much sun as possible. Twisting roads lead through forests and over hills from one village to another.

Houses in dry-field villages are often neglected. Craft touches in their design and construction are rough and few. The houses are scattered in a disorderly fashion. Interior plans are clumsy. Specialized work, like the cultivation of tea, tobacco, or silk worms, produces certain local architectural characteristics. The houses serve limited social functions; but, in general, they are rough and coarse. Dirty clothes and houses are the life of the dry-field farmer.

In mountain villages, small paddies and dry fields are built along the banks of streams on sloping hillsides. Some villages have created surprising numbers of paddies and fields on the slopes. Whole mountainsides covered with terraced paddies held by retaining walls tell of the hardships of ancestors long gone.

Flat land is as precious as sunlight in mountain areas. It is available for houses in very limited quantities. Small, stagelike plots for houses are built behind stone retaining walls. There plums and peaches bloom, and in the rear yards persimmon and chestnut trees add notes of cheer to the changing seasons. Mountain villages tend to be self-sufficient, and their inhabitants are skillful at making use of natural materials. Over long years, their architecture and other aspects of their way of life have gradually incorporated urban manners and styles. Since mountain people tend to be conservative, their way of life retains many things from the past.

In waterside villages below rocky cliffs are most clearly revealed the characteristics of the fisherman's house. No matter how steep the cliffs, there is invariably at least a potato patch on top. The men go to sea, and when they are at home they do almost nothing. In contrast, the wives and daughters never stop working. They gather edible seaweeds from the boulders at the shore, or they dive for abalone. It is the women who climb the cliffs to till small patches of garden. Because of the limited amount of flat land, small plots must suffice for houses. Stone retaining walls front along level areas, and there are built tightly grouped, sturdy, compact houses. There is no need for the large storage buildings and granaries found in farming villages. Necessities come from the local store. Since they do not need to accommodate numerous helpers at harvest time, nor are guest rooms necessary. Since there are no harvest crowds, it is the custom to share family rooms with guests.

Selected Examples

This is a representative wet-paddy farmhouse near Matsuyama, on the island of Shikoku. As is true of most farmhouses in western Japan, the buildings are placed on the periphery of the lot, which is surrounded by a clay wall. The arrangement creates a pleasing inner courtyard. The main residential building (*omoya*) and the storage shed (*naya*) adjoin each other. The roof is tile.

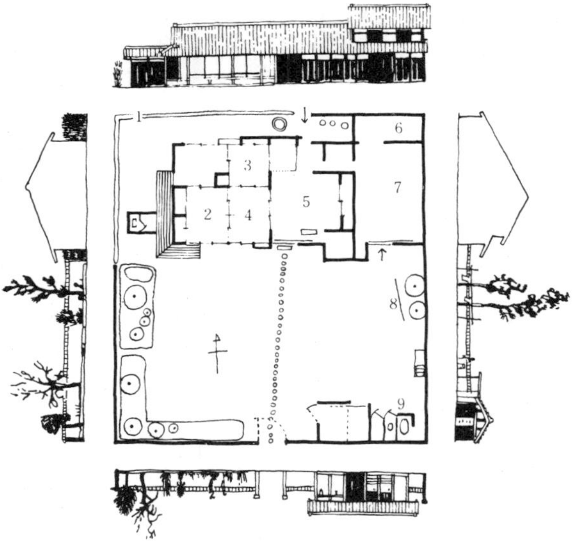

1. cedar hedge
2. guest room
3. family room
4. front parlor
5. earth floor
6. storage
7. storage shed
8. clothes-drying area
9. bathroom

[A] (*Nihon no Minka*, page 247, chart 110)

This is a dry-field farmhouse about two kilometers west of Urawa. In the daytime, when the family is working in the field, the house is as quiet as a Buddhist temple. The forest behind the house is of cedar and oak. In the front yard are plum and cherry trees. The part of the house that projects forward was once a stable; but, when the family stopped using horses, a loom was installed. Now the loom has been removed. In the center of the thatched roof is an opening for the escape of cobalt-blue smoke produced by the burning of straw in the hearth directly below. This house is typical of farmhouses in the Musashino region.

[B] (*Nihon no Minka*, page 147, chart 45)
1. godown
2. storage shed
3. stable
4. lavatory

This farmhouse is one of about fifty in a settlement in the mountains of Chichibu (Saitama Prefecture). Since there is only a limited amount of land for residential and agricultural uses, everything is carefully tended. Stone retaining walls create a stagelike projection of flat land next to the house. A vegetable called *udo* (*Aralia cordata*) and cucumbers are grown in the garden, where there are peach and oleaster trees. Mood and customs and manners suggest life on a small island.

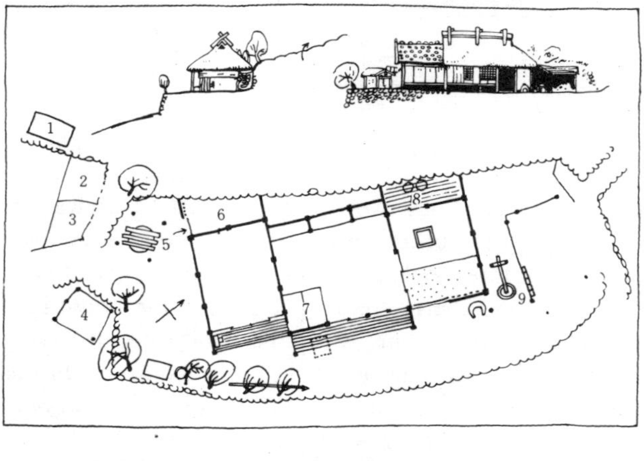

1. granary
2. udo
3. cucumber
4. manure
5. lavatory
6. storage
7. tatami
8. pickles
9. stone mill

[C] (*Nihon no Minka*, page 149, chart 46)

This is the home of a fishing family in southern Tokushima Prefecture. The shore is lined by cliffs, and the houses are built behind a mountain for protection from the strong Pacific winds. They are very small and have low ceilings. Everything is arranged with the orderliness of a ship's cabin. When the men are at home, they spend much time repairing nets in the wood-floored front room.

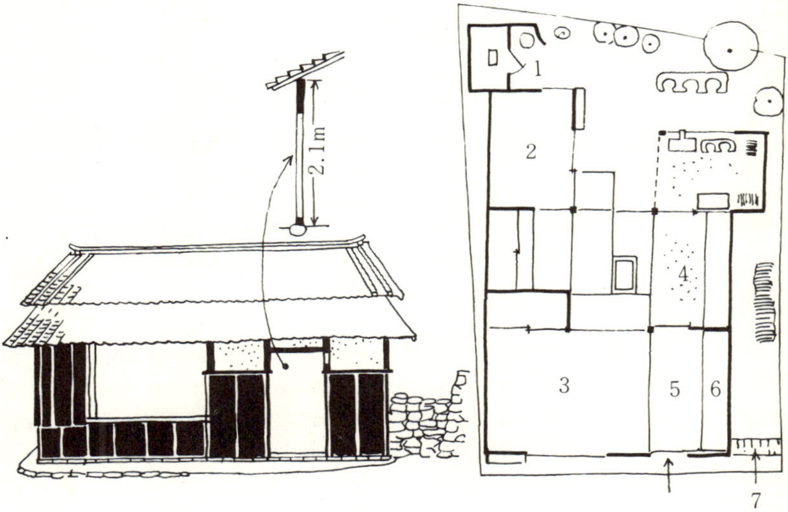

[D] (*Nihon no Minka*, page 242, chart 107)
1. lavatory 2. rear room
3. wood-floored front room
4. kitchen 5. earth floor
6. fishing implements 7. stone wall

Commentary

The first edition of this book appeared in 1922. With the rapid economic growth of Japan in the period following World War II, the appearance of the traditional folk dwelling has altered drastically. It is now as difficult to find a thatched farmhouse in rural Japan as it is to find a steam locomotive. Today farmhouse roofs are gleaming and colorful, their kitchens are bright, with running water and hot water provided by gas heating, and petroleum heating for the rooms. The developments in the Japanese folk dwelling in the past thirty years represent, on the one hand, enrichment and modernization, and, on the other, loss of local color.

This book is not a systematic study of the Japanese folk dwelling. The author, who styled himself a modernologist, described it as a sketch of the folk dwelling. His evaluations and criticisms are relatively subjective and arbitrary. But the book contains many examples from all parts of the country. It provides an opportunity to study the forerunners of the modern Japanese house.

38. THE WORLD OF THE JAPANESE PERFORMING ART

Nihon Geinô no Sekai By Hayashiya Tatsusaburô
Tokyo: NHK Books #184, Nihon Hôsô Shuppan Kyôkai, 1973.

True history is a tracing of mass movements. Thus it is important to consider the workings of the body politic and the aristocracy in terms of the general populace. Even in ancient cultures, which at first glance seem the exclusive property of the nobility, especially in the performing arts, a study of origins reveals a popular nucleus. This is particularly true in Japan. Here we will discuss the tea ceremony which developed in the Middle Ages.

Establishment and Development

References to tea begin to appear from the ninth century. Nobles enjoyed their tea, seated comfortably in chairs on the verandas of their resplendent villas, fishing in their private ponds while listening to koto music, in the style of T'ang China. The custom of drinking powdered tea was brought from Sung China by the Zen priest Eisai at the end of the twelfth century, and introduced into the regimen of Zen temples as a medicinal guard against sleepiness. In the thirteenth and fourteenth centuries, it became popular as an elegant pastime of the military and agricultural classes. It must be noted that their "tea parties" were more occasions for conversation than for the drinking tea, even though there were tea-judging contests. Among the upper classes, Toga-no-o tea (which was presented to the abbot Myôe by Eisai, and planted in the Toga-no-o district) was considered the finest and only true tea.

Only the wealthy could afford good teas, but this was no detriment to the spread of convivial tea drinking on all levels of society.

Along with the increasing popularity of a very informal style of tea drinking, a highly aristocratic tea ceremony developed as a means for viewing and appreciating hanging scrolls, tea bowls, and vases imported from China. This development took place mainly at the Higashiyama Villa of Yoshimasa (1435-90), the eighth of the Ashikaga shoguns, under the leadership of a priest from Nara named Murata Shukô. Earlier tea customs and the refined Higashiyama tea meetings were combined, and the term *sadô* or *chadô*, "way of tea," came into use.

In the following century Takeno Jô-ô (1502-55) and his famous student Sen no Rikyû (1522-91) developed the philosophy of the more subdued, meditational tea, served in the humble thatched hut, which stressed the natural aesthetics of *wabi* and *sabi*, far closer to the hearts of the common people.

On the other hand, Toyotomi Hideyoshi (1536-98) favored ever greater ostentation. He served tea in gold-encrusted surroundings, from solid gold cups. Under his influence, there arose a polite tea ceremony, led by Furuta Oribe (1544-1615), in which man-made beauty was prized. The tea cottages surviving from this period were built by Oribe and Kobori Enshû (1579-1647).

Rikyû's style was revived by his grandson Sôtan, and is perpetuated by the three Senke schools of the *Cha-no-yu* tea ceremony.

Is the Tea Ceremony an Art?

What aspects of the tea ceremony justify calling it a form of an art? First of all, while it takes the form of a "party" it is a total art that is in many ways similar to a theatrical performance. The host is the main performer, his tea house is the theatre, his guests are the audience, and his script is the Book of Tea Protocol (*Chakai-Ki*). Harmony among these four elements is the objective of the tea ceremony.

Secondly, the host and his guests must enter the tea house in a spirit of harmony. The guests are expected to read the feelings and intent of the host in the hanging scroll and flower arrangement, and the party is expected to proceed with elevating conversation.

And thirdly, it must be remembered that the quality of the tea is the highest possible. Rikyû was the first person to stress this point. He was careful to make friends with the Uji tea producers themselves in order to obtain the very best tea for his master Hideyoshi. It was Rikyû's unstinting efforts to perfect every detail that made it possible for him to bring the tea ceremony to the level of a pure and total art.

True Hospitality

The story is told that when Rikyû went with his students to visit the home of tea producer Kanbayashi, the host was so nervous that he broke all the rules of decorum, dropping his utensils and fumbling as he offered the tea bowl to Rikyû. Rikyû's students sneered at this clumsiness, but the master himself praised him heartily, explaining that in his eagerness to serve tea before it got cold he had no time for details of etiquette. In this, said Rikyû, was the essence of the tea ceremony.

Rikyû thus taught that a desire to serve and entertain is of utmost importance. Rikyû's association with Kanbayashi was first and foremost to provide the best tea possible for his guests. It is through the taste of the tea that truly human relationships are effected.

At the end of a meal, Japanese express gratitude in the phrase *go-chisô-sama*. The basic *chisô* means "to run with all one's might." Thus the guests are saying that they are appreciative of the labors of the host to prepare the meal for them. It is the giving of one's very best that makes the tea ceremony the rich experience it is and results in the pure harmony that is basic to the art.

Commentary

Hayashiya is a historian who is especially well-known for his work in the performing arts of Japan. Here he explores the background of Gagaku, Noh, Kyôgen, the Tea Ceremony, and Kabuki, and places them in historical perspective, in a clear and simple manner for the general public.

His insistence on viewing history from the standpoint of the masses is of particular interest. He considers the audience to be of at least equal importance with creators and performers, and believes the reasons for the founding of theatre identical with those that attract an audience.

Here we have introduced only the section of this book that deals with the Tea Ceremony. This art has become a highly formalized ritual, controlled by a strict system of masters and pupils, but Hayashiya points out that its original purpose was to provide a higher means of communication between host and guests.

39. ZEAMI

Zeami By Kitagawa Tadahiko
Tokyo: Chûkô Shinsho #292, Chûô Kôron-sha, 1972.

In 1908 the theses of Zeami, including the now famous *Kadensho* (or *Fûshi Kaden*), were discovered, and his name became known to the general public. Thus Zeami gained fame as an actor, playwright, director, and theoretician. His theoretical writings in particular focused attention on him as philosopher and theoretician. However, Zeami thought of himself mainly as a writer and actor, and the writing of Noh theory was clearly of secondary importance to him.

The two basic elements of Noh are "mime" and "dance accompanied by song." He said in his later years: "Sarugaku Noh, which is given for purposes of entertainment, has mime, or impersonation, for its most fundamental principle. Yet since Sarugaku finds its roots in, and is directly derived from Kagura [a religious dance], song and dance should be considered of primary importance." This statement makes it quite clear that the Noh of Zeami's day had a strong tendency toward mime. Mimetic Noh, in which all the characters are live human beings, has traditionally been designated the present (*genzai*) group. The Noh which Zeami created, and which is the mainstream of the Noh repertory today, has as its main character a supernatural being, and is known as phantasmal (*mugen*) Noh.

Zeami created and perfected this unique style and introduced it into Yamato Sarugaku, bringing materials from classical literature to the Noh stage for the first time.

Just who were the writers and what sort of plays were written before Zeami, and what was the situation in Yamato Sarugaku, in which Zeami was reared? The most important writer was Zeami's father, Kanami. Kanami's works were close to contemporary life, which he dramatized in a very free style. His plot development is rich in dramatic transitions.

"Jinen Koji" is a Kanami masterpiece. It tells of a young lay priest who rescues a girl from the clutches of a slave trader, through the dances for which he is famous. The theme is close to the life of the day, for slave traders were active during the Muromachi period.

The second most important writer of Zeami's day was Miyamasu. He spent most of his time touring the provinces, and his materials were chosen to appeal to his audiences. He paid close attention to the rural tastes upon which Kanami too placed much importance. Miyamasu was a contemporary of Zeami, but his style is based upon the older traditions of Yamato Sarugaku, which traditions were perpetuated by even later writers. Thus a rugged, more realistic Noh also continued to have its vogue.

Zeami was trained from childhood in the highly dramatic style of Yamato Sarugaku, but he was able to drive out the dominant mime elements almost completely, and transform Noh into an art of song and dance. His father had only succeeded in introducing music and dance and bringing about a generally harmonious merger with mime.

Before Zeami, there was one group of Noh plays with strong dance and song elements, the *waki* Noh (religious ceremonial pieces). Zeami's *waki* pieces are all dignified and sedate, and their dances are for the most part calm, majestic, and elegant. In comparison, *waki* pieces by other playwrights tend toward the showy and the spectacular. While Zeami never used set pieces or properties for such plays, other writers decorated their stages with palaces and ships and the like.

Using the *waki* group as his model, Zeami created the warrior-ghost (*shura*) group of plays, based on episodes from *The Tales of the Heike* (*Heike Monogatari*). In a word, Zeami strove for a static theatre, and placed great importance on artistic quality. This dramaturgical reform gave birth to Zeami's phantasmal style.

The following basic dramaturgical structure is uniquely Zeami's own.

Scene One: A traveling priest visits one of the ancient battlefields of the Genji and Heike clans. The ghost of a warrior appears, generally as a very old man, and tells of the battles fought there. He alludes to his real identity, and disappears.

Interlude: The priest questions a villager about the battles, and it becomes clear to him who the old man was.

Scene Two: As the night deepens and the priest begins to read his sutras, the warrior appears in his true form, dances and sings of his death in battle, requests prayers for his soul, and disappears once more.

The hero of the piece is from the world of classical literature, while the priest is a living person. Thus the priest exists in the same dimension as the audience, and is their representative. The world that unfolds on the stage is the dream world of priest and audience, through which they are drawn into the world of *The Tales of the Heike*. Zeami recreates the intense hatred, jealousy, and the obsessions of the ghost. With the *waki* pieces for his model he creates the aesthetics of extinction. Classical lyricism and religious precepts are combined.

Today the works of Zeami based on *The Tales of the Heike* are popular and often performed. With the general public of the Muromachi period, however, narrative tales of bravery, filled with bloody action, were of far more interest. Zeami's lyrical warrior-ghost pieces were appreciated by only a few intellectual aristocrats.

After his work with *The Tales of the Heike*, Zeami went on to dramatize episodes from such Heian classics as *The Tales of Ise* (*Ise Monogatari*) and *The Tale of Genji* (*Genji Monogatari*). It was at this point in his career that Zeami perfected the woman or wig (*katsura*) pieces, which are recognized as the flower of the Noh drama.

Kanami also wrote plays about women, but they are all about living contemporaries, or women of popular legend. Kanami's women were all driven mad by a ghost or by the treasured robes of a dead lover. Zeami's women go mad because of a lost child or lover. The two varieties are called "insanity through possession by a malevolent spirit" and "insanity because of love." The former is not completely wanting in the works of Zeami, but he passed them through the filter of the classics and his own phantasmal style to create an entirely new kind of theatre.

Zeami seems to have cared less and less for the general public as he grew older. In his later years, he expressed his great pride in his accomplishments and his sense of remoteness from the world when he said, "When I realize that in ages to come there will most likely be no one capable of truly appreciating Noh, it seems pointless to write any more plays of this caliber."

Commentary

Mention of the medieval arts of Japan brings to mind the beauty of quiet simplicity designated by the word *yûgen*, and this leads to thoughts of the Noh drama. However, the tastes of the Middle Ages tended toward broader, more colloquial elements. Noh first came into being as popular colloquial theatre. Zeami took it from its original context and raised it to new levels of elegance and refinement. In a single lifetime, he pointed the Noh in the direction it should ideally go, and because of which it lost popularity in his day. In later centuries it was revised as a classical art.

During the Edo period, a new theatre art called Kabuki appeared. Noh, which had been the mainstream of popular entertainment and contemporary theatre, gave way to the new form. Zeami's Noh became the property of the aristocratic warrior class. It was further polished and refined, and presently developed into the uniquely profound stage art we know today.

Such is the theme of this book. The author does not view the Noh drama through Zeami. Rather he discusses Zeami in the larger context of Noh history. He does not deny the greatness of Zeami, but he makes no attempt to glorify the aristocratic post-Zeami Noh.

Kawatake Shigetoshi, the great scholar of the theatre, observes in *An Outline History of the Japanese Theatre* (*Gaisetsu Nihon Engeki-shi*): "The popular audience is the soil in which all performing arts are germinated and nurtured. Folk arts are wild plants which have grown up in that soil. Later they are transplanted to the gardens of cultural arbiters and other influential persons, where they become sophisticated entertainment, and come to be known as the representative performing arts of their periods."

Kitagawa maintains that it is necessary to take a fresh look not only at the artistic Noh of today, but at the wild plant that was its ancestor as well.

40. THE WORLD OF KUROSAWA AKIRA

Kurosawa Akira no Sekai By Satô Tadao
Tokyo: Sanichi Shobô, 1969.

Kurosawa Akira wrote a large number of film scenarios before he gained fame as a director, most of which were never made into films. One of them, *The German of Dharma Temple* (*Daruma-dera no Doitsu-jin*), has attracted notice because it contains the seed of those special characteristics that later went to make the Kurosawa style. The most distinctive is his great love for the visual culture of Japan. Later he was to use the form of the Noh drama, an art for which he has always had a deep love, in such films as *The Men Who Step on the Tiger's Tail* (*Tora no O o Fumu Otokotachi*, 1945) and *Spider Web Castle* (*Kumonosu-jô*, 1957 generally known abroad as *Throne of Blood*). He was able to achieve a striking visual effect by using the plain earthen wall and white gravel ground cover of a traditional Japanese garden for the scene of an ancient trial in *Rashômon*. His taste for traditional images is further illustrated by scenic shots in his scenarios that call for "the graceful slope of the roof of an old Japanese building," "a beautiful arrangement of walls," or "the handsome structure of a pillar." A second characteristic is the pointing up of the contrast between the foolish, easily swayed masses and a hero who presses on after his own demands, refusing to be influenced by the conditions around him. This theme appears in *The German of Dharma Temple* in the contrast between the villagers whose attitude changes with the signing of the Russo-German Non-Aggression Pact, and the German Lange, an admirer of Japanese architecture, whose mind is not in the least swayed by this development. The fickle masses are a constant presence in Kurosawa's films. Two examples are the city officials in *To Live* (*Ikiru*, 1952), and the gangsters and townspeople in *Yôjinbô* (1961). The contrasting heroes are Watanabe, head of the Civic Affairs Section, and the masterless samurai.

Kurosawa's first work as a director was *Sugata Sanshirô* (1943). It is a highly original film, well-structured, melodramatic, and full of action. A judo master is the hero, in starkly simple fight scenes.

There is a famous scene in which the young hero, to prove to his teacher that he has "the courage to die," jumps into a pond and stays in the cold water all night long. As he observes the unfolding of a lotus blossom at break of day, he is suddenly aware of the fact that strength is not the only virtue. It goes without saying that such enlightenment derives from Zen. *Sugata Sanshirô* was made during the Second World War. Zen was popular, and was used by the government to forestall criticism and insecurity, and to promote tranquility in the midst of danger. Did Kurosawa actually believe in Zen himself, or did he use popular Zen ideas for visual effect? The answer is most likely both yes and no.

Since the war, Kurosawa has repeatedly pursued the theme of insecurity, in such films as *Quiet Duel* (*Shizuka-naru Kettô*, 1949), *To Live* (*Ikiru,* 1952) and *Record of a Living Being* (*Ikimono no Kiroku*, 1955). Such films are developments of and variations upon Kurosawa's war-time Zen. Such works as *Drunken Angel* (*Yoidore Tenshi*, 1948), *Seven Samurai* (*Shichinin no Samurai*, 1954) and *Red Beard* (*Aka Hige*, 1965) show a strong character who is capable of making clear decisions and taking appropriate action, in contrast with a young character who has a brilliant mind, but who is too impatient, too critical, and unable to take effective action. This is a variation upon the teacher-student relationship of *Sugata Sanshirô*. In Kurosawa's postwar films we no longer find the simple pattern of a hero attaining enlightenment, as did Sanshirô when he observed the lotus flower. Rather there is a unique idealism, with heroes struggling for their right to simple enlightenment.

Another characteristic of the works of Kurosawa is to be seen in the scenario for *Escape at Dawn* (*Akatsuki no Dassô*, directed by Taniguchi Senkichi in 1950), in which Kurosawa collaborated. It is the determination to subdue the weaknesses of a weakling. A servile soldier, who commits the sin of being deceived, is absolutely crushed by a sadistic officer.

Kurosawa has no sympathy for weaklings. Or perhaps it would be better to say that he does have sympathy for them, but none for a weakling who refuses to become strong. Kurosawa's contemporaries have attempted to maintain artistic continuity by setting great value on human weakness. Kurosawa created an entirely new film from servility and the attempt to drive it out. For him the greatest Japanese defect is submissiveness, which must be driven out before progress can be made.

Kurosawa's films are characterized by intense violence. His villains often have great charm. It is often the villain who has the strong desires. To Kurosawa, a villain is not merely shameless or impudent. He is not in pursuit of enlightenment, however, and he is not willing to bow to fate. A man fully aware that he is evil is for Kurosawa of far more worth than any slave-like "good" person.

Rashômon, which took the Grand Prix at the Venice International Film Festival of 1951, revealed the high level of Japanese cinema to the world. Released in Japan the previous year, it received no special acclaim, although the brilliance of the director was recognized. One critic thus explained the reason for this lack of recognition: "Disbelief and despair, distrust and doubt, deep within the fiber of this film, did not evoke a sympathetic response from the Japanese public. Yet it accorded with the mood of Western Europe, faced with all manner of deadlocks and crises."

But did *Rashômon* really express "disbelief and despair" and "distrust and doubt?" It is difficult to believe that Kurosawa, who had always preached a message of human trust and the victory of humanism, would suddenly make a plea for and maintain the exact opposite. Nor is he an artist who would waste time on paradox. After extremes of egotism and mendacity, the seemingly irrelevant conclusion to *Rashômon* shows a poor woodcutter taking in a foundling, and thereby showing once more that man is basically good. When the film was released in Japan, many critics protested that this conclusion was unnatural and sentimental. Kurosawa responded: "Fortunately I have no feeling for fashionable scepticism. I only desire to be simple in heart like the man in that last sequence."

Kurosawa has none of the scepticism of his critics. The scenario for *Rashômon* was originally written by Hashimoto Shinobu, based on the Akutagawa Ryûnosuke's short story *In a Grove* (*Yabu no Naka*), under the title *Three Confessions – a Bandit, the Rape Victim and the Husband*. Kurosawa completed the final scenario by adding a fourth episode in which a woodcutter who witnessed the incident reports what he saw. The addition of this final version of the story was not to complicate the plot yet further, but rather to indict the three principals, each of them having tried to make himself look innocent. Thus *Rashômon* makes a point of

Kurosawa's own basic trust in humanity and in the existence of objective truth. There would otherwise have been no reason at all for the fourth episode. There is, of course, a certain amount of falsehood in the story told by the woodcutter, but it is not meant to prove that truth is unknowable, but rather to show the woodcutter's charity when he takes in the abandoned baby.

Actually, it matters very little whether *Rashômon* was made to express belief or disbelief in humanity. It is a masterpiece purely for the brilliance of the directing. It is full of unforgettable cinematic images. The wife of a warrior (Kyô Machiko) is attacked by the bandit Tajômaru (Mifune Toshirô). She is forced to submit to his desires before the eyes of her husband (Mori Masayuki), who is tied to a tree. Her eyes remain open, and she stares directly into the glaring sunlight while the bandit kisses her. The simple action of the bandit's kiss is shown in fourteen separate shots that are interspersed with closeup shots of the sun, providing a rhythmical sequence, with strong accents. As Kyô Machiko's eyes glisten in the sunlight, the camera moves around for a shot of the perspiration on Tajômaru's back. The drops of sweat also glisten in the sun, giving the appearance of so many beautiful diamonds. Then the woman's hands caress the sweat-covered back, hinting at her ecstasy. And the scene when Tajômaru dashes shouting through the grove in the sun that filters down through the leaves, and ties up the man and goes after the woman, is probably the most beautiful example of the sheer beauty of movement in all Japanese cinema.

However, the sadistic pleasure of the assailant, depicted in this particular scene, is not the theme of the film. All during the confession, the violence of Tajômaru's evil joy, equal to the violence of his crime, is matched by a downpour of rain on the Rashômon Gate, shown in constant cutbacks, which seems intent upon washing away the intensity of the crime.

With this film, Kurosawa crystallized a style that is all his own. Through it he constantly reaffirms the idea that both ecstasy and atonement are voluntary. Violent wind and rain and the light of the sun often play an important part in the action. These violent natural images cut the hero off from society and leave him confronting his own inner voice. The hero stands in violent wind or rain or the light of the sun, that he may gaze at his own desires or entreaties or guilt. Kurosawa maintains that it is not through feelings of entrapment that the soul is uplifted, but that it surges up by passion or pride. His heroes do not repent after prosecution. They face into the blazing sun or the pounding rain to pour forth their guilt loudly and clearly. This is what is meant by soul-searching.

Commentary

The Japanese film world has produced at least three great directors – Mizoguchi Kenji (1898-1956), Ozu Yasujirô (1903-1963), and Kurosawa Akira (b. 1910). These three were the central figures of the postwar golden age of Japanese cinema. But Japanese critics, whose view was narrowed by their European complexes, were unable to grasp the international value of the films these men created. It is ironic that it was only after Kurosawa's *Rashômon* received the Grand Prix at the Venice International Film Festival, and the reputation of the great Japanese directors was established abroad, that the Japanese themselves began to give domestic films serious consideration.

This book is the first book-length monograph ever written about a Japanese director by a Japanese critic. The author has succeeded brilliantly in expressing the full spectrum of Kurosawa's works, through his own rich knowledge and sensitivity, by reexamining the films and all the early scenarios. He speaks most penetratingly of changes in Japanese society and in popular taste, which he finds reflected in the Japanese film, and especially in the works of the central creative force.

There is also an excellent work in English on this great director: *The Films of Akira Kurosawa*, by Donald Richie (Berkeley and Los Angeles: University of California Press, 1965).

X
Comparative Studies

41. CLIMATE

Fûdo By Watsuji Tetsurô
Tokyo: Iwanami Shoten, 1935.

The Concept of Climate

"Climate" is defined as "a general term to cover the climate, weather, geological features, soil, topography and scenery of a particular region." But the natural environment that surrounds man does not exist solely outside him. A certain degree of warmth and humidity in the atmosphere, for instance, creates within us a feeling of being refreshed. Man perceives himself in terms of climate, and a different climate leads to a different kind of self-perception. For example, a man's clothing, his food, his housing and his utensils all develop according to the climate in which he lives. It is through these objects that man defines himself, and the distinctive character of a climate inevitably affects both the social structure and the history of those who inhabit a given region. The climatic pattern is also the historical pattern. What follows is an attempt to comprehend the structure of human existence in historical and climatic terms, in particular the latter.

Three Varieties

There are three varieties of climate, the monsoon, the desert, and the meadow; and they are typified in Asia, Africa and Europe respectively. The main climatic indicator of the monsoon region is heat and humidity, and the people are characteristically submissive and resigned. The essential element of the desert, it goes without saying, is dryness, and the people who live in such areas are unusually practical and purposeful. They have a strong sense of belonging and of subservience to the whole, but they are most belligerent vis-à-vis the outsider. The climate of the meadow regions is exemplified by dryness in summer and humidity in winter, and especially in Greece, the cradle of European civilization, nature is amenable to man. Where nature does not act the tyrant it appears in a rational guise and renders up its secrets. Those who live in such regions are themselves rational.

The Distinctive Nature of the Monsoon Climate

The monsoon area includes Japan, China and India, and yet within this region Japan has an individual climate of its own. Compared with the regular nature of India's seasonal winds, Japan is under the influence of both the Asian Continent and the Pacific, and its winds are subject to great and sudden change. Typhoons, which are in a sense seasonal winds, are unpredictable and associated with violent wind and rain, whilst there are few places in the world which receive so much snow as Japan. Its climate is of a dual nature, tropical and frigid. The sight of snow on bamboo, a tropical plant, is frequently offered as an example of a scene unique to Japan.

The generally submissive, resigned nature of people living in the monsoon region takes on a rather special form in the Japanese. It is not simply the monotonous emotional perseverance one finds in the tropics; Japanese feelings call for sudden shifts of mood. There is no continental serenity, but a vital and nervous energy, and, as a result, a tendency to tire quickly and a lack of perseverance. Emotions can sometimes show unexpected violence, like a typhoon, but this power is not the strength of tenacity. So it is that Japan has often produced the historical phenomenon of complete social reform unaccompanied by any persistent struggle. The Japanese place great store by heightened emotions, but they dislike obstinacy. Thus they have great affection for the cherry, which blossoms in such profusion, suddenly as if in haste, only to fall, indifferent to its fate. Resistance and struggle are highly prized, but there must be no obstinacy. In the very midst of clinging to life the desire to live may suddenly be cast away. This is most clearly revealed if one examines the attitude of Japanese toward love. In classic Japanese love stories of every age there is a distinctive pattern, "a gentle love that conceals within it a violent passion, a love that is unselfish, resigned and yet militant" [*Fûdo*, page 139]. The best example of this is the love suicide, a favorite subject of the arts in the Tokugawa period. A love suicide is not simply based on a spiritual belief in the world beyond; it is the affirmation of love through a denial of life. The yearning for an eternity of love is crystallized in this moment of spiritual sublimation, this act of double suicide.

Human relations within the family differ greatly in the three areas, meadow, desert and monsoon. Meadow culture began with the piratical adventures of the Greeks. Adventurous men left their native lands and subjugated the islands and other coastal areas. They began to create primitive *polis*, and took the women of the conquered lands for their wives. So new families were formed by men who had escaped from their own families, and by women whose families had been massacred. Although the Greeks originally had a strong tradition of ancestor worship, the *polis*, once formed, took precedence over the family. The family meant husband and wife, and as far as the child's lineage was concerned his ancestry was rarely traced further than his father. In contrast, the desert-type family was conceived of as a traditional entity that inherited a lineage going back to the first ancestors. Even Jesus, born of a virgin, was "the descendant of Abraham and the son of David." And yet in desert culture the position of the family was inferior to that of the tribe; the unit of nomadic life was the tribe, not the family. It was among the families of the monsoon region, especially China and Japan, that family life was given greatest weight. As in the desert, it was a matter of lineage, but it never became absorbed into the tribe.

So the family signifies the whole entity. It is represented by the head of the house, but it does not exist purely for his benefit. Its main characteristic is that the present family bears responsibility for the whole family, past and future, from ancestor to grandchild, and it may even be that the head of the house is sacrificed when the future or honor of the family is at stake. The family is bound together by a gentle affection aimed at complete harmony. In the *Manyôshû* there is a poem by Yamanoue no Okura which illustrated this feeling well:

> How can silver, gold or jewels compare?
> This precious treasure, my child.

The Japanese commonly conceive of the family as "inside," and society beyond as "outside." This distinction is very strong; all the members of a family are known to each other as "those inside," and they are clearly distinguished from those outside. The same thing can be seen in the structure of Japanese houses. Rooms are never isolated by means of lock and key, and the distinction between individual rooms is done away with. Even if the rooms are partitioned off by screens, the division is based on a sense of mutual trust. In Europe the smallest unit is the room and the next unit of communal life is the walled town. The house, midway between these two units, is of relatively small significance; it is a place for social intercourse and communal life, but between distinct individuals. The Japanese have copied the European way of life in external form, but in the sense that they are unable to lead a social or public life as individuals but must define themselves in terms of the family, they remain untouched by European ways of thinking.

Commentary

The author of this book is well known as a scholar of ethical thought and cultural history, and this book is a collection of essays published in and about 1930 with later emendations. In the first chapter the author defines the concept of "climate" (*fûdo*), and in the second he discusses how cultural patterns are formed by climate in relation to the three basic varieties, monsoon, desert and meadow. In the third chapter he discusses the climate and culture of China and Japan in relation to the distinctive characteristics of the monsoon, and in the fourth chapter he discusses the effect of climate on art, comparing Eastern and Western art from the standpoint of certain "controlling factors." His conclusion is that Western art is controlled by the rational factor, whereas Eastern art is quite different. He here uses examples from gardens and art. The last chapter consists of thoughts on the history of climatology; he discusses its development from Hippocrates to Herder and Hegel, and further to Marx and Russell.

The author's basic attitude to his study of climate can be thus summarized:

"The man with the best sense of hearing recognizes musical talent most readily; and the one with the finest physique recognizes athletic prowess more readily than any other.... In just this way the beacon of reason shines most brightly in a meadow climate. In the monsoon zone it is the refinement of 'feeling' that is best recognized. In just the same way as we make music our own through the musician or are able to experience a game through an athlete, might we not learn to cultivate our own reason from the place where the light of reason shines the brightest and to perfect the refinement of our own feelings with the help of the places where such refinement of feeling is best realized?" (*Fûdo*, page 119)

This book was a pioneering work in Japan, a study of culture and man by a scholar of ethical thought. With the advance of such studies, some of the author's arguments are not beyond criticism, but this book has inspired many studies of Japanese culture by younger Japanese, and is often quoted. It is still worth reading as a classic in the field of comparative cultural studies.

Fûdo has been translated by Geoffrey Bownas under the title *Climate and Culture* (Tokyo: Hokuseidô, 1971).

42. THE MEAT-EATING PHILOSOPHY

Nikushoku no Shisô By Sabata Toyoyuki
Tokyo: Chûkô Shinsho #92, Chûô Kôron-sha, 1966.

The most conspicuous difference between European and Japanese dietary patterns is that the former is based on meat. Japanese eating habits are said to have become Westernized, but compared to Europe, where pigs' and calves' heads may appear on the dinner table, Japan can hardly be said to qualify as a meat-eating culture. In Japan rice definitely remains the staple food, with meat, fish, and vegetables served as side dishes. The corresponding staple in meat-eating Europe is less easily defined.

The high proportion of meat in the European diet since ancient times is due to the fact that Europe is far more suited to livestock breeding than Japan, thanks to unique climatic conditions that prevent the excessive growth of fodder grasses. Exaggerating somewhat, one could even say that livestock would flourish even if neglected altogether. But because pasture and forest land in a completely natural state were insufficient, people have cultivated the land to the extent of improving on already favorable conditions. In contrast, grain productivity is extremely low.

Around the thirteenth or fourteenth century, the earliest period for which we can ascertain the actual productivity of the various regions of Europe, excluding areas in which conditions were exceptionally favorable, the average grain yield was only three to four times the amount of seed planted. Even at the beginning of the nineteenth century, the yield did not in most cases exceed five or six times the amount sown. Comparing these statistics with those for Japan, we see that the average wet-rice yield in the Edo period was thirty to forty times the amount sown. Even today, land in Japan yields five times more rice per acre than in America and twice as much wheat as Europe or America, an indication of the efficiency of Japanese farming.

However, comparing European grain cultivation with Japanese wet-rice cultivation does not give us a complete picture. While theoretically grain cultivation can be considered apart from livestock breeding, in actual fact the two did not occur separately in Europe. The area as a whole comprised forest and pasture for livestock, with cultivated fields scattered here and there. Moreover, whether crops were rotated annually or whether land was divided into three fields rotated in succession among autumn wheat, spring wheat, and pasture, the bounds of the cultivated land itself were unstable, and so crops were always alternated with pasturage. Grain cultivation and stock breeding were similarly linked in the so-called agricultural revolution. Indeed, planting fallow land with clover or turnips served to increase soil fertility. These crops had high food value as fodder. The agricultural revolution did not merely increase grain productivity; it also revolutionized stock breeding.

The differences between Japanese and European eating patterns go beyond table manners to regulate the very bases of thought. First let us consider what fundamental ways of thinking result from a diet rich in meat.

In the past, when agriculture was the major industry, a meat diet meant that Europeans slaughtered their own cattle, horses, sheep, and swine for food. Although they have killed and eaten animals, yet they can advocate kindness to animals. Cruelty, to them, means the infliction of unnecessary pain; here they differ greatly from the Japanese, who think of kindness to animals as meaning to treat animals like human beings. In Europe, where love of animals and animal slaughter have existed side by side, a clear-cut line has been drawn between human beings and animals, and a "philosophy of discontinuity" has been generated whereby human beings are thought superior to all other creatures.

This is the viewpoint of Christianity. Human beings are created in the image of God, and they have been accorded the right to kill and eat other animals from the time of the Creation. It was necessary for Europeans continually to confirm their difference from the animals that were a part of their daily lives. The greatest problem concerned sexual conduct. The ideal was to live one's entire life having no contact with the opposite sex, an ideal that gave rise to the priestly celibacy of the Catholic Church. Failing this, the church made a sacrament of marriage, attempting to regulate sexual life.

Discontinuity between human beings and animals, or anthropocentrism, was linked to the discontinuity of Christian Europeans on the one hand and non-Christian peoples on the other. The Crusades, persecution of heretics and "heathens," colonial rule, and oppression of Jews, all arising from European anthropocentrism, are phenomena inconceivable to the Japanese, with their amiable commingling of indigenous gods and buddhas.

The logic of discontinuity also fostered among Europeans a class consciousness that set apart the "*real* human beings." At the time of the Meiji Restoration of 1868, when the modernization of Japan began in earnest, the ruling class comprised as much as 5 to 6 percent of the population, whereas in France at the time of the revolution the ruling class came to only 0.5 to 0.6 percent of the population. The ruling class was an isolated elite vested with special privileges, and separated by a clear line from the rest of society. And although the class system has been officially denied in recent times, class and status consciousness is extremely difficult to eradicate.

Under the Japanese system of compulsory education, the children of rich and poor attend the same primary schools, while in Europe the education of the upper and lower classes is treated differently from the start. It is much easier in Japan for children from poor families to work their way through school, graduate from a revered university, and climb from the lower to the upper ranks of society.

How was the formation of European thought conditioned by the fact that although the region was not naturally suited to grain cultivation, Europeans were not content with an exclusively meat diet but endeavored to raise grain as well? In the eleventh or twelfth century bread first entered the diet of the common people, making it necessary for groups of farming families to set up communal mills and baking ovens. This and the complex system of three-field rotation weakened the independence of the farmer.

Because of the unstable bounds of cultivated land, a concept akin to the Japanese "rice fields handed down by the ancestors" had difficulty taking root. In contrast to Japan, where communal irrigation and common use of fields and forests were secondary relationships adopted for the sake of individual farm management, European cooperatives regulated every aspect of farming, from the boundaries of fields and the choice of crops to planting and harvesting schedules. An extremely strong social consciousness developed as a result. It is to be seen in the logic of discontinuity as evident in the persecution of heretics among Christians themselves. Heretics and unbelievers were not merely inferior human beings but social outcasts.

The people of Europe and America are still bound by social and class consciousness. The fierce sense of individuality seen in the modern ideology of democracy serves to balance this consciousness, each of the two forces, society and class, functioning to check the excesses of the other.

Commentary

This book represents the attempt of a Japanese scholar of Western history to elucidate the history of Western thought from a Japanese standpoint. The meaning of "Europe" here is not confined to the western portion of the Eurasian land mass but in principle includes America, thus signifying Europe in the wider cultural sense.

Sabata Toyoyuki seeks to explain European and Japanese thought by dietary patterns. An aversion to meat as a young boy has colored his approach to the subject. Originally he was very fond of beef, but after being told one day, "Beef means the meat of cattle," he found that whenever he saw or smelled meat he envisaged the living animal and was nauseated. Why, he wondered, were Westerners not afflicted with a similar antipathy? It was this confrontation with his own sense of the strangeness of meat-eating that led him to explain European traditions of thought through dietary patterns.

Japan is said to have become rapidly Europeanized, but the diet has remained firmly based on rice. Christianity has gained very few followers in Japan. Industrialization has led to inevitable Europeanization in a number of social phenomena, but the same inevitability does not apply to those areas of society concerned with thought. The author sees a significant relationship between Japanese unwillingness to adopt a European meat diet on the one hand and traditions of thought on the other.

He succeeds to the theory of "climate" (*fûdo*) of Watsuji Tetsurô, who defines Europe as having a "pastoral climate." According to Watsuji, "The concept of climate includes the structure of social entities. It cannot be divorced from historical realities." (*Fûdo*, page 16) This is a typological concept, and the term "pastoral" is used as an index of European culture as a whole.

When Sabata speaks of the "stock-breeding" world of Europe, however, what he has in mind is the unique *climatic conditions* that naturally suited the region to stock breeding. His argument, postulating such natural factors and examining the inevitable relationships between dietary patterns and traditions of thought, is much more scientific than Watsuji's intuitive approach.

A meat diet necessitates a logic of discontinuity that firmly separates animals from human beings. This in turn determines European traditions of thought and is at the bottom of both Christianity and the class society. Nowhere do we find as direct a linking of dietary patterns and mental life as posited by this, Sabata's conclusion.

In the latter half of his book Sabata explains how the attempt to assimilate grain cultivation to a region basically unsuited to it influenced the formation of European thought. There is some truth in his assertion that reliance on communal efforts to produce bread led to a strengthening of social consciousness, but the discussion is less convincing than his argument in the first half of the book, where he singles out the logic of discontinuity as the basis of European thought.

43. A HISTORICAL VIEW OF THE ECOLOGY OF CIVILIZATION

Bunmei no Seitai Shikan By Umesao Tadao
Tokyo: Chûô Kôron-sha, 1967.

The Japanese have a feeling of cultural affinity with India. But it is doubtful that the Indians have any such feeling toward Japan. Is it not true that India has always been closer to Europe? The established theory of the racial origin of the Indian people is that they are a mixture of the original indigenous Dravidic tribes and the Aryan tribes who came in from the west; and the language of these Aryan tribes belongs to the Indo-European linguistic family. The history of India contains far more exchanges with the West than with the East. Both Tamerlane and Baber, who founded the Mogul Empire have long been thought to have been Mongols, but they were actually invaders from the West unrelated to the Mongols of east Asia. Most Mongoloid peoples live north of the Himalaya Mountains and east of Calcutta.

In other words, India is not a part of the Orient. It cannot, of course, be considered Occidental either. It is part of what we might call the "Intermedient." Japanese intellectuals have a tendency to split the world into halves and think of everything as either Oriental or Occidental, but it is necessary to add a third designation, for which we have coined the term Intermediental, to include the broad area of India and the Islamic countries.

[A]

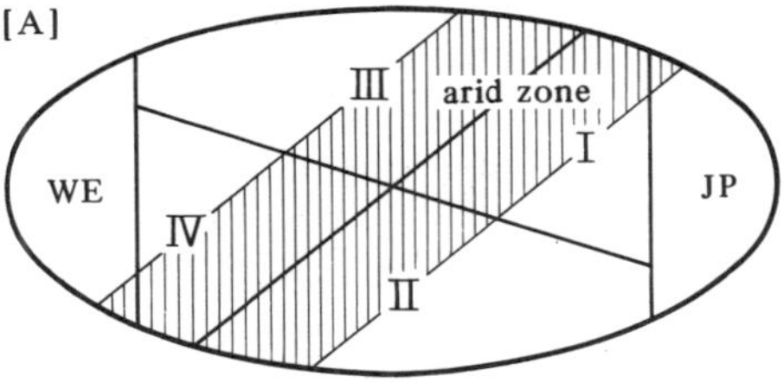

WE: Western Europe

JP: Japan

(*Bunmei no Seitai Shikan*, page 158)

Let us then divide the Old World into two areas (see diagram A). If we think of the Old World as an oval, Area One is the far eastern and far western tips of this oval, while Area Two is all the broad space between. The distinctive feature of Area One is a high level of modern technology.

Historically, Area One began as the home of wandering barbarians who made the civilization of Area Two their own and developed it through feudalism, absolutism, and bourgeois revolution to capitalism. Area Two is the home of all ancient civilization. It never went through a feudalistic stage, but created gigantic despotic empires. The weaknesses of this system caused Area Two to be colonized by Area One. In recent years, Area Two has made great strides toward modernization through a series of revolutions.

Area Two contains four huge communities, China, India, Russia, and the Islamic countries. Each is an enormous empire surrounded by satellite states. The internal development of each of the two areas has followed rough parallels.

It must be remembered that Japan after the Meiji Restoration was not necessarily striving for Westernization. Similar conditions in Western Europe and Japan resulted in parallel evolution.

Perhaps it would be well at this point to revise our terminology. The word "evolution" indicates lineage or genealogy, neither of which is what the author is attempting to describe. His aim is rather to examine cultural variations through the use of the term "evolution." The ecological term "succession" is probably more appropriate to our purposes. The author is attempting to show that both of the areas into which he has divided the Old World have their own characteristic succession, and that they are different from each other. The old view of history considers evolution to be mono-linear, with the same destination for all things. Thus variations were thought of as no more than deviations in the developmental process. With the adoption of an ecological viewpoint, we discover that development can also be multi-linear. We find it not at all strange that the development of Area One and that of Area Two have diverged.

Why have the two regions of Area One developed through such identical stages as to have been planned, in spite of their great distance from each other? We must take a close look at Area Two to find the answer.

The most striking aspect of the ecological structure of the Old World is the existence of an enormous arid zone that spreads across the continent at an oblique angle from northeast to southwest. It has played an important role in history. It is the source of violence and vandalism. Since ancient times, nomadic tribes have appeared repeatedly from this zone to attack the surrounding civilizations. In some cases, the destruction has been so great that the civilized society has been unable to recover.

On the other hand, the civilization of Area One has been able to mature in sheltered atmosphere, protected from destruction by a moderate climate, far from the source of violence. An application of the theory of succession reveals that Area One has progressed in a most orderly line of succession. We can think of history as a development brought about chiefly by forces within the community itself. This is known as autogenic succession. Conversely, the flow of history has been for the most part controlled by external forces in Area Two. This is called allogenic succession.

If we consider Southeast Asia a part of Area Two, where will we find it on Diagram A? If we think in terms of its actual physical position, we will find it in the lower right-hand corner of the diagram, in a corner of the Indian block. But this does not fit with the ecological facts. Historically, it has been deeply influenced by India, but it has always belonged in a quite different social category.

An aspect of Southeast Asia that never ceases to amaze the visitor is the great variety of cultures gathered there. India and China both contain vast numbers of small tribes, but a single large race dominates the country in terms of both population and culture. In Southeast Asia a great number of racial and cultural types live side by side.

[B]

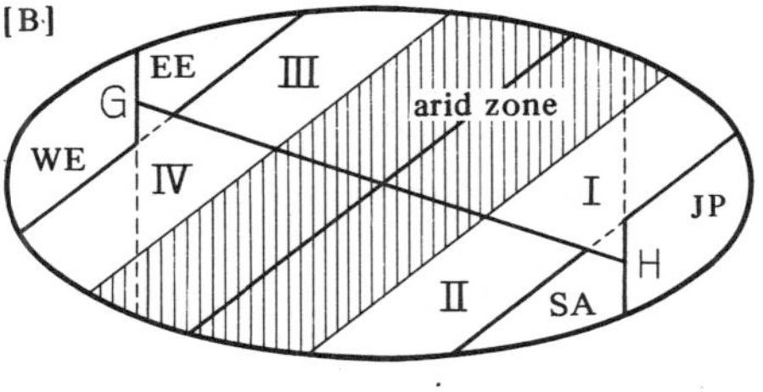

EE: Eastern Europe
WE: Western Europe
SA: Southeast Asia
JP: Japan

(*Bunmei no Seitai Shikan*, page 167)

If we revised our first diagram, taking this into consideration, we arrive at Diagram B, which shows the distribution of environmental factors important in shaping the history of the Old World. In purely geographical terms, we find the arid zone which includes the desert and the steppes running across the center, with semi-arid savannas lying along both sides, and humid forested areas along the outer edges of the savannas. The boundary lines are shown in Diagram B.

At the opposite end of our oval from Southeast Asia, we find the countries of Eastern Europe. A comparison between Southeast Asia and Eastern Europe may at first glance seem totally devoid of similarities, but a closer look in terms of comparative civilizations reveals correspondences. Both are collections of small nations. Both are intermediate zones surrounded by three of the world's huge communities. In Eastern Europe, as in Southeast Asia, numerous races, languages, and religions exist side by side. Historically they are also alike in that they have been repeatedly invaded by the larger communities surrounding them.

Commentary

This book is a collection of essays on subjects related to the central piece, "A Historical View of the Ecology of Civilization" (1972). All were written at about the same time.

In 1955, Umesao traveled to Afghanistan, Pakistan and India with the Karakoram-Hindu Kush scientific exploration party from Kyoto University. He says that the trip opened his eyes to the study of comparative civilization. He abandoned the theory of "one Asia" to consider the problem of the intrinsic cultural differences between Japan and India, and went on to maintain and develop the theory that the old idea that the world can simply be divided into two halves – the Orient and the Occident – is inadequate, and that there is an "Intermediental" world. As he went on to investigate these three large areas, he began to notice that while Japan and Western Europe are separated by a great distance, they have many historical similarities. "A Historical View of the Ecology of Civilization" is a theoretical development of this basic premise.

In this essay, the author divides the Old World into Area One and Area Two, and centering his discussion upon the arid zone running at an oblique angle across the center of the continent, he speaks in terms of an ecological theory of succession. He formulates his ecological view of history upon the idea that culture is more a problem of function and living habits than of descent and material civilization, and that the development of living habits are controlled by the environment. As he himself clearly states, he is applying the methods of botanical ecology to human society. In direct opposition to the static, non-historical application of botanical geography which created the cultural determinism of the past, he presents his ecological view as a new philosophy of history. The strength of this theory lies in the fact that the parallel phenomena of history can be explained without reliance upon a one-dimensional theory of evolution.

An ecological view of history was born when the author began field work in the arid zone. He rediscovered the meaning of the arid zone when he explored cultural differences between India and Japan. As this larger view of the world had not been a part of the traditional philosophy of civilization, Umesao's "A Historical View of the Ecology of Civilization" has been important in advanced thought on the subject.

44. MOZART

Mozart By Kobayashi Hideo
Tokyo: Kadokawa Bunko, green series #141, Kadokawa Shoten, 1959.

Twenty years ago, during a confused, vagrant period in my life, I was strolling along Dôton-bori in Osaka one cold winter night, when the famous theme from Mozart's G-Minor symphony began running through my head.

(*Mozart*, page 10)

I do not remember exactly what I was thinking about at the time, but it was probably something vast and insoluble, like life, or literature, or despair, or loneliness – meaningless words with which my head was always full to overflowing in those days. Whatever it may have been, I am sure that I was not making any conscious attempt to recall the music. It suddenly went through my head with crystal clarity as I walked along the crowded streets. I was shocked and excited, both at once. I dashed into a nearby department store and listened to a recording of the symphony, but the initial excitement was already gone.

I had a copy of an unfinished portrait of Mozart of which I was very fond. As a portrait it was of no great value, but it revealed a face with a somewhat feminine beauty and an almost frightening unhappiness. The large eyes were wide and slightly downcast. This is not the sort of expression one would wear in the presence of others. Mozart must have forgotten that he was sitting for a portrait. His eyes are looking out into space, the world has disappeared, the heart seems to contain a great agony. The eyes and mouth seem to have lost their usefulness. Only the ears seem expectant, awaiting something. One may almost imagine that they are moving, like the ears of an animal but they are hidden by his hair. I was convinced that the G-Minor symphony could only have been written by one whose face took on such an expression from time to time.

What agony he expressed through simple forms! It is impossible to express the greatness of his music in such terms as "perfect union of content and form." How can misfortune, unhappiness, and even agony take on such perfectly simple formal beauty? There is in it a miraculous union of two quite disparate states of the spirit. Even such depth and perfection Mozart's genius was constantly searching after. This, I began to believe, is what genuinely sad music is. This sadness quenched a thirst like clear cold water and gave me courage.

Always when I hear Mozart's music, the absolute freshness amazes me anew. It can make me feel that I am hearing it for the first time, no matter what mood may be at the time. No one can ever become completely a friend of such gentleness. It has in it the suppleness of finely honed steel.

Stendhal, one of Mozart's first admirers, said that the essence of his music is *tristesse*. It is particularly evident in the following allegro phrase (String Quintet, K.516).

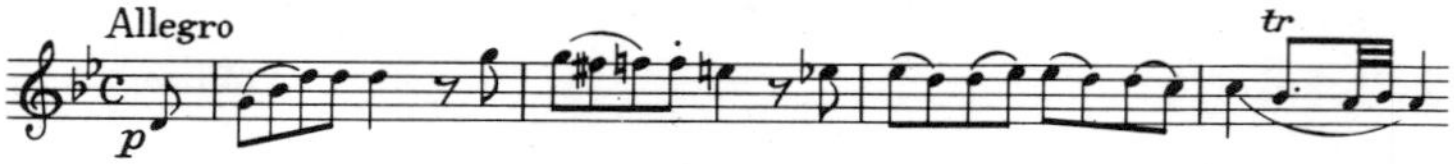

(*Mozart*, page 36)

When I read the Ghéon called this *tristesse allante* I was astonished to find in this single phrase all I myself had felt about the theme (Henri Ghéon; *Promenades avec Mozart*, 1932). Most certainly Mozart's sadness runs at such a pace that mere tears are incapable of keeping up with it. It is far too beautiful to be made a plaything of tears. It is like the blueness of the sky, the fragrance of the sea. It is the kind of sadness that the poets of the *Manyôshû* knew so well. No other composer has been able to write such an allegro. Mozart is not grieving, he is lonely, like a child playing at home alone. Loneliness is the real stuff of life.

The name of Mozart always brings the name of Haydn to mind. Everyone knows that they exerted a great influence on each other, but similar though they are, a careful listening reveals surprising differences. Wagner, one of the first who really understood Mozart's symphonies, found a distinct difference between them and the symphonies of Haydn, especially in the "extremely rich and melodious instrumental themes" of the former.

I entirely agree with him. The father of the symphony was not able to manage songlike melodies. But the point about Mozart's melodies that is missed by most listeners is their great brevity. Each of those lovely, much-loved melodies is but the length of a single breath. They are transformed by his unique modulation, extended and harmonized like magic to intoxicate the ear of the listener, until they sound as though they were being sung by a human voice.

Mozart would take the first tone from the cacophony of nature with inexpressible speed and grace. It is not that he tried to make his themes brief. It is just that nature seldom presents a lengthy theme, and long themes are usually the product of a contrivance. What was necessary for Mozart as he began work was a single present tone rather than an ambivalent theme. All he required was a single sound from a woman's voice or a random note from a clavecin. His ear would pick up the sound and hear all the nuances of resonance in it, which he would encase in exquisite form. Silence, which has no sound at all to most ears, contained numberless rich harmonies for him.

I like Haydn's music too. Haydn is incomparable in his perfection of form and clarity of expression. But after listening to Mozart, Haydn's music gives an impression of casual dalliance with decorations on empty forms. Mozart's music has an astonishing delicacy that makes such subtleties Haydn possesses seem extrinsic and superficial. Mozart has a subtle warmth that can be appreciated only by one whose heart is in his ears. Once fully experienced, the beauty and power of Mozart's intrinsic nuances make it impossible to forget his music.

What was Mozart striving for? Perhaps he had no particular aim at all. He was most likely oblivious to all the "purposes" and "intents" that poison the artists and thinkers of our day. In the world of art and thought, purposes and intents are entirely ineffective. They should be left to the world of science where hypotheses are developed.

Mozart was a great walker. A deep knowledge became a deepening of his genius. The import of his musical education is not easy to understand, for mental training was akin to physical training. He learned the form and method of the music of others by actual imitation. In his letters he averred that he could imitate any and all music. His basic education was in the imitation and composition of all sorts of music. He was never faced with the empty "intent" of a creator. Imitation was to him the only mother of creation. How can one know what one cannot imitate if one does not attempt to imitate everything? Amazed at Mozart's creativity, we must not underestimate his imitative ability.

Mozart did not decide upon a destination. His very method of walking through life was the force creating a destination. He was taken to unexpected places, and it was the places he was led that determined his purposes.

Commentary

Kobayashi is a representative literary critic. In his youth he studied French literature. His own view of literature was mainly formulated under the influence of such French symbolist poets as Valery and the Japanese writer Shiga Naoya. He made his debut in the literary world in 1929 when he was twenty-seven. He was recognized for his writings on contemporary literature and on Dostoyevsky. Later, while studying classical Japanese literature, he produced a series of "spiritual portraits" of such artists as Dostoyevsky, Mozart and Van Gogh.

The volume under discussion is one of the series. He was successful in drawing a portrait in words of a musician who was both a great craftsman and a great improvisationalist. It was based upon his own perceptions and upon extensive reading. The study represents a high print in Japanese understanding of the arts of the West.

About the Authors

The Map of Japan

ABOUT THE AUTHORS

1. dates
2. education and special field
3. current position
4. representative works

AIDA Yûji
1. b.1916 2. Kyoto University 3. Professor at the Research Institute for Humanistic Studies of Kyoto University 4. *Nihon Bunka no Jôken* (*The Conditions of Japanese Culture*). Tokyo: Banchô Shobô, 1965.

AKIYAMA Ken
1. b.1924 2. University of Tokyo 3. Professor at University of Tokyo 4. *Genji Monogatari no Sekai* (*The World of the Tale of Genji*). Tokyo: University of Tokyo Press, 1964.

DOI Takeo
1. b.1920 2. University of Tokyo 3. Professor at University of Tokyo 4. *Sôseki Bungaku ni okeru Amae no Kenkyû* (*A Study of Amae in Natsume Sôseki's Literary Works*). Tokyo: Kadokawa Bunko, white series #213-1, Kadokawa Shoten, 1972.

EGAMI Namio
1. b.1906 2. University of Tokyo 3. Professor at Sophia University 4. *Yûrashiya Kodai Hoppô Bunka* (*Culture of Ancient Northern Eurasia*). Tokyo: Yamakawa Shuppan-sha, 1948.

FUKUDA Hideko
1. 1865-1927 2. Shinsakae Girls' School 4. *Meiji Bungaku Zenshû* (*Collection of Meiji Literature*) vol. 84: *Meiji Shakaishugi Bungaku Shû* (*Socialistic Literature in Meiji Period*) No.2. Tokyo: Chikuma Shobô, 1965.

FUKUZAWA Yukichi
1. 1835-1901 2. Ogata Kôan's School 4. *Fukuzawa Yukichi Zenshû* (*Complete Works of Fukuzawa Yukichi*) in twenty volumes, ed. by Keio Gijuku. Tokyo: Iwanami Shoten, 1958-63.

HAYASHIYA Tatsusaburô
1. b.1914 2. Kyoto University 3. Professor at Kyoto University 4. *Chûsei Geinô-shi no Kenkyû* (*A Historical Study of the Medieval Performing Arts*). Tokyo: Iwanami Shoten, 1960.

HORI Ichirô
1. 1910-74 2. University of Tokyo 4. *Wagakuni Minkan Shinkô-shi no Kenkyû* (*A Study of the History of Japanese Folk Religion*). Tokyo: Tokyo Sôgensha, 1955.

IMOTO Nôichi
1. b.1913 2. University of Tokyo 3. Professor at Ochanomizu Women's University 4. *Haibungei no Ron* (*Essays on Haiku Literature*). Tokyo: Meiji Shoin, 1953.

ISHIDA Eiichirô
1. 1903-68 2. Vienna University 4. *Ishida Eiichirô Zenshû* (*Collected Works of Ishida Eiichirô*) in eight volumes. Tokyo: Chikuma Shobô, 1970-72.

ISHII Susumu
1. b.1931 2. University of Tokyo 3. Professor at University of Tokyo 4. *Nihon Chûsei Kokka-shi no Kenkyû* (*A Historical Study of Medieval State in Japan*). Tokyo: Iwanami Shoten, 1970.

ISHIMITSU Makiyo
1. 1868-1942 2. Japanese Military Academy 4. *Jôka no Hito* (*Man of a Castle Town*). Tokyo: Ryûseikaku, 1958.

KITAGAWA Tadahiko
1. b.1927 2. Kyoto University 3. Professor at Tenri University 4. *Kyôgen Hyaku-ban* (*One Hundred Kyôgen*). Kyoto: Tankô Shin-sha, 1964.

KITAJIMA Masamoto
1. b.1912 2. University of Tokyo 3. Professor at Tokyo Metropolitan University 4. *Edo Bakufu no Kenryoku Kôzô* (*The Power Structure of the Tokugawa Shogunate*). Tokyo: Iwanami Shoten, 1964.

KOBAYASHI Hideo
1. b.1902 2. University of Tokyo 3. Literary critic 4. *Kobayashi Hideo Zenshû* (*Collected Works of Kobayashi Hideo*) in twelve volumes. Tokyo: Shinchôsha, 1967-68.

KOBAYASHI Kunio
1. b.1918 2. University of Tokyo 3. Professor at Shinshû University 4. *Nihon Arupusu no Shizen* (*Nature of Japan Alps*). Tokyo: Tsukiji Shokan, 1958.

KOBAYASHI Tomoaki
1. b.1911 2. University of Tokyo 3. Professor at Ochanomizu Women's University 4. *Chûsei Bungaku no Shisô* (*Ideas in Medieval Literature*). Tokyo: Shibundô, 1964.

KON Wajirô
1. 1888-1973 2. Tokyo Academy of Fine Arts 4. *Kon Wajirô Shû* (*Collected Works of Kon Wajirô*) in nine volumes. Tokyo: Domesu Shuppan, 1971-72.

MARUYAMA Masao
1. b.1914 2. University of Tokyo 3. Professor at University of Tokyo 4. *Nihon Seiji Shisô-shi Kenkyû* (*A History of Japanese Political Thought*). Tokyo: University of Tokyo Press, 1952.

MATSUMOTO Shigeharu
1. b.1899 2. University of Tokyo 3. Chairman of the board in the International House of Japan 4. Ed. *Sekai no Meicho* (*Great Books of the World*) vol.33. Tokyo: Chûô Kôron-sha, 1970.

MINAMOTO Ryôen
1. b.1929 2. Kyoto University 3. Professor at Tôhoku University 4. *Tokugawa Shisô Shôshi* (*A Brief History of Tokugawa Ideology*). Tokyo: Chûô Kôron-sha, 1973.

MIYAMOTO Tsuneichi
1. b.1907 2. Tennôji Normal School 3. Professor at Musashino University of Arts 4. *Miyamoto Tsuneichi Chosakushû* (*Collected Works of Miyamoto Tsuneichi*) in twenty-five volumes. Tokyo: Miraisha, 1967-(continuing).

NAGAHARA Keiji
1. b.1922 2. University of Tokyo 3. Professor at Hitotsubashi University 4. *Nihon no Chûsei Shakai* (*Medieval Society in Japan*). Tokyo: Iwanami Shoten, 1968.

NAKAMURA Hajime
1. b.1912 2. University of Tokyo 3. Professor at University of Tokyo 4. *Nakamura Hajime Senshû* (*Selected Works of Nakamura Hajime*) in twenty-two volumes. Tokyo: Shunjûsha, 1962.

NAKANE Chie
1. b.1926 2. University of Tokyo 3. Professor at the Institute of Oriental Culture of University of Tokyo 4. *Mikai no Kao, Bunmei no Kao* (*The Face of Primitive Society, The Face of Civilization*). Tokyo: Chûô Kôron-sha, 1959.

NAKANISHI Susumu
1. b.1929 2. University of Tokyo 3. Professor at Seijô University 4. *Manyôshi no Kenkyû* (*A Historical Study on Manyôshû*). Tokyo: Ôfûsha, 1968.

NAKANO Takamasa
1. b.1920 2. University of Tokyo 3. Professor at Tokyo Metropolitan University 4. *Nihon no Heiya* (*The Plains of Japan*). Tokyo: Kokon Shoin, 1956.

OKA Yoshitake
1. b.1902 2. University of Tokyo 3. Professor emeritus at University of Tokyo 4. *Kindai Nihon no Seiji-ka* (*Modern Japanese Politicians*). Tokyo: Bungei Shunjû-sha, 1960.

OKAMOTO Tarô
1. b.1911 2. Tokyo Academy of Fine Arts 3. Artist 4. *Nihon Sai-hakken* (*The Rediscovery of Japan*). Tokyo: Shinchôsha, 1958.

ÔNO Susumu
1. b.1919 2. University of Tokyo 3. Professor at Gakushûin University 4. *Jôdai Kana-zukai no Kenkyû* (*A Study of Ancient Japanese Kana Usage*). Tokyo: Iwanami Shoten, 1953.

SABATA Toyoyuki
1. b.1926 2. Kyoto University 3. Professor at Kyoto Prefectural Medical College 4. *Yôroppa Hôken Toshi* (*The European Feudal City*). Osaka: Sôgensha, 1957.

SATÔ Tadao
1. b.1930 2. Niigata Industrial High School 3. Freelance writer 4. *Nihon Eiga Shisô-shi* (*A History of the Ideology of the Japanese Cinema*). Tokyo: Sanichi Shobô, 1970.

SUZUKI Daisetsu
1. 1870-1966 2. University of Tokyo 4. *Suzuki Daisetsu Zenshû* (*Collected Works of Suzuki Daisetsu*) in thirty volumes and two appendixes. Tokyo: Iwanami Shoten, 1968-71.

SUZUKI Takao
1. b.1926 2. Keio University 3. Professor at the Keio Institute of Cultural and Linguistic Studies 4. *Tozasareta Gengo: Nihongo no Sekai* (*The Closed Language: The World of Japanese*). Tokyo: Shinchôsha, 1975.

TAKEDA Chôshû
1. b.1916 2. Kyoto University 3. Professor at Dôshisha University 4. *Minzoku Bukkyô to Sosen Shinkô* (*Folk Buddhism and the Ancestor Cult*). Tokyo: University of Tokyo Press, 1971.

TOYAMA Shigehiko
1. b.1923 2. Tokyo University of Literature and Science (present: Tokyo University of Education) 3. Professor at Ochanomizu Women's University 4. *Homo Mentiensu* (*Homo Mentiens*). Tokyo: Misuzu Shobô, 1972.

UEYAMA Shunpei
1. b.1921 2. Kyoto University 3. Professor at Kyoto University 4. *Dai Tôa Sensô no Imi* (*The Meaning of the Greater East Asian War*). Tokyo: Chûô Kôron-sha, 1964.

UMEHARA Takeshi
1. b.1925 2. Kyoto University 3. President of Kyoto University of Arts 4. *Kakusareta Jûjika* (*Hidden Cross*). Tokyo: Shinchôsha, 1972.

UMESAO Tadao
1. b.1920 2. Kyoto University 3. Curator of the Museum of Japanese Ethnology 4. *Mogôru-zoku Tanken-ki* (*A Mongol Exploration*). Tokyo: Iwanami Shinsho #253, Iwanami Shoten, 1956.

WATSUJI Tetsurô
1. 1889-1960 2. University of Tokyo 4. *Watsuji Tetsurô Zenshû* (*Collected Works of Watsuji Tetsurô*) in twenty volumes. Tokyo: Iwanami Shoten, 1976-(continuing).

YANAGITA Kunio
1. 1875-1962 2. University of Tokyo 4. *Teihon Yanagita Kunio Shû* (*Complete Works of Yanagita Kunio*) in thirty-one volumes and five appendixes. Tokyo: Chikuma Shobô, 1961-72.

YASHIRO Yukio
1. 1890-1975 2. University of Tokyo 4. *Suiboku-ga* (*Suiboku Painting*). Tokyo: Iwanami Shinsho #736, Iwanami Shoten, 1972.

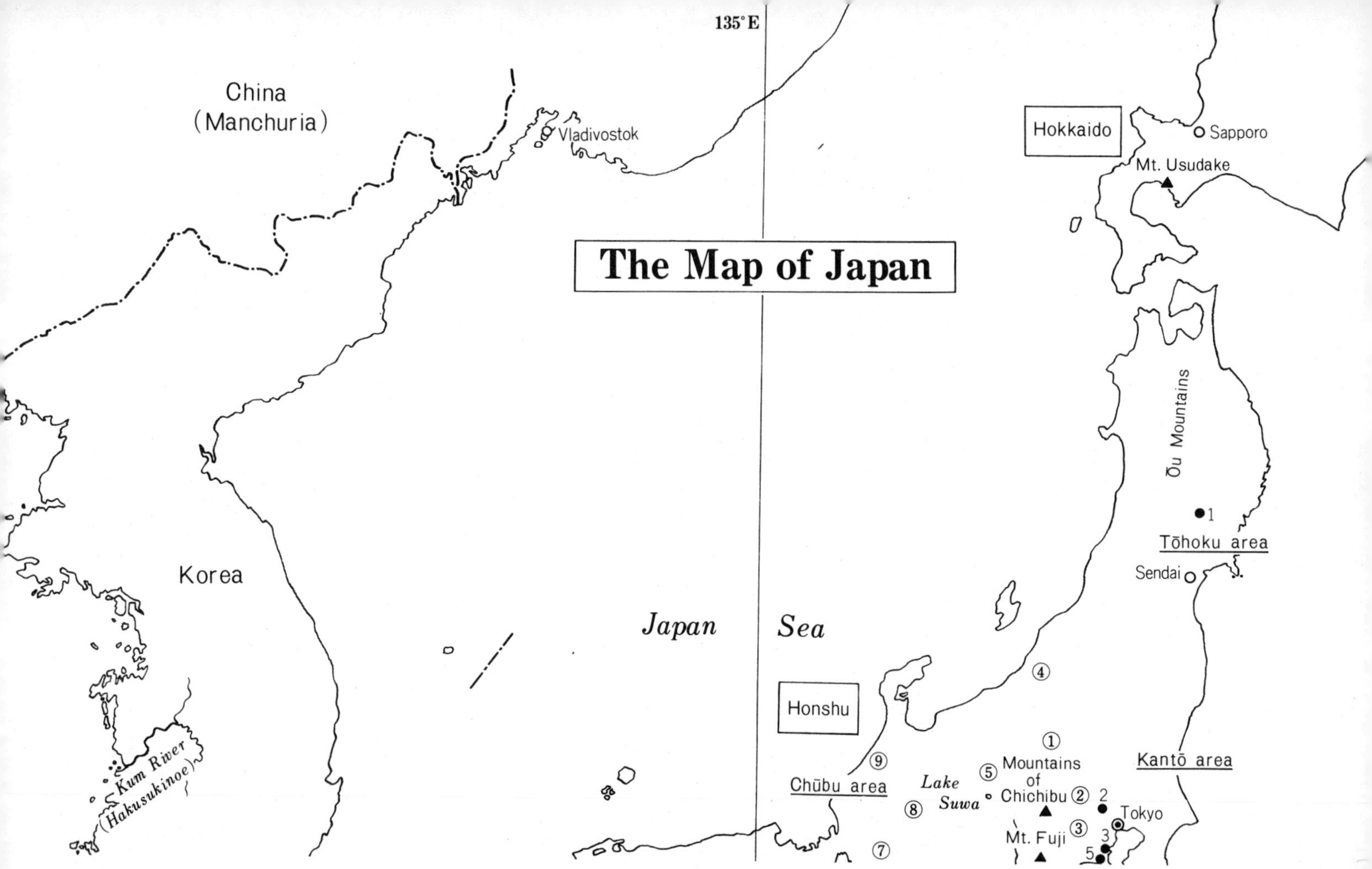

The Map of Japan
135° E
China
(Manchuria)
Vladivostok
Korea
Kum River
(Hakusukinoe)
Japan
Sea
Hokkaido
Sapporo
Mt. Usudake
Ōu Mountains
1
Tōhoku area
Sendai
Honshu
④
①
⑨
Chūbu area
Lake
Suwa
⑤
Mountains
of
Chichibu
②
2
Tokyo
Kantō area
⑧
③
Mt. Fuji
3
5
⑦

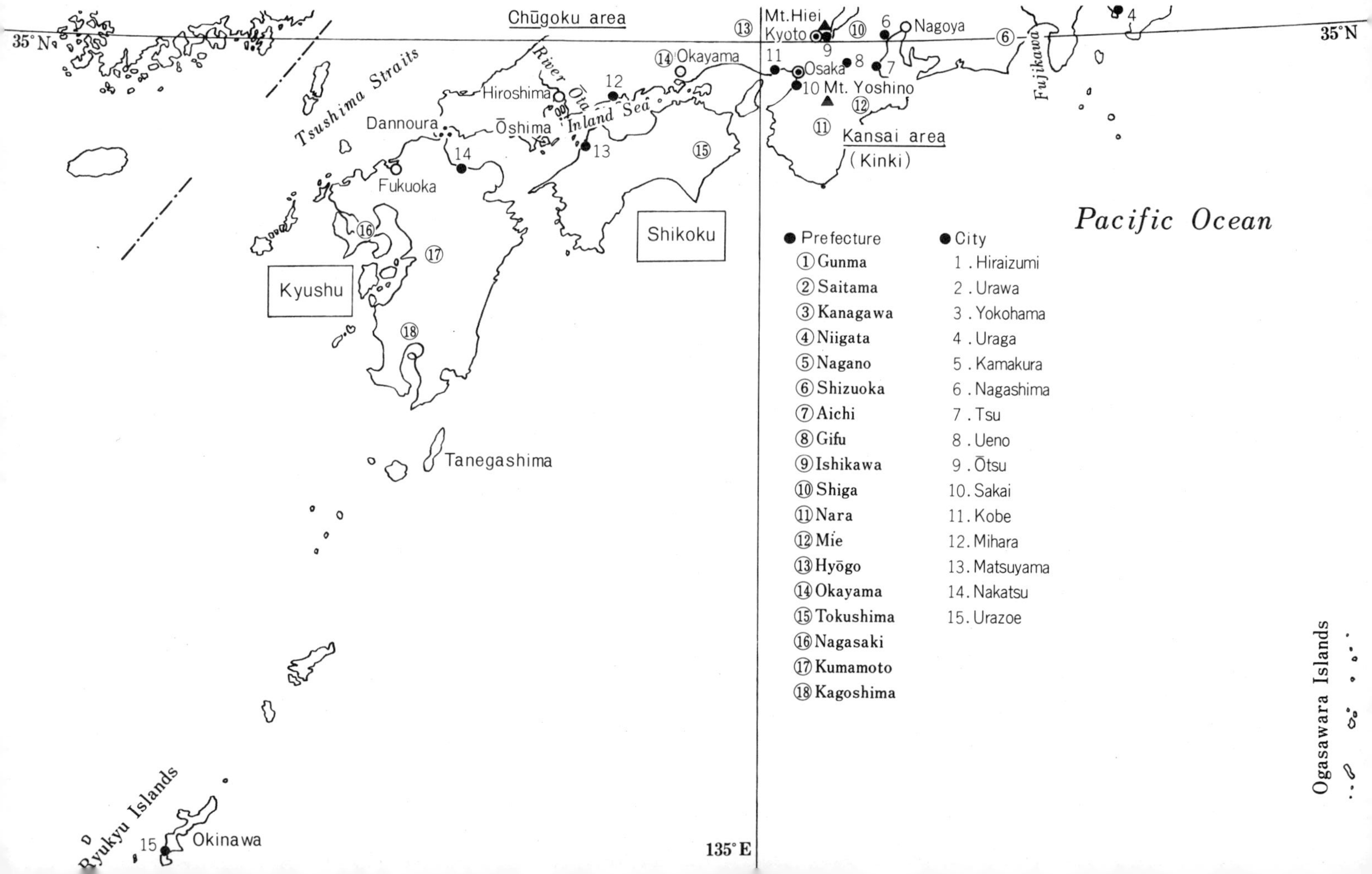
35°N
Chūgoku area
Tsushima Straits
Dannoura
Hiroshima
River Ōta
Ōshima
Inland Sea
Fukuoka
Kyushu
Shikoku
Okayama
Mt.Hiei
Kyoto
Osaka
Mt. Yoshino
Nagoya
Fujikawa
Kansai area
(Kinki)
Pacific Ocean
Tanegashima
Ryukyu Islands
Okinawa
Ogasawara Islands
135°E
● Prefecture
① Gunma
② Saitama
③ Kanagawa
④ Niigata
⑤ Nagano
⑥ Shizuoka
⑦ Aichi
⑧ Gifu
⑨ Ishikawa
⑩ Shiga
⑪ Nara
⑫ Mie
⑬ Hyōgo
⑭ Okayama
⑮ Tokushima
⑯ Nagasaki
⑰ Kumamoto
⑱ Kagoshima
● City
1. Hiraizumi
2. Urawa
3. Yokohama
4. Uraga
5. Kamakura
6. Nagashima
7. Tsu
8. Ueno
9. Ōtsu
10. Sakai
11. Kobe
12. Mihara
13. Matsuyama
14. Nakatsu
15. Urazoe

This book was published through a grant from the Commemorative Association for the Japan World Exposition.